Spices, Seasonings, and Herbs

Sylvia Windle Humphrey

SPICES, SEASONINGS, AND HERBS

THE DEFINITIVE COOKBOOK

Formerly *A Matter of Taste*

Collier Books, New York, New York

Collier-Macmillan Ltd., London

TO *Rosy*

Roses.

Acknowledgments

The final accomplishment of finishing a book causes every author to look back on the experiences both fortunate and exasperating that went into the making of the volume. The principal feeling is one of overwhelming gratitude to the people and circumstances that made the book possible. It seems more than one lifetime ago that the famous chemist and sensitive gourmet Wallace Carothers first opened my mind and palate to the joys of taste. Since then my friends all over the world have seemed to take pleasure in helping me to develop that taste and to increase my knowledge of their countries and of their national cuisines.

Even so, my knowledge would have stopped far short of the extraordinary without Anna Vidissoni, the genius of our kitchen, whose magic hands and ethereal ways with seasoning have refined my palate and educated my taste for nearly seventeen years.

Then Rosy—Elmer or Joseph Roessner he was christened— with kind but uncompromising discipline, taught me to write it down.

I am most grateful to Bernard Lewis of the American Spice Trade Association for putting me in the way of writing this book, and to Marshall Neale in the same office for his knowledgeable help.

Mr. John F. Angeline of Arthur D. Little, Inc., in Cambridge, Massachusetts, opened my eyes to new concepts of seasoning and was most patient and cooperative about allowing me to pick his brains for hours at a time. Dr. Jean Caul was also most helpful.

Mr. Robert Shinnagel treated me to a very informative tour

of the Dodge and Alcott flavor laboratories, and has given me much valuable information about the values of flavor.

Mimi Ouei has been unusually patient and helpful in explaining Chinese seasonings, giving of her great knowledge of the Chinese cuisine, and letting me use her recipes in this book.

To Anne Sekeley of the Artistic Cooking School in New York City I give many thanks for her true Hungarian recipes.

I am much obliged to the chef of the Spanish Pavilion and Granada Restaurant for his interesting recipe for Perdiz en Chocolate a la Navarra.

I would never have got the book to the publisher without Florence Bergin's help and advice in editing the recipes section.

To artist Bernard Langlais, appreciation for taking time from important works to put his mind on how to fit Nicholas Culpeper's lovely old drawings into this book. Gratitude also to Mr. Culpeper, may he continue to rest in peace.

Thank you, Dr. Karl Landes, for knowing absolutely everything about cinnamon and other spices, and for being absorbingly interesting on the subject.

Heartfelt thanks to H. J. Rietbergen for giving of his deep fund of knowledge about food and the serving of it.

Ford Madox Ford, writing in *Provence,* guided me to find there my own small hectare of olives and herbs. I am happy that Miss Janice Biala has given us permission to quote extensively from the book.

We lift a glass to Sir Alan Herbert, who was kind enough to allow us to use the "Recipe for a Martini" from *Two Gentlemen From Soho.*

I want to thank Mr. David Watkins of the Yale University Library for opening to me the facilities of the library and its excellent cookbook collection. Most of all I am deeply grateful to Miss Esther Wynne for the friendly corner of the library's Rare Book Room which she kept protected for my work.

Condolences and gratitude to the series of sympathetic editors who have seen this book through untold vicissitudes—to Bram Cavin, Herb Cohen, Bruno Fischer, and finally, to John Burton Brimer, who triumphantly carried it "home."

Contents

HERBS

SPECIAL SEASONINGS

RECIPES

Rosemary.

The Wild Pear

BASIC SEASONINGS

Sweet Marjoram.

Garden Rue.

1. What Seasonings Are

In 1740 in France a Jesuit priest named Father Brumoy wrote the preface to a cookbook which had been composed by his friend Marin, who was then chef to the Duchesse de Charlnus. *The Gifts of Comus,* once a remarkable cookbook, is forgotten now, but Father Brumoy's introduction is still up-to-the-minute after 200 years.

"Modern cookery," wrote Father Brumoy, "established on the foundations of the ancient, possesses more variety, simplicity and cleanliness, with infinitely less of labour and elaboration, and it is withal more knowing. The ancient cuisine was complicated and full of details. But the modern cuisine is a perfect system of chemistry. The science of the cook consists of breaking down, in rendering ease of digestion, in quintessing (so to speak) the viands, in extracting from them light and nourishing juices and in so mixing them together that no one flavor shall predominate, but that all shall be harmonized and blended. This is the high aim and great effort of Art. The harmony which strikes the eye in a picture should in a sauce cause in the palate as agreeable a sensation."

Father Brumoy, with his knowledge of chemistry, his consideration for nourishment, his interest in saving labor, seems more a part of the mid-twentieth century than of the early eighteenth. Such a man seems to make time stand still. In his day all France was engrossed and excited by the new cooking that was a perfect system of chemistry. Under the influence of two French queens, Catherine and Marie de Medici, both from Italy, and the impetus of an earlier age of science, the seventeenth century had seen the greatest development in the culinary arts that France has known; it was then that the great French cuisine began to take its modern shape.

But in 200 years how much of this science of the cook has filtered down to the amateur? How many know why lemon is served with fish? Why hot lobster takes butter, but mayonnaise goes with cold lobster; why horseradish makes shrimp taste better; what happens when wine is added to the gravy; why ginger is the outstanding seasoning in China; what effect has a marinade on meat? For that matter, who can explain the effect of salt on flavor? Or pepper?

Modern American kitchens have everything. The "everything" includes a shelf of herbs and spices arranged in neat tins or in graceful clear-glass bottles, bottles which are not the proper containers for spices and herbs whose color fades in the light. Most cooks are baffled by seasonings. Herb charts confuse with such recommendations as: use either fresh or dried for fruit cups, fruit salads, sauces, stews, soups, veal, pork, lamb, chicken, fish, duck, beans, cauliflower. Somewhat clearer but insufficient instructions now appear on the bottles.

Our ancestors both near and remote used herbs lavishly, and spices, too, when they could afford them, in part to disguise bad tastes, in part to contrive good ones, but mostly because herbs were always there—in the gardens and in the fields—and familiar because they were part of daily life, in constant use as medicines and deodorants, as seasonings and as perfumes. Perhaps it is the drugstore that has spoiled our cooking.

The objective of this book is to try to make seasoning less baffling to amateur cooks, the "high aim and great effort" being to bring a few of the findings of science into the ordinary household kitchen, working toward that harmonious blending of foods and condiments which causes so agreeable a sensation in the palate. Salaries have been paid in salt; wars have been fought for spice, and armies have mutinied to win a tasty "mess," so seasonings evidently fill a need—in fact, they are a spice of life.

The first thing to make clear is what seasonings are. After I was asked by a widow who for too long had been cooking little meals only for her children, "How can you? . . . a whole book . . . a book about salt and pepper?" it became evident that a definition should be included.

Seasonings are edible products of nature and man which have the power in one way or another to effect a change in other foods and in the organs of taste—to modify, to point up, to synthesize—achieving as a result a blended flavor more pleasing to the taste than unseasoned flavor.

The word *seasoning,* in all its meanings, implies that something special has been added—the acquired wisdom and spice that seasons a spare old man, the rich mellow patina which gives depth to well-seasoned wood (Oliver Wendell Holmes said that "knowledge and timber shouldn't be much used until they are seasoned"), or the relish of a salty speech seasoned with wit.

Well-seasoned food is no different: the basic character stands out, smoothed but imbued with quality, with spirit. Some of the truly great seasonings—lemon juice, ginger, vanilla—have an extraordinary capacity to pull together a variety of flavors into a fused oneness while adding little or no flavor of their own, rather like the unique effect of musk or ambergris on perfumes, blending odors and fixing them in fragrant permanence. Of course, the same seasonings are used in larger quantity to impart their own delightful flavors to a dish, as in lemon soufflé, gingerbread, or vanilla ice cream.

Well-seasoned verse, like this one by A. P. Herbert, telling how to blend the dry martini's venerable ancestor, could overturn the habits of a Third Avenue bar:

> Pluck me ten berries from the juniper,
> And in a beaker of strong barley-spirit
> The kindly juices of the fruit compress.
> This is our Alpha. Next clap on your wings,
> Fly south for Italy, nor come you back

Till in the cup you have made prisoner
Two little thimblefuls of that sweet syrup
The Romans call Martini. Pause o'er Paris
And fill two eggshells with the French vermouth.
Then home incontinent, and in one vessel
Cage your three captives, but in nice proportions,
So that no one is master, and the whole
Sweeter than France, but not so sweet as Italy.
Wring from an orange two bright tears, and shake,
Shake a long time the harmonious trinity.
Then in two cups like angels' ears present them,
And see there swims an olive in the bowl,
Which when the draft is finished, shall remain
Like the last emblem of a deserted love.

Call this drink "Angels' Ears" and the extra dry martini will be a thing forgotten.

But Mr. Herbert's recipe is in the realm of art, and in cooking, as in everything else, understanding, which is science, comes first, before creativity, which is art.

The civilized gratification of our senses is what makes art: sight and hearing, taste, smell, and touch, the "avenues of knowledge of the world." The culinary art travels mainly through three of the senses: taste, smell, and touch. The first-year biology offered in every high school teaches about the senses, the taste buds and the olfactory organ, but I have never heard that this course was used as a take-off to a much-needed Teen-Age Cordon Bleu.

Although our organs of taste and smell are quite simple compared with the complicated eye and ear, surprisingly little is known about how they actually work. Far more than enough has been discovered, nevertheless, to inform anyone who wants to be a better cook.

In the mouth are our taste buds, receptors for hot and cold, the nerve endings and mucous membranes that are sensitive to touch—the latter liking or disliking things which are rough, slippery, grainy, crisp—demanding that food feel right.

The olfactory organ, which detects odors and transmits its detections to the brain, is housed in an inch-square space in the back of the nose.

Since long before Father Brumoy's palate enjoyed a sauce, the palate was popularly believed to be the seat of taste. Even the language has recognized its use as a synonym for taste, as George Eliot's "I heard a little too much preaching . . . and lost my palate for it." Even so knowledgeable a wine taster as Victor, sommelier at New York's estimable Brussels Restaurant, gives credit to his palate (a superior one, he says, endowed him by a kindly nature) for his success. Though Victor's reputation as perhaps the most discriminating wine taster in this country is not undeserved, it is not his palate that has been helping him pick and choose; it is his nose.

A wine taster does not need a fine palate, or even a special nose. Much like anything else—training a bear, building a bridge, making fine wines—those who work hard enough at it, learn—anybody, well, almost anybody. Nature evidently considered the taste-smell senses important for man's survival in the primitive forests where other creatures seemed much better equipped than clumsy Man, who had no snout, no claws, no fangs, no speed, no poisoned bite, and whose young were weak, helpless, slow-growing. So Nature endowed us all fairly equally and quite well, too; the taste organs of individuals vary little, far less than those for sight and hearing.

Most normal, healthy individuals have quite similar capacities for taste and smell. The few really weak spots that are known are usually hereditary, and seem to pertain only to certain synthetic chemicals. It is evidently the pigmentation, the deepness of color, of the olfactory organ which determines the capacity to smell. Albinos, for instance, man and beast, completely lack this sense. Perhaps it is this pigmentation, or perhaps it is some completely unknown factor, that gives women a somewhat keener sense of smell, becoming even more acute just before the menstrual period. Which shows that fifty million Frenchmen and the chefs they have trained and the male population of the known world, all of whom have asserted for centuries that the female has an inferior palate, can be wrong.

If it is not his palate that causes him to excel as a wine taster, Victor of the Brussels nevertheless must have something unusual that allows him to find important differences in such subtle, delicate, complicated liquids as fine wines. Like everyone else, he has

taste buds on his tongue, around the edges and in the front and
back of the tongue, on the soft palate, and in the gullet.

So Victor pours a little wine; he sniffs it; he takes a sip; he
gargles with it (touching it to the palate); he swishes it around
the taste buds, and says, "This is an unusually fine example of the
1953 vintage from the vineyards of the Château Haut-Richeville-
Baron, probably from the slope in back of the château." But ask
Victor to hold his nose. With his sense of smell cut off, every wine,
whether red wine made from backyard Concord grapes or a renowned vintage beloved by emperors of France—all will taste
alike. Victor's palate will tell him only that he has in his mouth a
slightly sour liquid. It was his sense of smell, his olfactory organ,
that was giving him information. E. H. Starling, in *Principles of
Human Physiology* says, "The epicure with a fine palate has really
educated his sense of smell and would be little satisfied with the
simple sensations derived from his tongue."

The simplicity of the olfactory organ (yellow pigmented cells
with long tender delicate filaments extending into an air passage)
gives few clues as to how it detects odors. Yet no machine yet
invented can approach the sensitivity of these simple receptors.
The olfactory receptors can detect odors of one part in two billion.

It is not unreasonable that the palate has been given so much
credit in the past. The soft palate hangs where the nasal passage
joins the throat; the wine Victor is tasting, warmed in the mouth,
reaches the palate and the warmed, blended bouquet ascends the
nasal passage to the little room at the rear of the nose that houses
the delicate golden filaments of the olfactory organ. The taste buds
and the organ of smell (which are acting rather like the aerials
to a wireless set) then send their findings to the brain, which
identifies, then sends out messages to act on the signals of danger
or pleasure that it has received. Victor's intelligence, interest, and
experience translate his brain's messages into "This is a fine
Château Haut-Richeville-Baron. . . ." Victor's intelligence and
interest have trained his senses. Although the scientists say that
our chemical senses have lost much of their acuteness over the
centuries, I'll bet on Victor's well-trained nose to help him find
his way out of the woods.

With children it's different. They don't have what it takes to be wine tasters—the nose. Children are children, and their taste equipment is quite different from that of their parents. In the young, the olfactory organ is much underdeveloped in every way; taste buds, on the other hand, they have in exuberant quantities, not only in those places described before, but all over the mouth, on the insides of the cheeks and even on the roof of the mouth.

"Taste as we usually speak of it," R. W. Moncrieff writes in *The Chemical Senses,* "is a complex perception which takes into account odor, temperature, and touch. . . . All taste is experienced in the mouth. . . . The grading of tastes into each other is due principally to odor, from which sensation practically all 'flavor' is derived, and if odor and temperature-tactile complications are removed, we are left with four tastes—salt, sour, sweet, and bitter." Although the sensitive areas of all four overlap to a certain extent, the general pattern of distribution is: sweet-sensitive on the tip and front edges of the tongue, salt-sensitive and sour-sensitive along the sides, and the sophisticated bitter-sensitive taste buds have a groove to themselves across the back of the tongue.

The bitter taste is the most sensitive and longest lasting, and with the sweet taste is found in the greatest variety of compounds. It is also the most misunderstood and maligned. Experiments are being conducted to try to raise the threshold of the bitter taste so that people would notice it less—so that the other tastes, sweet, salt, and acid, would tend to overwhelm it. Taste perceptions would then change for some of the most characteristic and best-loved flavors: for coffee, beer, vermouth, quinine water, grapefruit. After-dinner coffee would never be the same!

Scientists report that the sweet-sensitive buds are the newest in the evolutionary scale, and the bitter ones the most sensitive. Both are somewhat more complex than the more simple salt and sour buds, and were developed perhaps more to encourage nourishment than to guard against danger. They also think it likely that children are not able to taste *bitter.* This may be true. Nearly all small children like beer, for instance; then, perhaps as their bitter taste buds develop, most of them decide, at least for a few years, that they don't like it!

There is no doubt, however, that children have numberless sweet taste buds; no doubt, too, that they need them. It takes a lot of sugar to keep up all that energy. One sees, however, that children are ill-equipped to experience flavor, their sensations of flavor being, I imagine, very much like those of an adult with a bad cold.

Nature's old-fashioned ways do not seem to encourage mixing of the generations; the very young and the mature usually enjoy different things. That the years are long between mud pies and mince, between tree-climbing and social-climbing, between fairy tales and the daily newspaper is a truth which carries over to the dinner table. What misery is caused, misery that frequently sets patterns for a lifetime, by treating children at the table as young adults, which they are not, the charming creatures—the more charming when they are not forced to eat what they are not yet equipped to enjoy.

What usually happens is this: Mother feeds the whole family the same things, leaning toward foods she thinks are good for the children. So the parents find the food dull, which it is; their satisfaction comes from full-bodied flavors, and the children—they wouldn't like it even if it were good.

Part of the trouble comes from lack of knowledge, in spite of Biology I, of how the taste equipment works. Mouth sensations are of first importance to young children: crisp vegetables and fruits, crunchy nuts, cold ices (hot things seem hotter to children than to hardened old grownups). The sweet acids of fruits find appealing responses in children's taste buds. Those seasonings which strongly affect the taste buds—salt and sugar and acids such as lemon juice and vinegar—seem much stronger to children than to adults. With children, hundreds more taste buds are involved. This does not necessarily mean that they do not like these things; often they do.

The idea that children should have and like only bland, innocuous things to eat—pap—is a result, perhaps, of confusing their size and comparative helplessness with a weak digestion. They can and do eat anything. Seasonings are not harmful; they improve the flavor and frequently the digestion also. Ralph Pfister, chef at the Kollman Home for Children in Brooklyn,

New York, has had great success with seasoned foods (herbs and spices) for children; they eat much better. He reminds us that they don't like to see the little leaves and such; he uses spice bags.

Children are conservative. Now and then one is encouraged by an experimental child who will bite anything that doesn't bite her first (it is usually female), but generally the reaction is "I don't like it. I never tasted it. I don't like it." The best way out of this impasse, to encourage children to branch out, is by imitation. But if mother and father have condemned themselves to a children's diet, how can the children grow up, gustatorially speaking? Because a child's olfactory organ develops, an appreciation of flavor gradually becomes noticeable until "Gee, Ma, what's cooking? That smells *good*." He has a good chance of becoming a gourmet by the time he's forty.

If he is lucky or well taught, he will rejoice in his sense of smell and make the most of it; its quick reactions and unequaled sensitivity protect him from danger and unpleasantness, delight him with the scents of nature—the garden, the woods, the sea—lead him to nourishment and are largely responsible for his enjoyment of it. And no other sense so gathers up the associations of the past, to be recalled by a chance odor half a lifetime later.

The importance of odor in nutrition—pleasurable nutrition—cannot be exaggerated. Bread baking, bacon frying, coffee roasting, a tangerine opened . . . odors are the invitation to dinner, and no dinner is satisfying without them. Odor stimulates the appetite and the flow of digestive juices which guarantee a salubrious feeling of comfort after dinner; even the natural vitamins in foods are now thought to have odors which attract. Moncrieff says in *The Chemical Senses,* "It is only natural that vitamins should have an olfactory attraction. It may be that the vitamins themselves are odorous or that they are always associated by natural design with odorous constituents. The attractive odors of citrus fruits, lemon, lime and orange, rich in vitamin C, come to mind." Actually, vitamin A, abundant in the sweet, pungent carrot, is known to improve, and even to repair, the sense of smell, increasing the pigmentation of the olfactory organ.

Cold takes away odor and flavor. Even the olfactory organ

reacts more slowly when it is cold. Several times the normal quantity of flavoring must be added to iced foods and drinks. Perhaps people will eventually learn how to use the refrigerator, instead of serving forth from it cold tasteless meals accompanied by chilly relishes: cold lettuce topped by frigid mayonnaise, icy fruits, their delicious aromas trapped by the cold—and the inevitable ice water.

It is heat that brings out the goodness. Moncrieff recommends that foods taste best at temperatures between 68 degrees and 104 degrees Fahrenheit, though they can be eaten in comfort as hot as 130 degrees.

Dishes which are not supposed to be hot, such as fruit and cold meats, are best served at room temperature—about 68 degrees.

So the cook who aims to please exercises skill and intelligence principally toward one end: the production of a pleasing aroma. This is what seasonings are for.

2. Seasonings—How They Work

"Epicurean cooks sharpen with cloyless sauce his appetite." Antony, as the whole world now knows, was in too far over his head to care what he ate; nevertheless, Cleopatra knew that there are few troubles that a tasty dish won't lighten.

The odors that stimulate the appetite are built up by blending together all the sensations of taste, including the nerve endings and receptors that feel touch and temperature. The inexperienced cook is not accustomed to thinking about these factors, except in the most general way, like, Is it slippery? Will it burn? Yet these receptors have much to do with bringing out the whole full flavor. Black and white pepper, the mints, vanilla, ginger, and many other seasonings irritate nerve endings in the mouth—and elsewhere—making them more alert to flavor, making them feel more sharply. Heat means not only degrees Fahrenheit, but also the effect of seasoning on hot and cold receptors.

Taste notes come in at different times. Learning the cause of this physiological fact, and how to take advantage of it, is one of the tricks of good seasoning. Different tastes do not react at the same speed. The acid taste is the most sensitive and will feel things first; salt, the most primitive taste, will come in next; and the sweet buds are the slowest—unless the sweet is saccharin (a chemical with a bitter reaction which, in fact, turns to bitter as the taste finishes). Bitter actually is the quickest, the most sensitive, but since it is in a groove at the back of the tongue, it stays on the edge of the picture. (The bitter taste can be overcome by raspberry, and by cocoa, and by vanilla, too, I think; sour by sweet, saltiness by syrup of orange, cinnamon, or sarsaparilla.) The main groups of taste buds arc located: sweet at the tip of the tongue, sour and salt at the sides, and bitter at the rear. Therefore it is useless to taste for saltiness at the tip of the tongue or for sweetness on the sides. Sweet reacts slowly, too. The wise cook, therefore, tastes a sufficient amount, puts it into the mouth and leaves it there about fifteen seconds. It is well, also, to rinse the mouth with warm water between tastings.

The Flavor Laboratory at Arthur D. Little, Inc., in Cambridge, Massachusetts, suggests that people's ability to taste doesn't differ as much as one might think, that there is at any rate an accepted flavor pattern: (a) There should be an early and good first impression. (b) There should be a rapid growth of a full, blended flavor, indicating usually that a full-bodied aroma has reached the olfactory organ. (c) There should be pleasant mouth sensations; (d) absence of isolated unpleasant notes, and (e) anticipation of the next mouthful.

To reach this ideal state of affairs the cook is daily finding out more about the flavor values and potency of her ingredients and their effect on the taste.

VARIATIONS ON A PEACH

A rose is a rose is a rose,. and a peach is a peach is a peach. A peach is also an almond. The fruit is a complicated arrangement of esters and minerals, calories and vitamins, that combine

in unique ways to make the luscious fruit look and taste like
peach.

Brillat-Savarin, whose observations on the *Physiology of Taste*
have been good for nearly two centuries, analyzes the pleasurable
act of eating a peach.

He who eats a peach is first agreeably hit by the odor which
emanated from it; he puts it in his mouth and tests the sensation of
freshness and acidity which attracts him enough to continue; but it is
not until the moment of swallowing, when the mouthful passes under
the nasal cavity, that the perfume is revealed to him which completes
the sensation that a peach should cause. Finally, it is not until when
he has swallowed, that, judging what he has just tried, he says to himself, "How delicious this is."

It was more for entertainment than for the enlightenment of
other gastronomes that Dr. Brillat-Savarin, scientist, cosmopolitan,
bon vivant, wrote these meditations about taste. Nevertheless,
one would rather have expected the doctor to explain how the
enticing odor of the peach starts all the right juices flowing that
make for a happy digestion, to have mentioned the sweetness
that goes along with the freshness of the fruit; to have marked
the note of bitter-almond which comes in just before swallowing.
Nor does he call attention to the temperature of his peach which
was cool—not warm—so that the completed sensation that a peach
should cause came to him *after* swallowing, as he exhaled, so
pushing the warmed, therefore stronger, peach fragrances into
the all-important nasal cavity.

COOKS' NOTES AFTER BRILLAT–SAVARIN:

The raw peach, unadorned, had been tried and found delicious. Its acidity, sweetness, and bitterness found response, favorable enough, in corresponding taste buds; the consistency and
temperature were appealing; the final perfumed flavor was delightful. What more had the peach to give? What tempting tones
of flavor might be composed about a peach? Simple tests resulted
in the following observations:

WITH A SPRINKLE OF SUGAR AND CREAM: Odor agreeable, less freshness, little acidity, sweet; whole sensation changed; cream coats peach and tongue with sweet butteriness; fat smooths sweet peachy taste and permits taste to cling longer; volatile acids in cream make flavor sensations pleasant.

WITH WHITE WINE: Perfume as usual, perhaps evaporation of wine enlivens odor slightly; freshness noticeable; sensations in mouth attractive—sweet, acid, and bitter are felt, but toned down and blended a bit by salts, sugars, and other flavoring qualities of wine; the infinitesimal amount of alcohol vaporizes in the warmth of the mouth, carrying to the nose a strong blended peachy flavor; no aftertaste.

FRUITY LIQUEUR ADDED (about 1 teaspoonful): New flavor sensation now felt; acid and bitter reduced. Greatest virtue vaporization of alcohol carrying greater flavor to the nose. Should try almond liqueur to bring out rather than suppress bitter-almond quality of peach.

LEMON OR ORANGE ADDED, WITH SUGAR SPRINKLE: Small amount of lemon or orange juice added with squeeze of oil from rind. Points up peach flavor, aromatic oil in rind blends flavors, its vapors carry flavors to nasal cavity. Would be better with added vanilla.

VANILLA, a few drops only, with above: Sweetens and blends peach flavors; opens receptors to receive tastes. Reminds of the role of irritation—even of pain—in stimulation of taste. Vanilla irritates membranes of mouth and nose, which stimulates perception of flavor, enhances odors.

WITH VANILLA ICE CREAM AND RASPBERRY SAUCE (Peach Melba): Odor lessened by cold; more appeal to eye; has acquired characteristics of sweetening, cream, vanilla; raspberry contributes interesting sweet-tartness as well as raspberry taste. Raspberry subdues bitter entirely. Aromatic oils in raspberry and vanilla—after the composition has been warmed in the mouth—greatly enhance final blended flavor with fruity highlights.

PEACH TORTE

Here the almond flavors in the peaches, in the nuts, and in the macaroons blend together to make an excellent dessert.

2 *pounds peaches*	*almond macaroons*
1 *cup flour*	*(small Italian amaretti,*
2 *cups sugar*	*if available)*
salt	*about ½ cup liqueur*
1 *lemon*	2 *tablespoons bread*
½ *cup butter*	*crumbs*
3 *eggs*	2 *tablespoons peach jam*
1 *vanilla bean or*	20 *shelled, blanched*
2 *teaspoons vanilla*	*almonds*
1½ *cups milk*	20 *pistachio nuts*

Mix together most of the flour (saving out 2 tablespoons for the custard, ½ cup of the sugar, a pinch of salt, and the grated rind of the lemon, after peeling off 1 curl to use in the custard. Add the slightly softened butter, broken into pieces, and 1 whole egg. Mix well. Shape into a ball, wrap in waxed paper and refrigerate for 1 hour. Cut peaches in halves, stone and peel; put into a pan with 1 cup of the sugar, a vanilla bean or 2 teaspoons vanilla, and water to cover. Bring to a boil and then simmer for 5 minutes. Allow to cool in syrup; chill in refrigerator. To make custard: Heat the milk with remaining sugar and a piece of lemon rind. In a bowl mix 2 egg yolks with the remaining flour; add the hot milk mixture slowly, stirring well. Pour it back into the pan; bring to a boil, stirring constantly; remove from heat and pour back into the bowl. Soak the same number of macaroons as peach halves in about ¼ cup of liqueur, make crumbs of the rest. Add the crumbs to the custard, and 2 tablespoons of liqueur. Mix well and chill.

Butter a torte pan and sprinkle it with bread crumbs, shaking the pan to cover well. Roll out the crust and spread it on the bottom and sides of the pan. Prick it with the prongs of a fork and cover it with paper weighted down with dry beans or rice. Bake in a 400-degree oven for ½ hour; cool. Put on serving plate.

Pour in custard. Take out peach halves and put a macaroon soaked with liqueur in each. Arrange the peaches hole side down on the custard, so that the macaroon is hidden. Mix 3 tablespoons of liqueur with the peach jam and brush over the peaches. Sprinkle with finely chopped almonds and pistachio nuts.

But no matter in how many different ways they are fixed, day after day, peaches will pall. Man needs variety. Neither taste nor emotion can always be held at the same level.

> And it's not in the range of belief
> That you could hold him as a glutton,
> Who when he is tired of beef
> Determines to tackle the mutton.
> But this I am willing to say
> If it will appease her sorrow,
> I'll marry this lady today,
> And I'll marry the other tomorrow.
> —GILBERT: *Trial by Jury*

In the case of the taste perceptions, they tire. After the first rapture, the delightful impression gradually fades away. Whether this phenomenon should be called "fatigue" or "adaptation," the result is the same. The nerves of the several taste receptors tire of one stimulus. They need a change, either a rest or a different stimulus, to restore sensation.

The smell of the first lilac is alluring; one cannot get enough of it; the nose buries deep into the flower as it breathes in the lovely odor. The scent fades; it has gone away—more accurately, the sense of smell has had enough lilac for the present. A strong stimulus exhausts the receptors in about two or three minutes, and recovery seems to take place in about the same time. People who are exposed to the same odor, even quite a disagreeable one, nearly all the time, at their work, for instance, get so they can't smell it at all.

A wine taster, after each wine, eats a bit of biscuit or a bite of mild cheese "to clean the palate," he says; actually it is to restore the nerves, the ability to taste wine again. Cheese tasters in Scotland take a nip of whisky between tastes.

It is doubtful if the whisky system would work at the dinner table; the chances are that the taste for both food and whisky would fade. Nevertheless, it is evident that meals should be planned, seasoned, and consumed in such a way as to keep the taste nerves on the *qui vive*.

Perhaps the Chinese, whose knowledge of food begins where all others leave off, have known this for centuries. Even ordinary dinners in the houses of families of good class include several dishes of contrasting color, texture, and flavor on the table simultaneously. Nor is the diner expected to finish one, then go on to the next; he dips, birdlike, from one to the other to appreciate the contrasts. In long Chinese banquets with as many as thirty-six courses, a delicate soup is brought out every now and then in order to clean the mouth for the next series of tastes.

This tends to argue against the French way of eating—each dish a separate course—well-illustrated by this menu given by Alice B. Toklas for an ordinary family dinner in the home of people of social standing:

Lentil Soup
Mirrored Eggs
Cold Ham with Lettuce Salad
Puree of Spinach with Croutons
Cheese
Berries and Fruit

I, myself, have been served, at one of the most famous restaurants in France, three separate courses of pâté one after another; each one was a little different, of course, and one had a thin crust around it. Nevertheless, as all pâtés are similar in texture and seasoning, they lapsed into dullness. The famous chef did not seem to know the principles of fatigue.

In a discussion of food tastes, the psychological factors cannot be ignored. It takes courage and curiosity—or a knowledgeable friend—to depart from the eating habits learned at home. In a publishing firm in Oslo I knew a young Norwegian secretary in her twenties who finally saved enough for a long-dreamed-of trip to Paris. When she came back to her beloved smøbrød and fisk pudding she was happy. "Yes, Paris was nice," she said, "very interesting. But I couldn't find anything to eat."

Although there are Frenchmen, even French chefs, who will admit that Chinese cuisine is the best in the world, there are few French people, including those rare ones who travel, who like to depart from their own habits of the table, which are to us cumbersome for everyday life.

I think of a French family I watched at a hotel in Holland where I always make my headquarters, the Hotel Heidepark, a pleasant home-away-from-home in the small centrally located town of Bilthoven. Its menus are interesting and the food good. Evidently it was well received by the French family. They—mother, father, three quite small children, and a mademoiselle—sat down to dinner a little before seven o'clock, and at a quarter to ten, when I went upstairs, they—children, too—were just finishing their fruit.

It may be true, as some say, that only psychology forms our likes and dislikes; that the pleasure, pain, or boredom associated with childhood meals makes the gourmet or the gulper of the future. The manufacturers who now mass-produce nearly all our foodstuffs attach so much importance to the psychological factors, which they call "interest" and "awareness," that they consider it uneconomical to try to interest the uninterested.

Even a few years ago it was possible to feel one's way around in this mass-production phenomenon. But it is increasingly frustrating. The grocer's shelves are stocked with so-called "gourmet dishes"—collections of expensive cocktail snacks, canned things, imported biscuits which are frequently rancid, some good jam. But attitudes such as "it doesn't pay to keep that" or "there is not enough demand" make it hard to find good wholesome foods that have taste: flour (in *large* bags) that has flavor and texture; sugars in various colors, flavors, and textures; different varieties of potatoes, labeled; good breads that go stale; fruits that have been bred for flavor instead of for shipping qualities. Small wonder that we have a nation of undernourished teen-agers!

The most hopeful sign in this rather desolate picture indicates that people—lots of people—can be interested. Although many GI's were homesick for the good old home-style cake mix, thousands of them came back having acquired tastes for all sorts of different and exotic foods, tastes which they have kept and enlarged.

Rather than spoil the fun for the rest of us, the provincial characters, like the middle-aged Viennese Babbitt that Joseph Wechsburg wrote about in *The New Yorker*, might carry their own food around with them wherever they go. He writes that on an Adriatic cruise, Mr. Qualtinger, a playwright, found the Viennese Babbitt in the deck chair next to him "complaining that he didn't like the ship's food and that unfortunately he had run out of the supply of cold homemade Wiener schnitzel and potato salad that he had brought along in jars."

3. *Salt*

Homo sapiens didn't notice his need for salt until he began to cook. Primitive man and not-so-primitive man, eating raw meat, milk and fruits, had a diet containing sufficient salt to replenish the body salts. As late as the thirteenth century Marco Polo found tribes living on a raw-meat diet in the midst of the plenty of the Mongol Empire, where standards of luxurious living were high and where highly prized salt formed a part of their financial system. Even today nomads and Bedouins do not salt their food.

Salt, therefore, is intimately associated with one of the greatest forward steps in the civilization of man—the advance from a static nomadic society to a constructive, inventive, agricultural society. Man learned to make and to use tools, he settled down to build dwellings, worked the fields, cooked his meats and added cereals and vegetables to his diet. Salt was needed now, as a preservative for the meats and as a seasoning for taste and for health. Those who lived near the sea were well off, but the peoples who had no nearby salt deposit suffered great hardship and expense. Salt became more precious than gold.

Inevitably, such a gift of the gods took on both religious and social symbolism: salt was associated with offerings to the gods;

a "covenant of salt" (Numbers 18:19) was an enduring pact; the phrase "bread and salt" in all nations represented the good life; salt became the symbol of fidelity and loyalty—"there is salt between us" is an Arab expression; a Persian phrase "untrue to salt" means to be disloyal or ungrateful; "salt as incorruptible, was the Simbole of friendship."

Salt was money; salt blocks actually were currency in some countries. The *salarium*, the allowance of salt given officers and men of the Roman army, was doubtless hauled up the Salt Road, the Via Salaria, along with the quantities of salt needed to make the *liquamen*, the seasoning that went into nearly everything the Romans ate—a sort of Roman MSG.

Now in the twentieth century there seems to be enough salt for everyone, except perhaps in parts of Africa where only the rich can afford it. But we still have the same trouble they had in the time of Matthew (5:13), the "salt which has lost its savour." Because of oppressive salt taxes, the Biblical salt was adulterated with earth—now it is cut with cornstarch. Fortunately, it is not impossible to find salt with savor; most supermarkets carry good Kosher salt, a salt with character. A salt mill with rock-salt to grind in it is nice, too. In France packages of fine sea-salt can be bought in every grocery. The satisfying taste of good salty salt is worth a little trouble.

By the time the food is on the table, it is too late to reach for the salt. Why? What does salt do to flavor? The Flavor Laboratory at Arthur D. Little, Inc., writes about the effect of salt on mashed potatoes: "Unseasoned mashed potatoes have a thin flavor composed of the following factors: raw starch, sour, earthy, peel-like, and astringent. Each of these characteristics is readily detectible because each seems to arrive separately. When salt is added, the mashed potatoes no longer have a thin flavor and their astringent quality has gone; starchiness is reduced and is no longer characterized as raw; sour, earthy, and peel-like flavors also seem to have been depressed. All this has occurred without salt having become a dominant note in the flavor impression. The net result is that flavor has become full-bodied and blended."

Someone has said that salt is what makes things taste bad when it isn't in them. The effect of salt is not to give notes of interest—highlights—but to lift the whole taste from one plane to another; it gives what the Arthur D. Little Flavor Laboratory calls "bloom," which means the sensation of a pleasantly full mouth.

My own theory is that salts, which increase the flow of saliva, then inundate the many salt buds which, though most plentiful on the sides, are all over the tongue, causing the feeling that one holds a very satisfactory, tasty mouthful. Any seasoning which drenches the whole tongue in this way would tend to spread a similarly agreeable sensation of a hearty mouthful: monosodium glutamate, another salt, does; meats, which contain their own salts, have a similar effect; sugar, appealing to the diffuse sweet buds, causes a like reaction; lemon juice and vinegar, touching acid buds which are all over the tongue, for the same reason are great seasonings too.

Although the addition of salt at the table is an insult to the cook, and can do no more than make an uninteresting dish slightly less unpalatable, nevertheless saltiness in hors d'oeuvre or coarse salt used as a topping on salt rolls opens the taste buds and piques the appetite.

4. Sugar, Honey, Molasses

Sugar and other sweets, such as honey and molasses, are indeed seasonings. They are seasonings that bring forth response from a basic sense, the sweet buds. This means, of course, sugar used not as a sweetening, but used in the same way as salt and other seasonings, only a little being added to achieve the desired result: drawing out flavor.

Sweetness works in more than one way. Most foods have some kind of sugar lurking in them—fructose in fruits, lactose in milk, maltose in grains, dextrose in grapes—often in almost unnoticeable amounts. It is a unique contribution to the taste of the whole.

The small quantity of added sugar combines with that which is part of the food, appeals to the sweet buds, and another component of the whole taste is built. Many vegetables profit noticeably from a sugar accent: the root vegetables, legumes, and corn. Also some fish and meats seem to like a taste of sugar.

The Arthur D. Little Flavor Laboratory reports the following findings on sugar as a seasoning: "In practically all cases, we have found that a low level of sucrose augments the flavor body of the food to which it has been added, even when sweetness itself is not notably increased . . . and frequently acts as a blender of flavor notes.

"Specifically, our studies have shown that sweetness and saltiness blend with each other: that sweetness reduces sourness and bitterness, that sucrose depresses metallic notes and those described as stem-like and seed-like in canned tomato juice . . . that the amine-type and indolic-type notes of shrimp can be reduced by small amounts of sugar (in the water in which they are cooked), while large quantities alter the shrimp flavor."

Although it has been grown in India for 2,000 years, sugar has been used, except medicinally, in the Western world only since the fourteenth and fifteenth centuries. Honey was the principal sweetener, and, surprisingly, in the Far East (India, China), molasses, too.

Honey is more than a sweetener. Its composition is interesting, consisting not only of sucrose but also of dextrose and fructose. Honey contains esters described by science as "rosy." From its perfumed sources come small amounts of aromatic oils and traces of acids. Only the bees can make it; so far its delicious, complicated constitution has eluded synthesis.

In the ancient recipes honey appears in seemingly odd places, though we have only the vaguest idea how much they put in; but this honey had the pungency of all outdoors. Even now, the honey from Mount Hymettus in Greece and from Provence in France holds the rich taste of herbs in the sun.

Obviously, some of the interesting honeys—basswood, buckwheat, avocado and many more—are tricky seasonings when used in place of sugar with meats, fish, or vegetables. But they are well worth a try since the aromatic oils give honey a seasoning dimension that sugar does not have, a direct contribution to aroma.

In breads, cakes, cookies, and confections, honey adds both

flavor and keeping quality. Substituted for half the sugar called for in desserts and jellies, or substituting for corn syrup in candies, honey contributes flavor and smooth texture.

Molasses was first made from sugar cane in India. Marco Polo found the Chinese making sugar and molasses by open-kettle methods. Here in the New World molasses is used principally not as a sweetening, not as a seasoning, but as a flavoring. In China and India, molasses is a seasoning, used in small amounts with meats, as in Chinese spareribs.

CHINESE SPARERIBS

1 to 1½ pounds meaty spareribs, cut almost apart
2 teaspoons salt
4 tablespoons molasses
2 teaspoons brown-bean sauce (may be omitted)

4 tablespoons (or more) soy sauce
2 cloves garlic, crushed
½ teaspoon ground cinnamon

Marinate spareribs in other ingredients a half hour or longer, turning occasionally. Broil slowly, turning once, for about 30 minutes. Makes 3 to 4 servings.

HONEY DRESSING

To 1 cup French dressing (3 to 4 parts pure olive oil, 1 part wine vinegar, salt, and freshly ground black pepper) add:

1 tablespoon honey
1 tablespoon chopped parsley

1 tablespoon chopped chives
1 teaspoon horseradish

Excellent on fruit salads—sliced orange salad, for example—and with avocado.

HONEY WITH TOMATO

A little honey or sugar on tomato brings out its flavor better than salt. Tomatoes lightly spread with honey and sprinkled generously with freshly ground black pepper are delicious.

Caramel or burnt sugar is a reliable old seasoning and coloring agent for soups, stews, goulashes, gravies, sauces, and glazes.

Sugar melts at 320 degrees. Cooled at that point it is barley sugar, beyond that it is caramel (356 to 374 degrees).

Boil 1 cup of sugar with 1/3 cup of cold water until dark brown. (Use in this stage for glazing.) Then add another cup of cold water and boil again until it acquires the consistency of thick syrup. Bottle it and use as required.

Sugars of different consistencies and colors—both for drinks and cooking—make for a pleasant variety in taste and texture—coarse beet or cane sugar for crunchy toppings, hard lumps of brown sugar for coffee and for decorating.

Foreign cookbooks often call for sugars by names unfamiliar to Americans: castor sugar is fine granulated, verifine, or berry sugar; Demerara sugar is light yellow; Barbados sugar is dark brown.

5. *The Acids*

An acid by any name—lemon juice, orange juice, verjuice, or vinegar—is a great seasoner.

Science in its joyless way asks us to believe that the primitive acid buds are for the prosaic purpose of protection from dangers. Acids save us from a danger greater than poisoning—monotony. The exhilarating response to the cleanness of the acid taste, its refreshing contrast to the ingratiating, ubiquitous sweet is pure pleasure.

Like the character of a good woman, food, too, wants the foil of acidity. The French, whose metaphors run to the kitchen, have expressed this quality in culinary terms: *"Soupe à la bonne femme,"* where the unctuousness of cream combines with the acidity of sorrel to symbolize a desirable disposition in woman.

SOUP À LA BONNE FEMME

Melt most of ½ pound of butter in a pan; put in 1 pound of sorrel (first cut into narrow ribbons, then cut slantwise the other way into diamonds) and a little salt and sauté for a few minutes on a low flame. Then pour in 4 pints of heated chicken broth and simmer for ½ hour. Beat 5 egg yolks a little and add to them, still stirring, some of the broth. Over very low heat, stirring continuously, add the egg yolks to the soup, being careful not to boil the soup. Stir in ½ cup of cream and what is left of the ½ pound of butter. Serve with hot French bread or Melba toast. Serves eight.

In New England they liked their women to have a dash of vinegar.

Scientists also write such things as "acids are tactile, not gustatory," meaning that acids pertain to the sense of touch, not to the sense of taste. This is evidently a scientist who was thirsty and who was quenched or slaked or refreshed by a glass of lemonade or orange juice, but he is not a cook.

Acid is one of the basic seasonings not because it cleans or burns or puckers up the mouth, but because the acid taste buds respond to acids in foods and have the capacity to lead flavor over quite a large surface. The vinegars usually have some aromatics of their own; the juice of citrus fruits does not. The aromatic oils of citrus fruits are in the rind.

Lemon juice is a salubrious seasoning having none of the unhappy side effects sometimes associated with salt. Those on salt-free diets have been delighted to discover how lemon juice and the other flavorsome acids also give character and fragrance to foods.

Acids have many valuable, interesting, and delightful characteristics. They do many things, chemically, to foods, but the appeal to the acid buds is fundamental, a basic block in the building of blended flavor.

One of the best illustrations of the blending-accenting aptitude of acids is its use in canapé spreads, dips and hors d'oeuvre. In these a certain amount of saltiness is good; more than a pinch of sugar is out of place. It takes an acid—lemon or lime juice or a fine, well-seasoned vinegar—to blend the ingredients and to accentuate the crisp, piquant nature so desirable in appetizers.

Any meat gravy, most especially of veal or chicken, likes a tablespoon or so of lemon or lime juice, or even a good wine vinegar. In fact, "when the lemon's lawful, but the grape's a crime," lemon can often be substituted in a recipe calling for wine as seasoning. Use instead of wine an equivalent amount of water called for in the recipe with the juice of half a lemon.

Fruit cups have more flavor if a small amount of lemon, lime, or orange juice or a mixture of citrus juices is stirred in. Auguste Escoffier, the famous Parisian chef, says all fruit ices must include both lemon and orange juices.

Many vegetables—artichokes, asparagus, broccoli, mushrooms, spinach, all leafy greens, string beans—like to be dressed with lemon butter (1 tablespoon lemon juice to ¼ cup melted butter). Potatoes seasoned with lemon juice, butter, and parsley, or a white sauce made with lemon juice, are excellent.

The seasoning appeal of sour cream, sour milk, yogurt, ricotta, for instance, is in the contribution made by their acids. The acids also are responsible for their wonderful digestibility; the acids, combining with the casein in the milk or cream, have already begun the digestive process.

Spinach, when dressed with vinegar or lemon juice, remains the good old body builder it was always thought to be. Both these acids act on the oxalic acid in spinach which is said to reduce the body's supply of calcium.

Lemon juice and vinegar cut oil in gravies, fish, fried food—the list is long! A wedge or a slice of lemon might be served with almost everything.

Acids are always welcome in salad dressings. In the mixing the acids form an emulsion with the oil, and with the fat in the egg, they make a smooth delicious sauce. There is no substitute for homemade mayonnaise, though there are some good ones on the market. With a blender it is easy, and it keeps nicely in the refrigerator.

LEMON JUICE HINTS

Lemon or lime juice "cooks" raw fish, as in South America's *seviche,* and in several Hawaiian recipes.

Lemon juice added to jams and jellies when they have finished cooking will help them to jell.

Lemon juice is a mild bleach; lemon juice and/or a piece of lemon in the water keeps mushrooms, celery, or vegetables such as artichokes from discoloring.

Lemon juice or a dash of vinegar added to boiling rice or potatoes keeps them white and fluffy.

Lemon juice or vinegar or white wine added to poaching fish keeps it white and firm.

Lemon or lime juice sprinkled on fresh fruit keeps it from discoloring when exposed to the air.

A few drops of lemon juice sprinkled on dried fruit before putting it through the chopper prevents the chopper from clogging.

Two teaspoons of lemon juice added to a cup of fresh cream turns it sour for sour-cream recipes, and two tablespoons added to a cup of fresh milk turns milk sour.

A few drops of lemon juice added to chilled cream speeds up the whipping process. A tablespoon of lemon juice added to every two-thirds cup of evaporated milk which has been chilled in the freezer speeds whipping and makes the whipped cream hold its shape longer.

Orange juice is much milder, much less acid than lemon and lime juice and vinegar. Nevertheless, it is an excellent seasoning on the same principle as the others, and worth experimenting with. The great virtue of orange with duck is that it cuts the fat, as well as blending in a wonderfully complementary flavor.

It is essential to bear in mind that there is vinegar and vinegar; a well-made, well-seasoned vinegar is a fine seasoning. The best is a true red-wine vinegar, but all pure, unsynthetic vinegars have their place as seasonings.

In citrus fruits the essential, aromatic oils are in the rind; gratings or small pieces of the rind impart delicious flavor to a dish, and carry the flavors quickly to the nose. If quite a bit of rind is wanted, and the rind is bitter, it may be blanched a few minutes in boiling water, carefully separated from the white part, and cut into strips or other shapes.

A twist of lemon or orange peel in after-dinner coffee—espresso —is a pleasant finis.

Health Hint: Lemon and orange juices are important sources of vitamin C, which helps to combat colds and other infections. Doctors are finding many incidences of scurvy, a disease caused by a vitamin C deficiency, among diet fadders and among people living alone, who often don't take the trouble to eat properly.

6. *Monosodium Glutamate*

Mei jing has long been a miracle seasoning in China, but Westerners have been a little slow about catching on. Everyone uses this wonderful seasoning without knowing it when he adds mushrooms to a dish; mushrooms were once a principal source of glutamate.

Now on grocers' shelves under many trade names—MSG, Accent, etc.—monosodium glutamate as a seasoning is so misunderstood by most cooks that many hesitate to take advantage of it.

Although there exists no flavor that is pleasing to people all over the world (orange is the most universally accepted), it is not entirely true that taste is only a matter of individual preference. There are certain principles of seasoning—that which brings out flavor—to which most people react in a similar way. Seasonings act on three senses: smell, which makes known the presence and identity of foods and is the embodiment of their flavor; taste, which excites the tongue; and feeling, which includes consistency and temperature. When the smell, taste, and feeling of a food is pleasant and appropriate, making one look forward to the next mouthful, it is generally said to have a good flavor. Monosodium glutamate acts powerfully on all three senses, with more potency than table salt (sodium chloride); its effect on odor, not yet understood by chemists, is unusually strong.

Monosodium glutamate itself has a taste that is both slightly sweet and slightly salty; it tastes like meat, like meat extract, like bouillon. Its taste is evident only when glutamate is sprinkled on solid foods or is used in excessive amounts. If used correctly as a seasoning, it cannot be tasted.

Some people object to the sensations produced by monosodium glutamate. These are the same sensations which help glutamate to accentuate the natural flavors of foods: it stimulates the flow of saliva, producing a greater sensation of succulence; more than any other seasoning it causes taste to spread more rapidly in the mouth, and sends a full-blended odor to the nose.

Monosodium glutamate has salt value. Although it cannot replace salt in foods, it usually increases the saltiness of salt. Glutamate can also have sweetening value. Again it cannot replace sugar, but it does accentuate the sweetness of small amounts of sugar. It is not good in deserts, however.

Sourness is usually reduced by glutamate, as in tomato juice, catsup, sweet pickles, and salad dressing.

Bitterness, as in spinach and liver, is often smoothed by the addition of glutamate.

Aroma in foods is extremely complex and the effect of glutamate on aroma is not yet, understood. Nevertheless, it seems to blend and to modify aromas, and to make things taste better. Sometimes it seems to suppress the rawness of cereals, the earthiness of potatoes and other root vegetables; it has an especially favorable effect on cooked carrots.

Monosodium glutamate is a super-seasoning. It acts as a blender of seasonings. It accentuates the natural flavor and blends in any other seasonings which have been added to meats, seafoods, and vegetables. Its effect on beef is unusually beneficial. The total impression of good flavor is better with glutamate than without it.

It is well to bear in mind that monosodium glutamate also accentuates bad flavors, and is best used with good, fresh foods.

Mace Tree.

SPICES

Cassia fistula

Saffron.

Nutmeg Tree,

7. Spices—Aromatics

"The bloodiest wars in the world have been fought for spices," Ford Madox Ford writes in his book about Provence. "For spices and religion, it being difficult to know which comes first. . . . The civilized races are those that use spices and cook their food, barbarism being denoted by the eating of barely singed meat or matter out of tins.

"The sequence is inevitable. A diet without spices causes indigestion. Indigestion causes religious and homicidal mania. Religious and homicidal mania are at the root of religious war.

"Of that Provence is the great exemplar. It is true that she does not grow the nutmeg nor the clove, nor yet cinnamon. But with mint, thyme, tarragon, verjuice, verbena, fennel, lime-flowers, bitter oranges, lemons, absinth—the plant, not the beverage—olives, basil, garlic, and an innumerable company of minor potherbs down to pimento and the peppers—and mustard, all growing in profusion and without cultivation over her rocks . . . the Provençal digestions are tranquilised and her populations content to stay at home."

The crusade for spices that began in the Middle Ages is like a continuous showing of a Cecil B. DeMille epic melodrama. It has everything: banners flying, masses moving. From all Europe thousands of men, in most unsuitable costumes, romantically took off to see the world—spices, religion, exploration and adventure, indigestion—any excuse would do. Some of them even used their own money. Many a Crusader did a good business turn and many an adventurer lost his life.

If spices and the new Mohammedanism—"The Infidel"—hadn't existed, the Middle Ages would have invented them. Religious ecstasies (the church tried to subdue these unwholesome manifestations), simple beheadings, and courts of love were too little outlet for the extravagant emotionalism of the Middle Ages, when, for more than two centuries, it is doubtful that one person had his foot on the ground.

The epic saga doesn't lack villains. Frail barques laden with precious pepper encounter not only tropical monsoons, but also Persian pirates. The great ships of India impressed Marco Polo as being tremendous; they held 200 to 300 mariners, 5,000 to 6,000 baskets of pepper, and fifty to sixty private cabins for merchants.

Of these ships in the harbor at Zayton (probably Amoy) in China, Marco Polo says they "bring thither spicery and all other kinds of costly wares. And I assure you that for one shipload of pepper that goes to Alexandria or elsewhere, there comes a hundred such, aye, and more, too, to this haven of Zayton, for it is one of the two greatest havens in the world for commerce." According to Marco Polo the daily consumption of pepper in the Chinese city of Kinsay (Shanghai?) alone was nearly 10,000 pounds.

Life-size heroes, too, appear on the screen as the search for sea routes to the Orient spurs seamen and adventurers to new explorations: Columbus, sailing westward to India, finds the New World, and with it allspice and red peppers. Soon Cortez will taste vanilla and chocolate, also.

Vasco da Gama, sailing under the Portuguese flag, reaches India by circumnavigating Africa; one of Magellan's ships survives the trip around the world to bring back enough spices to finance the entire expedition. Overnight little Portugal becomes one of the richest nations.

As other countries join the race, new villains flicker into the picture: sinister Arabs, sinister Portuguese, sinister Dutch, sinister British, all ready to stop at nothing to clinch a monopoly of the spice trade—money, then colonies, more money—for cloves and cinnamon, for the nutmeg and its mace, for ginger, for cubeb and spikenard and galingale and pepper; pepper was money itself.

So little did they know about their spices, only about money, that when the price of mace soared, a Dutch order went out from Amsterdam: "Burn down half the nutmeg trees and plant more mace."

It was four centuries before the struggle was over—even the young United States of America had its fling at it—and at last the contest settled down to spice trade for all.

Why the Middle Ages? Why did the wars for spices begin so late in our history?

As far as we know, spices always have been with us. The ancient world knew and desired and used spices as we do today: in food and drink, in perfumes and disinfectants, in medicines and preservatives. There was no more priceless, more welcome gift—the kings of the Orient bearing gifts to the Christ Child gave frankincense and myrrh. Myrrh included possibly nutmeg, which comes also from a myrrh tree (*Myristica fragrans*).

In the sixteenth century B.C., the first of Egypt's handsome, intelligent queens sent her dainty ships down the Red Sea to the Land of Punt. They came back loaded with the marvels of the country, "all goodly fragrant woods of God's-Land (the East), heaps of myrrh-resin, with fresh myrrh trees, with ebony and pure ivory, with green gold of Emu, with cinnamon wood, khesyt wood, with two kinds of incense, eye cosmetic, with apes, monkeys, dogs, and with skins of the southern panther, with natives and their children." (Breasted: *The Conquest of Civilization*.)

It is reasonable to suppose that the Pharaohs, with seagoing ships sailing in the same direction, brought back similar things more than 1,500 years earlier.

As the civilized world grew to include Greece, then Rome, there continued to be a regular, though slow, trade with the Orient in spices and many Oriental luxuries.

The Han dynasty in China, shortly before the beginning of

the Christian era, working for direct trade relations, sent emissaries to Rome, but they never succeeded in reaching there. There is evidence in both countries, however, that by the first century A.D. there had been some exchange—Roman glass and Greek motifs found their way to China and Korea and in Rome peaches and apricots from China beguiled the tables of the rich. Possibly emigrants, it has been suggested by historians, unsuccessful generals and diplomats, succeeded in reaching Rome from China.

With the gradual disintegration of the Roman Empire into a multitude of petty states in the early centuries of the Christian era, there no longer existed over half the known world Roman law, Roman money, Roman protection, and Roman peace, encouraging the exchange of trade and ideas.

While Europe quarreled through the centuries known as the Dark Ages, the Oriental world prospered. In 570 Mohammed was born, a gifted man who established a new religion among the Arabs. Within a few years after his death, Moslem leaders had organized the desert nomads, who now added religious zeal to the wild courage of barbarian Arabs, and had taken both Egypt and Syria away from the feeble Roman ruler in Constantinople. By 750 the Arab world extended from Spain (where it gave to Spain the highest culture it has known) across Northern Africa, Persia and Arabia to Samarkand and India. While Europe sank deeper into ignorance, the Arabs led the world in science, algebra (an Arab word), and grammar.

Obviously the Arabs held the key to Europe's spices. And these necessities of life became more expensive than ever. So, as Europe began to stir after centuries of apathy, it found a powerful new Empire, motivated by a vigorous new religion, in its way —the way to the spice-growing countries. The propaganda was easy: "Take back from the infidel; Jerusalem—and our spices," resulting in four centuries of bloodshed, the discovery of a new continent, the end of Arab power, and plenty of fragrant spices for all at a reasonable—even low—price.

The aromatics, edible plants containing aromatic oils, have been called by Grinod de la Reynière, who is described as the father of the French cuisine, the "hidden soul of cooking." It follows that, like most blessings from the spiritual realm, their cultivation has been neglected.

> The mouse that . . . trusts to one poor hole
> Can never be a mouse of any soul.
> —ALEXANDER POPE

These blythe spirits of the kitchen are, in the case of the true spices, from _tropical_ plants:

Nutmeg, seed of the fruit (about the size of a peach) of a handsome evergreen shrub;

Mace, the fleshy covering of the nutmeg;

Clove, the unopened flower bud of a magnificent tropical tree;

Ginger, the root of a perennial tropical plant, which displays a highly prized flower, its siren-scent intoxicating even sailors at sea;

Cinnamon and _cassia,_ the inner bark of an evergreen tree;

Cardamom, "grains of Paradise," the seed of a plant of the ginger family;

Allspice, the berry of a handsome tropical evergreen;

Pepper, the berry of a climbing perennial vine of the tropics;

Vanilla, the seed pods of a tropical vine; and

Turmeric, the root of a tropical plant of the ginger family.

The _herbs_ we use come from the _temperate_ zone. It is usually the leaves that hold the most aromatic oils, though it may be the seeds or roots or bulb; in some herbs, angelica, for instance, the whole plant—leaves, stem root, and seed—is aromatic.

Nutmeg and mace, cinnamon, clove, ginger, and cardamom are known as the sweet spices, not because they go well in desserts and sweet pastries, though they do, but because they carry their own sweetness. Pepper, too. Pepper, a hot spice responding to the hot receptors in the mouth, also has an endearing sweetness; possibly it is this unbeatable combination that has made it the world's most popular spice.

There are many spice blends, too, of which curry powder is the best known to us.

The aromatic oils of spices and herbs are contained in microscopic sacs, waiting to be released by heat (of the fire or of the sun) or friction (grinding, pounding, even being brushed against).

Large firms extract and refine these "essential oils," and it is in this form that most large-scale producers of foods, perfumes, etc., use them. Forty per cent of the spices now used in this country go into manufactured products—foods, perfumes, and such.

Quite obviously whole spices, ground when needed, are much more full-flavored than containers of ground spice which sit for months on the shelf.

Grinding one's own spices is a pleasure, not a duty. The busier, the poorer, the more alone one is, the more the act of grinding, the rising pungency perfuming the house as well as the meal to follow, gives not only a lot of pleasure for a penny, but the splendid aromas also revive tired spirits and stir up anticipation of things to come.

The trappings for grinding spices should be kept handy, of course. A mortar and pestle is one of the most satisfactory appliances in the kitchen. But other ways are good, too. My grandmother always kept a row of jars or canisters for ginger root, nutmeg, allspice, etc., each with its own little cloth and strainer; alongside the jars she kept a flatiron—for crushing spices only.

Nutmeg mills, like pepper mills, which have been used for years in Europe, are now available here. Pepper mills can be used to grind allspice berries, although the perfume of allspice or cinnamon or cloves being ground in a mortar is too good to miss. Dried ginger root, though not difficult, is something of a nuisance to make usable. Nevertheless, it is well to keep on hand some whole ginger for yellow tomato jam, Chinese foods (fresh ginger can be found in Chinese groceries), and many wonderful dishes. French housewives have a trick of sprinkling freshly ground cloves on the stove to eliminate unpleasant cooking odors, or freshening the house by carrying a pan with burning cloves from room to room.

For those housewives who can't be persuaded to get into the spice-grinding routine, here is a reminder that the already ground spices lose their oils, lose their fresh quality in exactly the same way that coffee does. No American housewife would keep coffee around the house for months and expect it to retain its good fresh coffee flavor; its oils evaporate and deteriorate. Ground spices are the same.

What are the properties of aromatics? What do they actually contribute to foods that they can be called the "soul of cooking"?

The pungent or perfumed oils of spices and herbs, liberated by the heat of cooking, insinuate their way among the other ingredients, helping their flavors to merge; they contribute their own fragrance, usually hardly noticeable but giving spirit to the whole; and most important, they carry the completed flavor to the nose where it will be appreciated.

Aromatics are complicated compounds, containing not only their aromatic oils, but sugars and salts, and chemicals which irritate, chemicals which soothe (clove oil has the ability to anesthetize, so it is used to deaden the pains of toothache). In keeping with Moncrieff's theory that nature tends to wrap vitamins in attractive packages, though most spices and herbs have not yet been analyzed for vitamin content, it is known that paprika contains more vitamin C than lemon juice, and it is thought that turmeric has a higher vitamin-A content than a golden carrot.

A few recipes will illustrate what a fillip of spice does to meats or vegetables.

CHICKEN À LA CONTADINE
(from Alice B. Toklas)

1 2- to 2½-pound chicken	*1 tablespoon tomato jam*
4 tablespoons butter	*A good pinch of*
½ cup sweet vermouth	*cinnamon*
	A pinch of cayenne

Cut chicken into 8 pieces; salt and pepper them. Lightly brown them in the butter over medium heat. Lower the heat, cover the pan and let them cook for 20 minutes, shaking the pan frequently. Remove from heat and pour over them the contents of the pan. Pour into the pan the vermouth and light it. While still lighted, replace the pieces of chicken. Add 1 tablespoon tomato jam, a good pinch of cinnamon, and one of cayenne. Stir the chicken for 5 minutes to heat and to coat each piece with sauce.

CHARCOAL–BROILED STEAK

3 pounds sirloin steak,   freshly ground pepper
   1½ inches thick   2 cloves garlic, sliced
1 teaspoon salt   2 branches rosemary
¾ teaspoon monosodium
   glutamate

Rub steak well with salt, glutamate, pepper, and garlic. Allow to set to absorb flavors for a half hour or longer at room temperature. Grill over charcoal; toss on the coals one branch of rosemary for each side of the steak. For a rare steak grill about 5 to 6 minutes on each side.

CUCUMBER SALAD   (Liang Pan Huang Kua)

1 cucumber   1 teaspoon chopped ginger
2 tablespoons vinegar   2 tablespoons sesame-seed
3 tablespoons soy sauce   oil (safflower oil may be
1 tablespoon sugar   substituted)

Slice cucumber very thin. Salt and refrigerate ½ hour. Pour off liquid. Add vinegar, soy sauce, sugar, and ginger. Allow to marinate for a few hours in the refrigerator and then add the sesame-seed oil. Serve in a shallow dish.

MARY GARDEN PEARS

3 large pears, peeled, cored,   2 inches vanilla bean or
   and halved   1 teaspoon vanilla
1 small box frozen rasp-   syrup (1 cup water cooked
   berries, thawed   with ¼ cup sugar)
1 tablespoon lemon juice   whipped cream
1 tablespoon orange juice   a few fresh cherries,
   sugar   stoned

Make raspberry sauce by passing raspberries combined with juice through fine sieve; add sugar. Poach pears in vanilla-flavored syrup 10 minutes. Cool. Spread sauce in a shallow dish. Place pears on sauce. Decorate with whipped cream and cherries which have been lightly sugared. Makes 6 servings.

GENERAL INFORMATION

Aromatic spices and herbs—*aroma* is the Greek word for them —should be bought from a reputable dealer who will supply spices with a rich fresh color and a strong fresh pungence. They should be pure spices, unadulterated by the addition of cheap waste products.

For best results, spices should be stored in a dry, airy space. Heat robs them of their flavor and dampness cakes spices that are already ground. The containers should be kept tightly closed in order to conserve their volatile oils.

In order to preserve the green color of herbs, they should be kept in opaque containers or in a dark closet. Whole spices and whole leaf herbs keep better than powdered ones. They should, however, be tested periodically for freshness—the nose is a keen judge.

Spices, except when they are used as *flavors* not as *seasonings,* are expected to improve the existing flavors of a dish, not to smother them. Spices and herbs have no effect on the chemical composition of foods, so they may be added or subtracted at will.

Ground spices give up their flavors more quickly than whole ones, so it is recommended that in long-cooking dishes they be added near the end of the cooking period. A good time to add ground spices is with the salt. An excellent method for this type of seasoning is to make and have ready your own spice mixture to which salt has been added. (See *Spice Blends.*)

There is no way to become a good cook overnight; the difference between a good cook and an indifferent one is a good head for seasoning. With some knowledge of the flavor values of the various seasonings, the effects they have on foods, and the responses they elicit from the taste receptors, combined with the examples given in several recipes gathered from diverse cuisines, any interested person should have the courage to make a start; it is unlikely that dinner will be ruined. Voltaire said, "Cooking is one of the arts, and the basis of all art is discipline."

8. *Allspice*

ALLSPICE (*Pimenta officinaus*). As if to make up for giving the Western Hemisphere only one true aromatic spice, nature made three spices in one. Allspice tastes like a mixture of cloves, cinnamon, and nutmeg. The powerful clove dominates, with the cinnamon a poor second and the nutmeg quality least.

Allspice is the fruit of a tropical American tree of the myrtle family, remarkably showy with shiny green aromatic leaves. The berry is picked green, and after being sun-dried for about a week, looks like a plump California-size peppercorn. Explorers of the early seventeenth century hopefully named the berry *pimenta,* Spanish for pepper. Pepper meant real money in the pocket in those days, but apparently they went back home without the new spice, because it was more than a century later before it came into popular use in Europe.

This warm, sweet spice has no history of greed, thievery, and bloodshed, and as yet only a little culinary history. Brought in from the West Indies along with the great cargoes of rum and molasses, allspice brought happy relief to Colonial housewives, whose precious store of spices from the Orient had to be kept locked up and used sparingly. And good use they made of the versatile new spice, in their pies and in Indian puddings, in spiced and pickled meats, and it helped to dress up the inevitable pumpkin:

> We have pumpkins at morning and pumpkins at noon,
> If 'twere not for pumpkins, we should be undoone.

so ran the lament of a Plimouth Colony housewife.

In Jamaica, where the evergreen allspice tree grows abundantly, the berries, mashed or whole, go into almost everything—soups, stews and sauces, and the curries, which were introduced by English settlers.

New World allspice blends well with New World foods: tomatoes, sweet potatoes and yams, the yellow squashes and pumpkins, spice cakes and pickles, and chocolate. Allspice is indispensable in mincemeat, and good with ham.

Because of the strong clove oil which dominates allspice, the whole berries will give their best effect when tied in a cheesecloth bag and used in long-cooking (pot roasts) or long-soaking (pickling liquids or marinades) dishes.

Although allspice blends pleasantly with other spices, it is well to leave out the cloves.

BOSTON BAKED BANANAS

3 apples	*2 tablespoons brown sugar*
2 tablespoons sugar	*mixed with*
1 tablespoon lemon juice	*½ teaspoon allspice*
1 teaspoon grated lemon	*2 tablespoons dark rum*
rind	*2 tablespoons water*
½ teaspoon cinnamon	*2 tablespoons butter*
4 bananas	

Wash and slice apples. Cook until soft (about 10 minutes) in as little water as possible, stirring from time to time. Put through food mill. Season with sugar, lemon juice, rind, and cinnamon. Grease a fireproof serving dish with butter. Cut bananas in halves crosswise, then lengthwise, and arrange in the dish. Sprinkle with the brown sugar-allspice mixture. Spread with apple sauce, pour on rum and water. Dot with butter. Bake in a preheated 375-degree oven for 20 minutes. Serve with whipped cream flavored with 1 tablespoon brown sugar, a pinch of allspice, 1 teaspoon rum, or with fruit sauce. Makes 4–5 servings.

FRUIT SAUCE

grated rind ½ lemon	*2 eggs, separated*
juice ½ lemon	*1 teaspoon vanilla*
½ cup orange juice	*1 teaspoon rum*
⅓ cup sugar	
pinch of salt	

Mix fruit, sugar, salt, and beaten egg yolks. Cook over low heat, stirring constantly, until thick. Add seasonings. Fold in stiffly beaten whites. Serve warm or cool.

SPICY BLUEBERRY PIE

1 cup sugar	1/4 teaspoon grated lemon rind
3 1/2 tablespoons quick-cooking tapioca	1 tablespoon fresh lemon juice
1/4 teaspoon salt	1 quart unsweetened blueberries, frozen or fresh
1/4 teaspoon ground cinnamon	2 tablespoons butter
1/4 teaspoon ground allspice	pastry for a two-crust 9-inch pie
pinch of mace	
1/3 pound white grapes, halved	

Combine sugar, tapioca, salt, spices, and lemon rind. Mix with the lemon juice and blueberries. Turn into a pastry-lined 9-inch pie-pan. Arrange white grapes over berries. Dot with butter. Top with pastry rolled to 1/8 inch thickness. Cut 2 or 3 gashes in top crust to allow steam to escape or top pie with a lattice of pastry cut into 1/2-inch strips. Bake in a 425-degree oven for 40 minutes or until crust is brown. Remove from heat. Cool before serving. Makes 6 servings.

PUMPKIN PANCAKES (from Jamaica)

3 cups mashed pumpkin	1/2 teaspoon baking powder
For each cup pumpkin:	1/2 teaspoon allspice
1/2 cup flour	1 beaten egg

Mix ingredients and beat well. Drop by spoonfuls onto pre-heated, greased griddle or into hot deep fat. Dry, sprinkle with powdered sugar, and serve at once.

9. Cardamom

CARDAMOM (*Elettaria cardamom maton*), sometimes spelled cardomon. A jewel of a spice, it is the second most expensive spice in the world (saffron comes first), so dear because every delicate little seed pod has to be snipped off the plant by hand with scissors. The yield is low, too, only about 250 pounds per acre. It is native to India, but most of our supply now comes from Guatemala.

Cardamom, a clean flowery-spicy breath sweetener, is put up by nature in handy little-fingernail-size, bleached-white capsules, each containing ten to twelve pungent black seeds, easy to fit into pocket or purse. As a member of the ginger family, it has some of the properties, but not the taste, of that invaluable plant. It is sweeter than ginger, with less edge, yet has authority. Like ginger, it awakens the whole tongue, making it, in moderation, a good ingredient in a spice blend which is to be used to bring out the flavor of *main* dishes. Like ginger, it belongs with fresh melon. Like ginger, it is good for the stomach.

Cardamom is most familiar in sweets. Fine Danish pastries and coffee cakes are frequently seasoned with cardamom, both in the dough and in the filling. In all the Scandinavian countries it has been both a favorite seasoning and flavor ever since Viking sailors first carried it home from the markets in Constantinople more than 1,500 years ago. In Norway, the Christmas season reeks of cardamom, and the Swedes consume fifty times more cardamom per capita than does the United States.

STUFFED CABBAGE ROLLS (*Kåldolmar*) with cardamom seasoned cream gravy, is a fine old Scandinavian dish. Maybe the Viking sailors also brought back this recipe for "dolma" from Constantinople.

Discard wilted outer leaves from 1 large (3 to 3½ pounds) head of cabbage; rinse and cut out the core. Put in kettle with boiling salted water to cover; cover and simmer about 5 minutes, or until leaves are softened. Carefully separate cabbage leaves and set aside on absorbent paper to drain.

FILLING

1 pound veal, ground 4 times	⅔ cup fine, dry bread crumbs
1 pound beef, ground 4 times	4 teaspoons grated onion
1¼ cups milk	2½ teaspoons salt
	1 teaspoon nutmeg

Mix together lightly in a bowl.

CABBAGE ROLLS

Place small cabbage leaf in the center of each large leaf. Drop about ½ cup of meat mixture onto center of each small leaf. (Meat mixture will drop more readily from moist cup or spoon.) Roll each leaf, tucking ends in toward center. Fasten securely with wooden toothpicks or tie with clean string.

Bring to boil in a large kettle salted water (1 teaspoon per quart) to cover rolls. Add cabbage rolls one by one so that water continues to boil. Reduce heat, cover and simmer until tender, about 20 minutes. Carefully remove rolls with a slotted spoon. Remove toothpicks or string. Place rolls in serving dish and serve with cream gravy.

CREAM GRAVY

3 tablespoons butter	½ teaspoon ground cardamom
3 tablespoons flour	
¾ teaspoon salt	2 cups hot milk

Heat butter in saucepan over low heat, blend in dry ingredients. Stir until mixture bubbles. Remove from heat. Add milk gradually, stirring constantly. Return to heat and bring rapidly to a boil, stirring constantly. Cook about 2 minutes longer. Makes about 15 cabbage rolls with gravy.

SOUR CREAM WAFFLES (Vafler)

In Norway, these tender sweet waffles are served cold at teatime (though good coffee will probably be the drink) with ham or thin slices of goat cheese (*gjietost*). Norwegian waffle irons make pretty heart-shaped waffles, but more prosaic American ones will serve.

2 *eggs, separated*	1 *teaspoon ground*
¼ *cup melted butter, set*	*cardamom*
aside to cool	½ *teaspoon salt*
1 *cup sifted flour*	1 *cup thick sour cream*
2 *tablespoons sugar*	1 *cup buttermilk*
1 *teaspoon baking soda*	

Beat yolks until thick and lemon-colored. Add melted butter, cream, and buttermilk gradually. Continue to beat until well-blended. Add liquid mixture all at one time to dry ingredients; mix only until batter is smooth. Do not overmix. Beat egg whites until rounded peaks are formed. Fold gently into batter. Bake according to waffle-iron directions.

The distinctive flavor of cardamom is like a spice blend—a perfume blend, rather—in itself. As such, it perfumes a fruit salad or a macédoine of fruits. In a vegetable salad the little seeds give contrast of texture as well as flavor. Cardamom is good with winter vegetables—sweet potatoes and squash—that like a bit of sweet and spice as accent. It shines in sweets: cookies, cakes, and pastries. Its perfumed spiciness is pleasant in pumpkin, apple, and other fruit pies.

In Indian curries, cardamom is one of the essential ingredients. Then after dinner, the Indians sensibly chew cardamom seeds to make the breath fresh and sweet again.

In India, cardamom is an indispensable seasoning. An ingredient of most curries, it also seasons vegetables, starches, yogurt, and sweets. Indians also like whole spices. Anyone who has the courage may try the following recipe for fried rice:

FRIED RICE

2 *pounds rice*	⅞ *teaspoon cinnamon*
4 *ounces onions, sliced*	½ *cup butter*
(½ *cup*)	*salt to taste*
⅜ *teaspoon cloves*	3 *pints water*
⅜ *teaspoon cardamom*	

Sauté onions in butter until golden brown. Remove. Sauté spices in the same butter until they crackle. Add rice and sauté a few minutes. Add salt and water, cover and cook until all the water has been absorbed. Serve hot, garnished with sliced fried onions. Makes 8 servings.

In Arab countries, where after-dinner coffee is almost a ceremony, a whole cardamom capsule is broken into the little cup of steaming black coffee, refreshing the room with its clean, warm aroma, and making the coffee flavor, for which it has an affinity, even more delicious.

10. Cinnamon and Cassia

CINNAMON (Cinnamomum zeylanicum) and CASSIA (Cinnamomum laurii), saved by a slight bitter-sweet authority from being insipid, are the true sweet spices.

Possibly the first spice known to man, the bark of the cinnamon tree brought such a spicy sparkle into the life of this poor creature that cinnamon became a sacred thing, to be burned at the ritual sacrifices to the gods. Still one of the fragrant spices blended in incense, cinnamon has been burned around the world for thousands of years—the biggest smell probably having been achieved at the funeral of Poppaea, Nero's unwanted second wife, when Rome's entire cinnamon supply for a whole year was burned, presumably as a show of grief.

It is not recorded that it made the slightest difference whether Poppaea's funeral rites were celebrated with Cinnamomum zeylanicum or with Cinnamomum laurii. Nowadays, however, there are people who would care. Depending on who is doing the talking, the one is better than the other.

Handsome evergreens of the laurel genus, the Cinnamomum family is large, producing trees in many shapes and sizes. Of these, the two varieties which produce all of the good cinnamon used the world over are Ceylon cinnamon (C. zeylanicum) and cassia (C. laurii).

Ceylon cinnamon, about 1 per cent of the world's supply, is

light tan in color, delicate in flavor. Mexico insists on having Ceylon cinnamon. Cassia comes from Vietnam (called Saigon cassia, the highest quality), China (not available at present), and Indonesia. Good cassia is strong in color and flavor; it is much preferred in the United States and in most of the world. Cassia is in greater supply than Ceylon cinnamon, and therefore cheaper.

What makes cinnamon—or cassia—good, better, best? The amount of essential oils and the incidence of flavor component (in this case, cinnamic aldehyde) are considered the most desirable qualities in a spice. On the average, essential oil content is as follows: Saigon—3.5 per cent; China—1 to 2.5 per cent; Indonesia—1 to 2 per cent; Ceylon—2.5 to 3 per cent. Of cinnamic aldehyde: Saigon—50 per cent; China—20 per cent; Indonesia—10 per cent; Ceylon—40 per cent. Saigon cassia has bite; Ceylon cinnamon does not.

Only cassia (*C. laurii*) grows in China. *Cassia* is the Chinese word meaning "sweet"—the true sweet spice.

It is the bark of the tree which is the spice. A cinnamon tree is rather like a birch tree with its loose bark. In a complicated system of rotation and pruning, the bark is peeled from the trees and rolled into quills, dried, and shipped. Best to use as cinnamon-stick stirrers are quills of Batavia (Indonesia) cassia, which are straight and smooth because they have been scraped.

Although it is usually cassia that one buys, we all call this delicious spice "cinnamon."

Versatile cinnamon goes from the sacrificial sublime to the breakfast table; it is the breakfast spice. Early colonists always kept a big shaker of cinnamon and sugar (called an "oomah") on the table for sprinkling on cereals, waffles, pancakes, and hot toast.

The sweetness of cinnamon responds to the sweet taste buds and its aromatic oil helps in the blending process, but generally, cinnamon is used in the Western world for the contribution its own pleasant taste gives to many dishes.

Although mostly used in fruit pies and coffee cakes and spiced drinks, cinnamon has value for other dishes as well:

A dash of cinnamon does wonders for chocolate—in ice cream or pie, devil's food cake or chocolate sauce.

- A cinnamon-stick stirrer gives a welcome lift to a cup of cocoa or chocolate.

- A piece of cinnamon stick always goes in pickles (it doesn't cloud the liquid as ground spice would) and is cooked with a compote of dried fruits. It is excellent sprinkled on fresh fruits, too.

- We have learned from the countries where spices are grown that cinnamon is good with meats and alone or with other spices lends itself to long-cooking meat dishes.

- It is a standard ingredient of the spice-salt blend which is regularly used in stews, stuffings, meat loaf, terrines, etc.

- The Pennsylvania Dutch sprinkle cinnamon and sugar on thickly sliced ripe tomatoes.

- Cinnamon and sugar sprinkled on sliced fresh oranges is good.

- A quick dessert is canned applesauce with cinnamon-flavored whipped cream and slivers of grated bitter chocolate on top.

- For tea: A half lump of sugar, sprinkled well with cinnamon, may be put in the center of small muffins, and baked.

- In an espresso, cinnamon is almost as good as cardamom.

CHICKEN FRICASSEE

3 tablespoons butter or chicken fat	*2 inches of cinnamon stick*
1 3½–4-pound chicken cut in serving-size pieces	*1 bay leaf*
	1 blade mace
2 tablespoons flour	*½ teaspoon peppercorns*
2 teaspoons salt	*4 tablespoons rice*
1 onion, coarsely chopped	*minced parsley*

Shake chicken in a bag with flour and salt. In a heavy kettle brown chicken, onion, and spices in the fat. Add 1 quart water and simmer 1½ hours, covered, until chicken is tender. After 1 hour remove spices and add rice. Sprinkle with parsley before serving. Good with hot biscuits and green salad.

CHINESE STEAMED PEARS

4 medium-size cooking pears	*8 teaspoons honey*
	2 teaspoons cinnamon

Cut off tops of pears, save to use later. Scoop out core from the center top. Do not core through the fruit. Fill the cavities with honey and cinnamon. Put the tops back on the pears and place in ovenproof individual dishes in which they will be served. Steam for half an hour or a little longer (depending on the size and ripeness of the fruit) until the fruit is cooked through. Serve very hot. Makes 4 servings.

FALSTAFF CAKES

1 cup flour	*3 teaspoons Dutch cocoa*
¾ cup butter	*½ teaspoon cinnamon*
3 tablespoons sugar	*2 egg yolks*

Work ingredients into a smooth dough on a lightly floured board (in Italy they mix it on the kitchen table). Roll into a ball and allow it to rest for about ½ hour. Roll out on lightly floured board to about ⅛ inch thickness. Cut with oval cookie cutter about 1½ inches long. Place on lightly buttered baking sheet and bake in a 350-degree oven for 10 minutes. When cold, put together like a sandwich with chocolate cream filling.

CHOCOLATE CREAM FILLING

Mix together ¼ pound slightly softened butter with the same amount of confectioners' (icing) sugar with a wooden spoon. Beat until light. When it is light and frothy beat in a heaping tablespoon of Dutch cocoa and 2 teaspoons of good rum. Before serving, powder the cakes with vanilla sugar (confectioner's sugar).

11. Cloves

CLOVES (*Eugenia caryophyllata*) are the spiciest of spices. The aromatic clove is known by a lowly nickname—"nail," a spicy nail, and moreover, the masculine clove is actually a pink, a bud of the pink family, picked before the petals unfold.

The history of cloves is the usual one of battle and bloodshed, but with a heartening twist. The natives of the Spice Islands (the Moluccas) who owned the handsome, fragile clove trees fought the Europeans for their own rights in the spice trade. They had no chance, but they tried. And today the finest, plumpest cloves of Amboisia are no longer exported; the people prefer to use them in their smoking tobacco.

The evergreen clove tree, bearing all year round the bright red blossoms of the pink, is money and life to the people of the islands. When a child is born, the parents plant a clove tree, hoping the tree and the child will grow and prosper together. The clove buds must be picked by hand one at a time, taking care for the delicate tree, and at exactly the right degree of maturity. Four to seven thousand of the dried buds make a pound. The United States now imports most of its cloves not from the Spice Islands but from Zanzibar and Madagascar.

As a spice, the virile and versatile clove contributes to every department of the menu. As a carnation—a pungent pink—it is essential in fine French perfumes. It flavors soaps and candies, medicines and fine tobaccos.

As a local anesthetic, the aromatic oil of the clove eases toothache and briskly stuns the taste receptors into paying attention to flavors. As one of the most useful spices, a little does wonders for flavor, blending even tobaccos, but too much smothers and alters the taste.

Don't be tempted to stud an onion with several cloves; one is probably enough when its pungency is released by the heat of cooking. Ham and other pork dishes can stand more. Uncooked marinades will not suffer if four or five cloves are added.

In all kinds of spicy cakes, hot drinks and punches, and spicy pickles, cloves are indispensable.

One or two cloves heated in a fruit sauce or a cream sauce—but carefully—then removed, add a subtle interest.

A good pinch of clove (perhaps $\frac{1}{8}$ teaspoonful to a cup) adds a fine fillip to chocolate. A dash of clove and cinnamon is good in apricot glaze.

A spicy sweetener of the breath as well as of the menu, cloves were known in China in the third century b.c. as the "chicken tongue spice." One of the Han emperors required his courtiers to hold cloves under their tongues while in his presence, giving them a kind of chickeny look.

Clove is also one of the essential ingredients in the spice-salt blend used for stews, stuffings, and other long-cooking dishes.

BANANA SAUCE FOR PUDDINGS, CAKE, OR ICE CREAM

2 *ripe bananas*	*pinch of cayenne pepper*
2 *cloves*	1 *teaspoon guava jelly*
1 *bay leaf (small)*	1 *cup water*

Cut up bananas. Put all ingredients in a saucepan and simmer for 10 minutes. Put through food mill or sieve. Serve hot or cold.

12. *Ginger*

GINGER (*Zingiber officinale*), a native Chinese, is known by those clever cooks to be the favorite son of the Kitchen god.

Ginger is a romantic plant. The beckoning perfume of its pure white flower leads needy man to its fabulous roots. According to Oriental legend, the flower lends some of its allure to whoever wears it. The plainest woman who understands the ways of the root of ginger will be sought by many husbands, for she will be the finest cook.

The most important seasoning, along with soy sauce, in the incomparable Chinese cuisine, slices of ginger root or, now and then, ground ginger, season every kind of food from hors d'oeuvre to sweet and fruit.

Ginger is one of the perfect examples of the power a seasoning can have. The properties contained in its ample, innocent-looking root have the capacity both to tone down and tone up the other foods in a dish; it smooths the edges, takes away the slightly raw taste from meats and vegetables and sauces, minimizes the bad points and accents the good. It acts as a catalyst; in its gingery way, it cheers every individual piece into teamwork. And although one does not actually taste it, ginger is also contributing its own zesty flavor to the whole.

Then, too, ginger acts on the tongue and mouth membranes, enlivening them and alerting them to the good flavors they are about to enjoy. And its aromatic oil fairly tosses the delicious flavor to the nose.

Most of the ginger used in the United States comes from Jamaica; it is available whole, cracked, or ground. Crystallized and preserved ginger are confections, not spices. Fresh ginger root can be bought in Chinese grocery stores. It will keep from two to three weeks in the refrigerator; even then, it only shrivels and can be restored by soaking in cold water. Dried ginger root should be rehydrated in cold water. It is best to soak it overnight. Steaming will rehydrate dried ginger root in about a half hour. These gingers, as well as ginger tea, are looked upon in ginger's native habitat as a carminative to ease an ailing stomach, just as good pediatricians recommend ginger ale today.

Ginger, of course, is familiar as a flavor in gingerbread and cookies, in pies and cakes, in pickling and meat processing and spice blends. How to use ginger knowledgeably as a seasoning has not yet been learned, however. Here are some Chinese recipes which open up new vistas:

B E E F   A N D   T U R N I P   S O U P (*Lo Po Niu Jo T'ang*)

1 pound lean beef	*2½ tablespoons soy sauce*
6 cups water	*½ teaspoon salt*
4 small turnips	*⅛ teaspoon black pepper*
3 slices ginger	

Cut the beef into 1-inch cubes, put in a saucepan with the water and bring to a boil. Skim off the scum as it rises to the top. Lower the heat and let simmer about 1 hour. Cut the turnips into cubes about the same size as the meat and add to the soup and simmer another 45 minutes. Add ginger, soy sauce, salt and pepper. When it comes to a boil again, serve immediately. Makes 6 servings.

STEAMED SEA BASS (*Chen Lu-Yu*)

1 2-pound sea bass	*1¼ tablespoons fermented*
1 tablespoon oil	*black bean, mashed*
¾ teaspoon salt	*2 stalks scallions, cut into*
1 teaspoon sugar	*1-inch sections*
1½ teaspoons sherry	*2 slices ginger*

Clean the fish but do not remove head and tail. Score both sides of the fish with diagonal slashes about 1½ inches apart. Drain the fish and dry it well. Rub the inside and outside of the fish with the oil, making sure that the gashes are well coated. Place a rack in a large pan which contains 2 inches of boiling water. Place the fish in a heated fireproof serving dish; sprinkle with salt, sugar, and sherry; cover with the black beans, scallions, and ginger. Place the dish containing fish on the rack in the pan, cover pan and turn up heat. Steam for 15 minues and serve very hot in the serving dish. Makes 4–5 servings.

JADE BELT DUCK (*Yu Tai Ya*)

1 4-pound duck	*2 tablespoons sherry*
4 cups water	*3 tablespoons soy sauce*
1 pound Smithfield ham or	*½ teaspoon salt*
prosciutto, sliced thin	*4 slices ginger, chopped*
2 bunches leeks	*fine*

Clean the duck well; cut off the tail and oil sacs and discard. Put the duck in a saucepan with about 4 cups of water or enough to cover it. Bring to a boil and simmer for 15 minutes. Remove the duck and reserve the broth. Bone the duck and cut meat into slices 2 inches by 1 inch. Wrap the ham around the meat and tie with the leek leaves; arrange attractively in a deep ovenproof dish. Add sherry, soy sauce, salt, ginger, and the broth. Place the dish on a rack in a large saucepan containing 2 inches of boiling water and steam for about 1 hour. Serve in the same dish. Makes 6 servings. (According to legend, Virginia traders learned how to make "Smithfield" ham from the Chinese.)

Hot Drink Note: Ginger in a hot drink is good on a damp evening. Ginger was kept on the shelves of English pubs, sprinkled into ale and porter, stirred with a red hot poker, and drunk sizzling hot.

13. *Mace*

MACE (Myristica fragrans houtt) always seems like a step-child; although it forms the outer coating of the nutmeg, it is a character in its own right.

The fruit which bears the mace and the nutmeg is about the size of a peach, and the fruits are so similar in structure that the peach will serve here as an example. Like the peach, there is a nut with a shell; this is the nutmeg. The next layer, which in the peach is its meat, is here the mace, fleshy, but much less thick than the meat of the peach. Then comes a fleshy husk, thicker than the fuzzy peel of a peach, which I understand the natives of the Spice Islands prize highly for use in preserves.

After the outer husk is removed, the mace is stripped off and put to dry. At that time it is a vivid red color which fades to a light orange shade in the drying process. This is called the "blade" of mace.

Although, like nutmeg, mace has a seductive sweetness, it is a bit more pungent, slightly more snappy. Its flavor is quite similar to the nutmeg, and they could be used interchangeably but for the mace's color, which is not always a virtue.

Mace peps up the taste receptors and its oil aids in blending. A blade, therefore, is a welcome addition to long-cooking casseroles, to court bouillon, or to marinades.

All fruit cups, fruit salads, and desserts of fruit, delicious as they are, taste even better for an unobtrusive sprinkle of spice, which gives the fruity flavors a lift to the nose. Mace is no exception, and for some reason it seems to do special credit to cherries.

Mace is the indispensable pound-cake spice, as it smooths the egginess of eggs and improves the taste as well as the color of the cake. It is also a pleasant seasoning for fish and vegetables.

OLD–FASHIONED POUND CAKE

(which is supposed to be 1 pound of butter, 1 pound of sugar, 1 pound of eggs, and 1 pound of flour)

2 cups butter, softened	*8 drops of rose water,*
2 cups sugar	*or*
9 eggs	*2 tablespoons brandy*
1 teaspoon vanilla	*4 cups sifted cake flour*
1 teaspoon ground mace	*½ teaspoon cream of tartar*
	½ teaspoon salt

Cream butter thoroughly. Add sugar gradually, creaming until light and fluffy. Beat in vanilla, mace, and rose water. Resift flour with cream of tartar and salt. Sift in dry ingredients gradually, blending well. (Use lowest speed of electric mixer.) Pour into 2 loaf pans. Grease only the bottom of the pan and flour it lightly, or line pan with heavy waxed paper. Place in a cold oven. Set control at 325 degrees and bake for 1 to 1½ hours, or until cake tester inserted in the center comes out clean. Leave in pan at least 20 minutes. Turn out on wire cake rack to finish cooling. Store in tightly closed tins.

POTAGE CRÉCY

3 cups sliced carrots	*⅛ teaspoon freshly ground*
1 cup diced potatoes	*black pepper*
6 cups chicken stock	*2 tablespoons butter*
1 teaspoon salt	*minced fresh parsley*
¼ teaspoon ground mace	*cooked carrot rings*

Cook carrots and potatoes in stock until tender, about 25 minutes. Press through sieve. Add seasonings. Serve hot, garnished with minced parsley and a few cooked carrot rings.

LAMB TONGUES IN MADEIRA SAUCE

6 *lamb tongues (1 per person)*	1 *teaspoon salt*
1 *bay leaf*	4 *tablespoons butter*
small blade of mace	½ *clove garlic*
sprigs of parsley and	4 *tablespoons flour*
celery	2 *cups retained stock*
	2 *tablespoons Madeira*

Cover the tongues with water. Add the spices and salt. Bring to a boil and simmer for ½ hour. Take the tongues out of the stock and trim the necks if necessary. Drain and cut into slices. Sauté these in butter with the garlic. Brown the flour in the butter, stir in stock to make a smooth sauce. Add the Madeira. Strain the sauce over the tongue. Serve with boiled rice.

CHERRY FLAN

1 *8-inch pastry shell*	½ *cup finely ground almonds*
1 *quart stoned cherries*	2 *eggs*
¾ *cup sugar*	3 *tablespoons jelly (goose-*
½ *teaspoon mace*	*berry, currant, apricot)*
6 *tablespoons softened butter*	*for glaze*
6 *tablespoons sugar*	1 *teaspoon rum*

Allow cherries, sugar, and mace to soak together ½ hour. Fill pastry shell with the cherries. Mix together the butter, sugar, almonds, and eggs and cover cherries with the mixture. Cook in a 375-degree oven. After the flan is cool, glaze with the jelly and rum which have been melted together.

PASTRY SHELL

¾ *cup all-purpose flour, sifted*	¼ *teaspoon baking powder*
pinch of salt	¾ *teaspoon cinnamon*
1 *tablespoon sugar*	¼ *cup butter*
	1 *egg, beaten*

Sift flour with dry ingredients. Work in butter with pastry blender. Lightly work in egg with the finger. Roll out on lightly floured board. Line pan with the dough. Fill with above mixture and bake.

14. *Nutmeg*

NUTMEG (Myristica fragrans houtt) is a charming, seductive spice, welcome everywhere. A small amount of charm is sufficient; in this case too much *Myristica fragrans,* like so much of the contents of kitchen and bathroom shelves, is good in small doses, poisoning in quantity.

The sturdy nutmeg tree, which yields its fruit for more than fifty years, is a tropical island plant; it likes to smell the sea, they say. The fruit is picked by means of long poles to which a basket (called a *gai-gai*) with prongs is attached. Like cranberries, nutmegs are tested for soundness by bouncing them.

The musk-nut's seductive perfume (in Latin and Italian it is *noce moscata,* literally "nut of musk") is enlivened by a bitter bite which hits the back of the tongue at the end of a taste. It is a most sophisticated and indispensable seasoning. Not only has it a strong, sweet aromatic quality, but its great virtue is that it plays with different taste buds, blending sparkle and contrast into foods.

Its sweetness blends with and its bitterness gives a snap to bland custards and light sauces. Nutmeg is a great favorite with chefs trained in the French school, possibly because what they consider their finest seasonings are in quite a low key. The best-trained chefs tend to look down on much of the heartily seasoned regional cooking in France and elsewhere.

Actually, the French, who had little to do with the battle of the centuries for spices, use them very little. They season with herbs grown in France. Alice B. Toklas tells of a pumpkin pie, similar to ours except for the omission of spices and currants, which is made in the Bugey region of France. (Do we put currants in pumpkin pie?) The farmer's daughter who brought the pie, when questioned about this, said that they did not grow spices, it was not hot enough, and that their grapes were not suitable for drying and becoming currants. They never *bought* any provisions except coffee and sugar.

The Dutch, whose lives were dug so deep into the East Indies and into the spice trade, are great users of spices (but not so familiar with herbs). Mace is used frequently in Dutch dishes, and a bit of nutmeg goes into everything. One never expects a Dutch vegetable to appear at table without its sprinkling of nutmeg.

Nutmegs had such value in Colonial times that they were sold as charms at county fairs. According to legend, Connecticut, the Nutmeg State, is so named because of the capacity of slick Yankee traders to sell a wooden nutmeg for the real thing.

The most useful nutmeg recipe yet to come to light is a gypsy one: Cut a whole nutmeg in four parts. Bury one segment in the earth; throw one on the fire; throw one in the water; and boil the fourth. Drink the nutmeg brew and carry the boiled segment around for a few days, sleeping with it under your pillow, and your wedding knot will never slip.

One nutmeg, grated, yields about 1 tablespoon.

Nutmeg is an essential ingredient of spice blends, both sweet and salt. A grating of nutmeg goes into almost everything, but the nutmeg flavor should not be apparent.

VEAL KIDNEY PIE (*Hertford*)

2 or 3 *veal kidneys with a little of their fat*
1 *tablespoon chopped parsley*
½ *teaspoon thyme*
1 *small bay leaf*
⅛ *teaspoon cloves*
1 *teaspoon nutmeg*
2 *tablespoons chopped celery*
salt and pepper
4 *hard-cooked eggs, sliced*
½ *cup bread crumbs*
¼ *cup dry white wine*
stock to cover
1 *crust short pastry*

Mince kidneys and fat. Add seasonings. In a deep pie dish put kidneys, sliced eggs, and bread crumbs in layers. Add wine and stock to cover. Top with pastry crust which is well-pricked to allow steam to escape. Bake in a 350-degree oven for 2 hours. Makes 4 to 6 servings.

15. *Pepper*

PEPPER (*Piper nigrum*), whose hot sweet bite lights up three meals a day, has sparked many a conflagration in the more than five thousand years of its peppery history. To know it is to love it; that's the trouble.

The world's most desired spice grows on a perennial climbing vine; its clusters of red berries look like currants both before and after they are dried.

Black and white pepper come from the same berry. For black pepper, the 14-to-1 American favorite, the berry is picked before it is fully ripe. The resulting dried berry is the familiar little black peppercorn, which is black outside and white inside. White pepper is the mature berry with its outer husk removed. The slightly milder white variety is preferred by European cooks, though all the world thinks it is hot stuff.

The Malabar Coast of India produces most of the world's pepper; the names of its many varieties roll off the tongue like the beats of a Kipling recessional: Alleppey, Calicut, Tellicherry. Sarawak supplies about seventy per cent of all white pepper.

Pepper is a masculine, no-nonsense spice. Like the ideal man, it is stimulating yet surprisingly sweet. It stings the hot receptors while soothing the sweet buds, then goes on to help the alimentary canal do its work of converting food into energy.

Though pepper is a universal favorite, it is not true that everyone knows it. Those whose only knowledge of pepper comes from the little containers of quite irritating dust have no idea of its delicious flavor. To grind fresh pepper from a good-looking pepper mill is the way to get the most good out of a peppercorn. When a pepper mill seems cumbersome in the kitchen, the excellent, coarse butcher's grind, called "mignonette pepper" in Europe, is delicious.

According to the great chef Louis Diat, good pepper is a great corrective, valuable for adjusting seasoning at the last minute. From hors d'oeuvre to cake, pepper is needed to stimulate, to blend, to contribute its peppy aroma. It also relieves the dullness of salt-free diets.

Whole peppercorns release their flavors slowly. They are essential in all long-cooking dishes, marinades, and court bouillon. Usually they are tied in a little cheesecloth bag with other seasonings, but many people like to bite into a nippy peppercorn.

Ground pepper spread on rugs or woolens is said to be an effective moth repellent, one that might be equally effective against burglars.

STEAK AU POIVRE

3½ pounds sirloin steak, cut 1½ inches thick	3 tablespoons butter
4 teaspoons coarsely ground black pepper	2 tablespoons olive oil
	¼ cup brandy
1 teaspoon salt	½ cup dry white wine
	2 tablespoons cream
	1 tablespoon butter

Slash fat edges of steak at 2-inch intervals so edges will not curl during cooking. Rub and press coarsely ground black pepper into both sides of steak. Sprinkle lightly with salt. Heat butter and oil in heavy skillet over high heat. Add steak and sear on both sides. Cook 6 to 7 minutes on each side, depending on the degree of rareness desired. Remove meat to serving platter. Add 1 tablespoon butter and scrape pan. Add white wine and cream to pan; boil briskly, scraping meat juices into the sauce, until reduced by two-thirds. Add brandy to pan; heat and light it and pour over steak. Makes 6 servings.

16. Saffron

SAFFRON (Crocus sativus), aromatic, edible gold, is, like the hard currency kind of gold, costly. It is worth its weight in gold, but this gold will grow easily in one's own backyard. The saffron crop comes from a beautiful flower, the daintily charming, purple-violet autumn crocus with a showy orange stigma.

There is a catch: to harvest one pound of saffron, you have to grow 75,000 pretty autumn crocuses. Worse still, somebody has to pick out from each crocus three golden stigmas, 225,000 of them to a pound. These stigmas are the saffron whose unique flavor—clean, distinguished, pleasantly bitter—perfumes and colors holiday cakes and breads, as well as many of the world's best rice dishes—hearty arroz con pollo, festive paella, incomparable bouillabaisse.

No wonder the dealers who adulterated saffron were in simpler times burned at the stake.

Americans have been missing the most important use of saffron, regardless of expense. Cookbooks of the fourteenth and fifteenth centuries show that more than half of the recipes contain saffron, no doubt because saffron gives a lift to the spirits. Francis Bacon said, "It maketh the English sprightly"; Christopher Catlan wrote, "The virtue thereof pierceth to the heart, provoking laughter and merriment." Such old names in England as "Saffron Hill" and "Saffron Walden" remind us that the English cultivated many of the pretty flowers that lifted the spirits. Gilbert White's *Natural History of Selborne* asks:

> Say, what impels, amidst surrounding snow
> Congeal's, the CROCUS flaming bud to grow?
> Say, what retards, amidst the summer's blaze,
> The AUTUMNAL BULB, till pale declining days . . .

It is worth knowing that saffron has an endless number of virtues. In ancient times the Babylonians, Romans, and Greeks used saffron as a flavoring, as a perfume, and as a dye; the ladies tinted their hair with it. An extract of saffron and wine was sprinkled on the streets, in the theaters, and in the baths of ancient cities.

Although saffron is of great significance in India, its use is more discreet. The top band of color on the flag of India is saffron gold, signifying courage, sacrifice, and the spirit of renunciation. Hindu monks wear saffron robes.

Most of the today's saffron comes in the form of dried stigma. This should be powdered before using in that most wonderful of utensils, the mortar and pestle. Only a small amount of the precious stuff is needed to color and season a surprisingly large amount of food. About ¼ teaspoonful will take care of three or more cups of food—one cup of rice and two cups of liquid, for instance; or two cups of flour and one of milk; one chicken with rice and two cups of broth. The saffron should be dissolved in liquid, preferably hot, or in hot fat. When adding to bread and cake, saffron may be mixed with the sugar, then dissolved in milk. Scandinavians heat the saffron-sugar mixture in the oven before mixing with liquid.

In Scandinavia, especially in Sweden, Santa Lucia's Day is made much of. On the morning of December 13, the day that marks the beginning of the Christmas holidays in Sweden, one of the young girls of the household, dressed in the traditional white robe, red girdle and stockings, and wearing a crown of evergreen leaves and lighted candles, brings saffron cakes and coffee to all the bedrooms of the house.

SANTA LUCIA SAFFRON BUNS

1 cup milk	1 package dry yeast
1 teaspoon saffron	about 3½ cups sifted flour
½ cup butter	1 egg, well beaten
⅓ cup sugar	2 tablespoons boiling water
1 teaspoon salt	raisins

Crumble saffron and dissolve in 2 tablespoons boiling water. Set aside to cool to lukewarm. Scald milk and combine with butter, sugar, and salt in a large bowl. Soften yeast in lukewarm water. Add yeast, egg, saffron to milk mixture and as much flour as can be stirred into the dough. Turn out on floured board; allow to rest 5 minutes, then knead. Place in greased bowl; brush top with cooking oil; cover with a clean towel and let rise in a warm place, out of drafts, until double in bulk. Punch down and allow to rise again. Turn onto lightly floured board and form into Santa Lucia buns in this way: Break off pieces of dough and roll into strips 4 inches long and ½ inch thick. Roll a coil from each end toward the center of strip. Place two coiled strips together so that coils are back to back. Press one on top of another to make a pinwheel shape; or coil ends in opposite directions. Place one raisin in the center of each coil. Place on greased baking sheets. Cover and let rise again until doubled. Bake at 375 degrees for 15 to 20 minutes.

PAELLA

PAELLA (pronounced *pah-ay-uah*), probably Spain's most famous dish, has a legend explaining its origin. A warrior, returning from the wars, hadn't eaten for days. On his way home he shot some game, fished a bit, and gathered a few vegetables. All these he took to his wife and told her to cook them together at once as he was starving. She complained but complied, added rice to the mixture, and so served to her man the first paella.

Ideally, paella should be made in large quantities. In Spain it is a favorite for large informal gatherings, such as country weddings, and should be eaten, it is said, with a wooden spoon, good health, and a good appetite.

Paella, native of Valencia, has long been made all over Spain, the recipes varying from town to town, the principle always the same: meat and fish mixed with rice, vegetables, and seasonings. Plump, pearl rice is excellent in this dish. Saffron is nearly always added to the rice, though many families who cannot afford solid-gold saffron substitute a cheaper yellow seasoning making the finished fare a great flat pan of golden rice, liberally interspersed with succulent morsels. The top is decoratively finished with red pepper which has been fried a minute in oil, shrimp, green vegetables, and mussels or clams in their open shells.

A lovely young woman from Barcelona, Gloria Rubiol, tells how to make paella. Her native Catalonia (somewhat north of Valencia, the home of Paella) is a cosmopolitan district which has been influenced by most of the Mediterranean peoples— Arabic, Italian, French, Greek.

In the Catalan language, the "paella" is really the saucepan in which the food is prepared and served. It is a large, round, quite flat, hand-wrought-iron pan with two handles. A pan of this shape with little depth allows the liquid to evaporate easily, leaving the rice exactly right: dry, not overcooked, not soupy, but nevertheless impregnated with oil.

The ingredients in a paella should never be extravagant or elaborate, or materials foreign to Spain. In Spain paella sometimes might contain several different kinds of meats, fish and vegetables, including such things as tuna fish, mushrooms, olives and capers, perhaps for a holiday meal. For everyday eating that would be too expensive. There is usually chicken (or rabbit), sausage for flavor, a bit of pork to make it tasty, perhaps the liver of the chicken, mussels or clams, shrimp (lobster is both sophisticated and expensive), green beans, and strips of pimento. And onions, of course. In Miss Rubiol's home they often use green peas instead of beans, but her aunt in Valencia is shocked at this departure.

In the paella the meat is browned in olive oil; then the onion (and usually a little garlic) is added and cooked slowly for about 5 minutes. The rice is now added to the pan and browned in the oil. Then the tomatoes and the beans (or other vegetables), which have been partially cooked, and the hot liquid are added. The liquid can be from vegetables or fish or chicken stock. A tiny bit of saffron is mixed into the hot water before it is poured into the pan. The amount of liquid should be 2 to $2\frac{1}{2}$ times the amount of rice.

Scrubbed mussels or clams may be put on top to cook with the paella, or they may be put on, already cooked, before serving. All is simmered very slowly, either on top of the stove or in the oven. (In the country there are no ovens in the houses.) The whole is cooked for about $\frac{1}{2}$ hour. The rice should be dry and tender on top, but slightly sticky on the bottom. Let it stand for 5 minutes before serving to allow it to set. Decorate with cooked mussels or clams, shrimp and/or crayfish and lobster in their shells. Quarters of lemon, which each person will squeeze onto his helping, edge the plate.

Eat it all. The Spanish are very particular about their rice and think that the rice in leftover paella would be inedible. In fact, before adding the rice to the rest of the preparation, the cook asks, "At what time do you want to eat?" Otherwise, "*Se pasa el arroz*," a somewhat slangy way of saying that the rice will have passed its best.

Red wine in a typical Spanish *porròn*, which looks like an un-usually fancy glass utensil from the chemistry lab, adds a festive note when paella is served.

17. *Turmeric*

TURMERIC (*Curcuma longa*), by its Arab name, Curcuma, would have no smell at all; this is named for its color, the bril-liant orange hue that has been used as a dye since centuries before Christ. It is as a member of the illustrious family *Zingiberaceae* (ginger) that it has made its name as an excellent but, in the Occident, a much neglected spice.

Although turmeric is familiar to us only as an ingredient in chowchow, prepared mustards, and chili powder, it is a season-ing of great interest and character which deserves closer attention. Marco Polo had never seen the turmeric root and was much im-pressed by it: "There is also a vegetable which has all the prop-erties of the true saffron, as well as the smell and the color, and yet it is not really saffron. It is held in great estimation, and being an ingredient in all their dishes, it bears, on that account, a high price."

It is similar to saffron in both color and its delightful clean bitter quality, so useful and rare in aromatic seasonings. While it is less delicate than saffron, as a member of the ginger family its valuable aromatic oil may be expected to give an outstanding performance as a stimulant and blender, as well as adding its own characteristic, the light bitter fillip at the finish.

Many Indian dishes combine all the ginger family—ginger, cardamom, and turmeric—so acquiring sweetness, bite, and bitter-ness, as well as an unusually fine aromatic quality. Many other Indian recipes, however, call for only a pinch or two of turmeric, thereby gaining color and a hint only of final interest—most often with delicate fish or vegetables.

With this background knowledge an interested cook should be able to put together an exciting range of newly flavored dishes, as well as the old ones, like rice dishes, saffron style.

CHICKEN SALAD

3 cups diced cooked
  chicken
1¼ cups diced celery
2 teaspoons salt
½ teaspoon poultry
  seasoning
1 teaspoon ground
  turmeric

⅛ teaspoon ground black
  pepper
1 tablespoon lemon juice
4 tablespoons mayonnaise
  lettuce
  ripe olives

Lightly toss together chicken, celery, salt, poultry seasoning, turmeric, pepper, lemon juice, and mayonnaise. Serve on bed of lettuce. Garnish with ripe olives. Makes 4–6 servings.

MASALA FISH

2 pounds fish fillets
¾ teaspoon crushed red
  pepper
1 tablespoon mixed garlic,
  ginger, and coriander,
  ground together

1 pinch turmeric
1 lemon—juice only
  butter (in India, clarified
  butter would be used)

Smear spices and lemon juice on fish. Sauté in butter on both sides until light brown. Serve at once. Makes 6 servings.

MURGH MUSALLAM

1 4- or 5-pound chicken,
  cut into pieces
  1-inch piece ginger
1 medium clove garlic
1 large onion
  butter
1 teaspoon turmeric
1 teaspoon cumin seed
  2-inch piece of cinnamon

4 cloves
  crushed red pepper to
  taste
2 cardamoms
1 teaspoon salt
5 large tomatoes, skinned
  and cut into small pieces
1 tablespoon molasses

Grind the ginger, garlic, and onion and rub into the chicken pieces. In a heavy pan brown chicken lightly in butter, add spices, tomatoes, and molasses. Add water to cover. Dot generously with butter. Cover pan tightly and cook on slow heat until tender, about 1½ hours. Serve with hot boiled rice. Makes 6 servings.

Note: Indians like to bite on whole spices. For Western tastes the whole spices should be tied in a cheesecloth bag, or if preferred, crushed in a mortar before adding to the dish.

18. *Vanilla*

VANILLA (*Vanilla planifolia*) is the Queen of Seasonings. Symbolized by the rare and beautiful lime-yellow orchid from which the fruit grows, vanilla is truly regal—majestic in influence; a sweetly benign sovereign, soothing here, strengthening there, promoting harmony for the whole.

Vanilla makes sweet sweeter; fruits more fragrantly good; brings out the flavor of chocolate and coffee; tames the taste of flour and of eggs; tones down the aggressiveness of acids; smooths the rough edges of flavor and blends them into the other ingredients.

A native of Mexico, this temperamental, handsome plant with the heavy shiny leaves of the orchid is now grown in many hot countries. Its exquisite blossom that lasts but a day gives way to the fruit, a cluster of long green pods, the vanilla bean. The finest vanilla beans still come from Mexico and Madagascar, however, the latter contributing about three-fourths of the world's vanilla beans. So valuable are these beans that they are branded by a pattern of pinpricks by each grower to prevent bean-rustling.

More precious than all the gold he plundered, vanilla and chocolate made their first voyage to Europe together with Cortez. It was in Mexico, Aztec empire of Montezuma, that the Spaniards first tasted a delicious drink made from the fruit of the cacao tree, chocolate, and the bean of *tlilxochitl* (black flower), which the Spaniards called *vainilla,* meaning "little scabbard."

"The favorite beverage was the *'chocolatl'*," William Prescott tells us in *The Conquest of Mexico,* flavored with vanilla and different spices. They had a way of preparing the froth of it so as to make it almost solid enough to be eaten, and drank it cold. An old Spanish soldier in his memoirs stresses the importance of "opening the mouth wide, in order to facilitate deglutition, that the foam may dissolve gradually, and descend imperceptibly, as it were." It was so nutritious that a single cup of it was enough to sustain a man through the longest day's march, the soldier claimed.

According to Prescott, this delicious beverage was so popular that 2,000 jars of it were allowed daily for Montezuma's household. "The Emperor took no other beverage than chocolatl, a potation of chocolate, flavored with vanilla and other spices, and so prepared as to be reduced to a froth of the consistency of honey, which gradually dissolved in the mouth. This beverage, if so it could be called, was served in golden goblets, with spoons of the same metal or of tortoise-shell finely wrought. The Emperor was exceedingly fond of it, to judge from the quantity—no less than fifty jars or pitchers being prepared for his own daily consumption!"

What a day it was when Emperor Montezuma's favorite drink was introduced in Spain! A craze for the new drink swept Europe. Brillat-Savarin tells us that Spanish ladies were not content to drink "chocolate caliente" several times a day at home, but even had to have it served to them in church.

Hot chocolate is still Mexico's favorite drink and the decoratively carved utensils that are rolled between the hands to fluff up the famous froth are almost too pretty to use. A prosaic rotary beater does quite a good job with this excellent recipe.

MEXICAN HOT CHOCOLATE

6 squares Mexican chocolate or
4 squares (1 ounce) chocolate and
1 teaspoon cinnamon
4 tablespoons sugar

1 teaspoon vanilla
6 cups milk
1 egg

Grate chocolate and dissolve in ½ cup scalded milk. If American chocolate is used, add cinnamon and sugar, as Mexican chocolate has cinnamon in it. Add the rest of the milk. Bring to a boil and boil about 2 minutes. Beat egg and vanilla in a large bowl and continue beating while pouring in chocolate. Return to the fire; heat but do not boil, beating with *molino* or egg beater. Beat to a froth before serving each cup.

It seemed an eternal marriage—chocolate and vanilla. For generations they were always used together until Queen Elizabeth I's apothecary, a man named Hugh Morgan, suggested that vanilla be tried alone, as a separate flavoring. So here begins the success story of vanilla, the world's prize flavor. And chocolate?—chocolate still needs its vanilla.

Vanilla is said to be the world's most popular flavor. But it is when you don't taste the vanilla that this unique gift of nature is doing its best work. The small bottle of vanilla extract that stands in most cupboards is destined to be measured out, teaspoon by teaspoon, into cakes and puddings. But it goes into many kinds of puddings and cakes, not only vanilla desserts; it goes into chocolate and cheese cake, with mocha and spice, banana or lemon. A little vanilla is added because the recipe calls for it.

When you understand the part that is acted by "one teaspoon vanilla" in a cake, a whole new cookbook comes into your kitchen, one that you may write yourself. Vanilla smooths the raw taste of flour and tones down the egginess of the eggs, but it doesn't stop there. It makes the sugar sweeter, the fruit fruitier while softening its acidity; it makes the chocolate give out all it's got. And it blends all the flavors into one harmonious cake.

Asking special climatic conditions, painstakingly pollinated by hand, cared for and even harvested by experts, cured by a lengthy, exacting process requiring many months, the vanilla bean, when at last well matured, aromatic, delicate, and mellow, can be compared to a fine wine. The most and best vanilla flavor is trapped in the vanilla pod, and many of the finest cooks still prefer to use the bean itself, rather than the extract.

Few American children have ever seen the funny, shriveled brown bean, nor lifted the lid of a cookie jar to sniff the fragrant goodness of spice and apple and vanilla, for buried deep in the jar is a tart apple to keep the cookies fresh and a piece of vanilla bean to accent the sweet-smelling contents.

Combining quality and economy, the best and surest way to buy vanilla is to buy the bean itself. Many pharmacies and specialty food shops carry beans, or they can be ordered from L. A. Champon & Co., Inc., 230 West 41 Street, New York 36, N.Y.

There is a lot of mileage in one 10-inch vanilla bean. Either whole or cut in pieces, it can be used, washed, and used several times.

You will discover that the bean retains its bouquet through months of use. Never throw away a vanilla bean; it is good to the end. When it really dries out, and doesn't come back in infusions, it is excellent grated to flavor custards and cakes, ice cream, fruit cups—even hot cereals. The little black speckles seldom detract from the looks of a dish.

Those who didn't learn at Grandma's knee how to use whole vanilla bean, now have a hard time finding directions:

Vanilla beans should be kept in a clean, airtight glass container. Vanilla sugar, easy to make and to have on hand, is one way to season with the whole bean. Put one or two beans in a sugar canister and let the fragrance permeate the sugar for a couple of weeks. If the bean is split lengthwise, it works faster. Many pounds of sugar can be flavored with the same bean or two.

Vanilla sugar has a strong flavor and should be used with care; part vanilla sugar and part unflavored sugar may be used in a recipe. Bear in mind also that vanilla makes sugar sweeter. In Escoffier's recipe for sweetened whipped cream (*Crème Fouettée*), vanilla sugar is only one-fifth the amount of sugar called for. Escoffier's authoritative chocolate sauce adds only one heaping tablespoon of vanilla sugar to one-half pound of chocolate!

An infusion of the vanilla bean and the liquid to be used in a recipe makes a smooth, well-mixed seasoning. The liquid—milk, for instance—is brought to a boil; the vanilla bean is added as the milk is taken from the fire and allowed to infuse for ten minutes or more, depending on the strength of the flavor wanted. A decided taste of vanilla is wanted in vanilla ice cream, for example, so a twenty-minute infusion is suggested.

A sugar syrup is often used for many desserts and ices. Vanilla, infused into this syrup, especially when the syrup is to be mixed with cooked or fresh fruits, heightens the natural flavor of the fruits.

Rice to be used for desserts is frequently infused with vanilla bean, orange and lemon peel.

In the West Indies a vanilla essence is made by soaking two or three vanilla pods in a half pint of rum. A strong essence is recommended as being more economical, as less will be required for flavoring.

Vanilla beans may be split to extract quicker flavor. Small pieces may be split and scraped; in this case, of course, they cannot be used again.

DESSERT RICE (*Escoffier*)

2 cups rice	4 egg yolks
1 cup sugar	1 vanilla bean
pinch of salt	peel of 1 lemon or orange
3 cups milk	3 tablespoons butter

Bring milk to a boil. Remove from fire and add sugar, salt, butter, vanilla bean, and peel. Allow to infuse 10 minutes, or more if desired. Remove vanilla bean and peel. Wash rice well. (Escoffier recommends blanching it by dipping it in boiling water, then rinsing again in tepid water.) Put rice and milk in covered casserole in a moderate oven. Cook without touching for about ½ hour until milk is absorbed and rice is cooked. Remove from oven; cool slightly, and add beaten egg yolks, mixing carefully with a fork in order to leave rice grains whole. The rice is then ready for any number of delicious desserts.

SAUCES FOR DESSERT RICE

APRICOT SAUCE

½ cup apricot jam   1 teaspoon vanilla
1 tablespoon butter   ½ cup brandy
½ cup water

Put jam, butter, and water on the fire and bring to a boil, stirring constantly. Add brandy and cook 2 minutes more. Remove from heat and beat in vanilla.

CARAMEL SAUCE

1 cup sugar   1 stick cinnamon
1 cup water   1 teaspoon grated lemon
1 tablespoon sherry   peel
¼ teaspoon ground cloves   ½ teaspoon vanilla

Put the sugar in a saucepan and let it melt and brown to a golden yellow. Add the other ingredients and boil 3 minutes. Remove cinnamon stick and stir in vanilla. Serve hot or cold.

CREAM SAUCE

1 pint heavy or all-purpose   1 teaspoon grated nutmeg
  cream   1 teaspoon vanilla
2 tablespoons powdered   1 teaspoon sherry or
  sugar   Madeira

Boil cream and sugar together until it thickens. Remove from fire and beat in nutmeg, vanilla, and wine. Serve warm or cold. Excellent also on stewed fruits.

PUNCH SAUCE

½ cup cognac or rum   grated rind of ½ lemon
½ cup powdered sugar   1 teaspoon vanilla
  grated rind of ½ orange   juice of 3 oranges

Put in a saucepan the cognac or rum, sugar, grated rinds, and vanilla; heat and set alight. Cover tightly and let ingredients infuse for about 2 minutes. Add the orange juice. Serve very hot.

A piece of vanilla bean is often cut off to season a small amount of liquid. The following proportions are reasonable suggestions (practice will soon tell if you prefer more or less): one inch to one cup; two inches to one pint; a half bean to one quart. The cut piece of bean is then washed, dried, and stored again.

It was the French, of course, who discovered that vanilla is far more than a flavor. They have long let it work its miracles as a blender and a booster. For generations the wisest French and Italian chefs have used vanilla to bring out the best in fruit. The vanilla serves only as an accent, not as a flavor. It accents the natural fruit sugars and flavors while toning down the acidity.

French cooks add a little vanilla when making jams and jellies; one-quarter to one-half teaspoon of vanilla for fruit pies; about one-half teaspoon for four cups of rhubarb; in fruit sherbets, fruit sauces; applesauce, fresh or canned; in fruit cups; fruit salad dressing; fruit molds; on broiled grapefruit; in grape stuffing for duck, or other fruit stuffings; in lemonade and fruit punches. It underscores the flavor of mincemeat.

Vanilla has a hidden value for weight-watchers. Doctors say that it is almost impossible for a seriously overweight person to stay on a reducing diet which doesn't provide some sweetness. A deep-seated craving for sweets must be satisfied enough to make it possible to stop nibbling. Vanilla itself counts but six calories for one teaspoon, but it can count out many calories of sugar. Vanilla brings out sweetness, making less sugar necessary. A small amount of some kind of sugar must be present, however, which the vanilla accents; vanilla is not a sweetener.

The natural sugars in dessert fruits and fruit punches are brought out by vanilla.

Cocoa made from nonfat dry milk will have a richer flavor with the addition of one-quarter teaspoon of vanilla per cup.

Well-beaten cottage cheese flavored with a little vanilla and grated lemon rind is excellent on gingerbread and other desserts. A teaspoon or so of sugar added to this gives the illusion of a quite sweet sauce.

With the addition of a half teaspoon of vanilla, the quantity of sugar may be reduced by at least three tablespoonfuls.

But even the French, master sauce-makers, have never applied vanilla's subtle influence to the great French sauces. Perhaps they thought the perfection of these culinary classics could not be improved.

Although the salubrious effect of vanilla on acids has long been known, it had never been tried in the delicate sauces that enhance meats, fish, and vegetables. New experiments show that Hollandaise, Béarnaise, poulette, and so on, the smooth delicate symbols of the haute cuisine, prefer a touch of vanilla. The blend of flavors is then complete.

Although the only perfect vanilla is contained in the bean, there are many times when vanilla in liquid form is easier to use. Then pure vanilla extract is excellent, pure vanilla extract only; a synthetic magic wand doesn't work magic. For baiting beetles or waging war against the fruit fly, synthetic vanillin gives excellent results, according to a U.S. Department of Agriculture bulletin, but it has no place in the kitchen.

The chemical composition of vanilla is still not thoroughly understood. Vanilla beans contain volatile oils, sugars, gum, fat, waxes, resins, vanillin, organic acids, natural coloring matters, and mineral constituents. The vanillin, one of the important components of flavor, is found in small amounts in the fully ripe beans. Yet of all the natural flavorful constituents of the cured vanilla bean, only vanillin is imitated in making the synthetic product. D. S. Correll, a distinguished orchid specialist, writes: "The delicate ephemeral essence of the natural product [vanilla], which leaves no unpleasant aftertaste, has not been completely captured by the test tubes."

19. Spice Blends

Many spice blends, considered suitable for several types of dishes, are now available on the American market, and more are coming out all the time:

Curry powder is in a class by itself and deserves long treatment at the end of the chapter.

Chili powder is an American invention which originated in the Southwest during the nineteenth century. It contains

chili pepper, red pepper, cumin, oregano, garlic and sometimes clove, allspice, and onion.

Poultry seasoning usually contains sage, thyme, savory, marjoram, white pepper, nutmeg, ginger, allspice, and perhaps
cloves and mace.

Apple-pie spice is a blend of the sweet baking spices, with a
predominance of cinnamon, also cloves, nutmeg, mace,
allspice, and ginger.

Barbecue spice is a blend of such spices as chili peppers, cumin,
garlic, cloves, paprika, salt, and sugar.

Pumpkin-pie spice is a blend of cinnamon, cloves, and ginger.

Mixed pickling spice is a mixture of several whole spices,
including mustard seed, bay leaves, black and white peppercorns, dill seed, red peppers, ginger, cinnamon, mace,
allspice, coriander seed, etc.

Seafood seasoning, tomato seasoning, cheese blend, and seasoned salt, and many others.

For traveling cooks, spice and herb blends are good com-
panions. In her original little book *My Fair Lady Cooks,* Emma
Dempster spins the culinary lore of six years on the road with
My Fair Lady. With 3 or 4 blends, dill weed, and a pepper mill
in her organized traveling kitchen, she was all set to season.

These blends are too standardized; they do not leave freedom
for variety and for different kinds of foods or for different seasons.
There is frequently too much in them. With the exception of
curry powder and chili powder (and these can be individual, too),
a personal blend will generally be found more pleasing.

The great Escoffier himself gives the proportions for a good
spice blend. It is used as a poultry seasoning for most stuffings, in
soups, braises, stews, casseroles, galantines, terrines, meat pies, and
cooking in buttered paper. His proportions may be cut to size:

5 ounces bay leaves	*3 ounces ginger root*
3 ounces thyme (half of it wild, if possible)	*3 ounces mace*
	10 ounces mixed pepper, half black and half white
3 ounces coriander	
4 ounces cinnamon	
6 ounces nutmeg	*1 ounce cayenne*
4 ounces cloves	

Put all ingredients into a mortar and pound them until they are able to pass through a very fine sieve. Put in airtight container and keep dry. It is recommended to put 1 pound of salt to every 3½ ounces of spices.

Boulestin and Hill, in *Herbs, Salads and Seasonings,* recommend the blend from the great French chef, Carême: 3 parts peppercorns (white and black in equal quantities); 1 part, in equal quantities, cloves, nutmeg, cinnamon, thyme, bay leaf. Add a small quantity of ginger and mace. Should be finely pounded, sieved, and tightly stoppered. No doubt Escoffier's proportion of salt would be equally good here.

It will be noticed that the spice blends of two equally famous French chefs, the blends to be used in exactly the same way, are quite different. Each chef also has said that this kind of seasoning must be exact, that it must not vary the least bit! The amateur, it seems, should not be afraid to try.

The Chinese blend of the five spices is available already mixed in Chinese grocery stores. This blend can be tried in equal quantities and adjusted if one spice stands out: cinnamon, clove, fennel, anise, and black pepper. This blend is used in exactly the same way as that of Escoffier.

In Morocco, a spice shop (an *épicerie*) might carry in stock some 200 "spices"; such perfumed products of nature as a basket of rosebuds, the fruit of the ash tree, belladonna, iris root, and cubeb (a gray, perfumed pepper) are strangers to Western kitchens.

The pleasant, light cuisine of Morocco favors seasonings that are grown at home—cumin, caraway, and coriander, the native saffron, wild ginger, and hot red peppers. Imported pepper (white is preferred) and cinnamon are much used.

The spice blend sold in each *épicerie* is called *Ras el Hanout,* literally, "the head of the shop." Each shop (and each good chef) blends its own. Actually, *Ras el Hanout* is similar to Indian curry powder or garam masala (in Morocco it is often called "the Indian spice") and a good, peppy curry powder can be substituted for it. I would suggest adding 2 or 3 freshly crushed spices to curry powder; allspice, a little lavender, and a few dried petals of damask rose would add a subtle Moroccan flavor.

Ras el Hanout is sold in France, and can probably be obtained through the Northwest Trading Company, 366 Broadway, New York City, which imports Moroccan couscous.

K E F T A (*Ground beef on a skewer*)

This is a famous Moroccan dish and should be very highly spiced.

1 pound beef, ground very fine	*3 to 4 marjoram leaves, minced or ¼ teaspoon dried*
½ teaspoon finely chopped coriander	*1 teaspoon salt*
3 to 4 sprigs parsley, chopped	*¼ teaspoon pepper*
5 to 6 mint leaves, minced	*½ teaspoon paprika*
	½ teaspoon Ras el Hanout
	½ teaspoon cumin
	1 onion minced

Mix all the ingredients well and allow to stand for an hour or more so that the spices may penetrate and blend. Take an amount of meat about the size of an egg, and mold on the skewer in sausage form, two or three to a skewer. Grill rapidly, turning often, and serve hot.

CURRY, the oldest spice blend, varies with each type of food, with the section of India in which it is made, and with each family. There are no cookbooks; girls learn from their mothers how to blend spices and arrange interesting and balanced meals.

Ninety per cent of all Indians are vegetarians, some so strict that they will not even eat eggs, and their principal source of protein is a bean or lentil paste called *dahl.* Vegetarianism is based on the principle of nonviolence. There are many excellent vegetable curries.

The *KORMA,* a rich, thickened, brown curry, is popular in the north of India. Poppy seeds and dessicated coconut along with other condiments are used for thickening. The outstanding principle of the korma, however, is that the meat is made tender by marinating in yogurt. *Ghee* (clarified butter) is the fat used in northern India.

In Bengal, mustard-seed oil (usually rancid, I have heard) is the preferred cooking medium. And fish is a *must* for all meals, often made into a soupy curry with fish, vegetables, possibly some raisins, and seasoned with spices and a little molasses. A shrimp curry is popular.

In the south of India the curries are hotter but not so rich. Coconut oil is used in cooking, and the curries are usually thinned with coconut milk (made from grated fresh or dried coconut mixed with water and squeezed through a cloth or strainer). In the Bombay district of western India vegetable dishes predominate. There is, however, a meat curry called "wide-mouthed curry," because so many different ingredients are in it.

There are sixty to seventy kinds of curry—mild or hot, light or dark, etc. Here are two curry formulas:

MILD AND LIGHT: 10 per cent cumin; 10 per cent fenugreek (available in our drugstores); 2 per cent fennel seed; 5 per cent white pepper; 32 per cent turmeric; 1 per cent cayenne; 12 per cent cardamom; 2 per cent cassia; 2 per cent cloves; 24 per cent coriander.

HOT AND LIGHT: 12 per cent cardamom; 26 per cent coriander; 2 per cent cloves; 10 per cent cumin; 2 per cent fennel; 10 per cent fenugreek; 5 per cent black pepper; 7 per cent ginger; 20 per cent turmeric; 6 per cent cayenne.

Housewives in India make a spice blend called "garam masala," which might be this: 3 tablespoons black peppercorns; 3 tablespoons whole coriander; 2½ tablespoons dark caraway seeds; 1-inch stick cinnamon; 1 tablespoon each cloves and cardamom seeds. Grind and store tightly covered. The mixture is good for seasoning vegetables and potatoes. Some cooks sprinkle a little of it on everything before serving.

The massala is also made in Jamaica. Recipes for making curries always specify "curry powder" or "massala."

6 *tablespoons coriander*	1 *heaped teaspoon*
1 *heaped teaspoon anise*	*cinnamon*
seed	1 *heaped teaspoon black*
1 *heaped teaspoon allspice*	*peppercorns*
1 *heaped teaspoon turmeric*	*1 teaspoon mustard seed
or saffron	3 *cloves garlic*
1 *heaped teaspoon*	1 *large onion*
cardamom	*red pepper to taste*

* Double quantity if used for beef.

Grind on a stone. Grind turmeric first and add enough water to make a stiff paste. Gradually add other ingredients, grinding very fine. Omit onion, garlic, and red pepper if it is to be kept overnight; add before using.

Cucumbers may be stuffed with massala, then braised in oil in a covered frying pan until soft and brown.

CHICK PEAS WITH MASSALA

1 pound chick peas (canned	*½ onion*
ones may be used)	*piece of red pepper*
1 tablespoon massala	*1 teaspoon salt*
2 tablespoons oil	

Soak peas overnight, then remove outer skin. Put in a bowl and sprinkle with salt. Grind onion and pepper with massala, and sauté in hot oil. Add peas, cover, and continue to sauté, stirring frequently, until peas are fairly soft. Makes 5 or 6 servings.

Most curries are started by cooking chopped onions and garlic in fat. The spices are then added and cooked thoroughly. The Indian palate can immediately detect the taste of "raw" spices. Whole spices are usually used in India, though frequently ginger is chopped, for instance, and the seeds, cinnamon and cloves, are ground.

Rice in the south and potatoes in the north are usually served with curries, as well as cool vegetable dishes made with yogurt or cottage cheese.

Indian foods are usually served with several chutneys. These are piquant relishes made with mango, lemon or tamarind rind, chopped mint, grated coconut, bacon crumbles, Bombay duck, sambals, etc.

If India has many kinds of curry, ranging from mild to very hot, there is even greater variation throughout the "curry belt." Malayans and Indonesians consider Indian curry harsh and rather uninteresting because it is mostly pepper, they say. The Chinese make what is called a "cold curry," and the amiable Malayan curry is only medium hot. Chicken curry is the national dish of Malaya, with prawn curry a close second.

CHICKEN CURRY OF MALAYA

1 2½-pound chicken, cut in
  serving-size pieces
4 tablespoons peanut or
  vegetable oil
1 onion, minced
2 cloves garlic, minced
1 tablespoon crushed
  coriander seed

1 teaspoon crushed
  caraway seed
1 tablespoon ground hot
  red pepper
1 teaspoon ground ginger
1 tablespoon curry powder
½ teaspoon salt
1 tablespoon lemon juice
2 cups coconut milk

In a large heavy pan heat oil; brown chicken, onion, garlic, and spices. Add lemon juice and coconut milk. Cover and simmer until chicken is tender, about 40 minutes. Serve with rice and condiments. In Malaya there would be a selection from the following condiments: dried fish, cube fresh pineapple, cucumber in coconut milk, tiny fried onions, very tiny fried fish, chopped peanuts, chutney, diced bananas, grated coconut, cauliflower, cabbage, and sometimes tomatoes, though Malayan tomatoes are too acid.

The curry powder we buy in America is a mixture similar to those listed above. It is an invention of the British settlers in India. Curry powder is good not only for curries and to dress up leftovers, but also to give a little nip and some color to many dishes: hôrs d'oeuvre; salad dressings; chicken gravy, cheese, and egg dishes.

Summer Savory.

HERBS

Baum.

Common Hyſsop.

Juniper.

Sweet Chervil

20. Herbs

The history of herbs is as benign as that of spices is belligerent. Marching armies passed blindly by the verdant bank where wild thyme blows; no daring ships were launched in search of a pot of basil, though basil itself is not without its own sinister history.

But if the herbs have not made history, they are none the less a part of our historical tradition, more closely associated with the daily life of our forebears than were the golden spices. Herbs are plants of the temperate zone, of our own environment. In our Western society herbs have been medicine and mythology; food and flavoring; drinks and decoration; they cured the dropsy and worms in the ears or the bites of mad dogs. They kept away snakes and fleas and witches and some of the stenches of medieval life.

The herb garden was pantry and medicine cabinet.

Thomas Tusser in his *Five Hundreth Points of Good Husbandry*, published in England in 1573, lists the herbs he considered essential for the garden:

1. Twenty-one kinds of strewing herbs; 2. Herbs and roots to boil and to butter; 3. Forty herbs, branches and flowers for windows and pots; 4. Twenty-two herbs and roots for sallads and sauces; 5. Forty-two herbs and seeds for the kitchen; 6. Seventeen herbs to still in summer; 7. Twenty-eight herbs necessary to grow in the garden for physic.

Gervase Markham, in *Country Contentments,* written about 1635, advises the English "huswife" about the "inward and outward Vertues which ought to be a Compleat Woman; her Skill in Physicke, Surgerie, Extraction of Oyles, Banqueting-Stuffe. Ordering of great Feasts, Preserving of all sorts of Wines, Conceited Secrets, Distillation, Perfumes, Brewing, Baking and all other things belonging to a Household."

In those days when the housewife was expected to be a doctor, pharmacist and gardener, baker, vintner, perfumer and textile manufacturer, there was no talk of women needing a career outside the home in order to use their talents and energies.

Practice of the domestic virtues now, as always, induces contentment in a household. Herbs are no longer required as home medicines. They are a part of the "conceited secrets" the wise housewife uses to promote the health and happiness of her family. Even the fragrance of herbs is said to diffuse health-giving qualities.

Today's housewife, instead of being surgeon, baker, pharmacist, and vintner, is chauffeur, cook, and maid; wage-earner, school director, and politician. Though she seldom brews the beer and is not at all clever at mixing a love potion, she will find that the culture of herbs fits well into her way of living, with the terrace and barbecue, with simple informal entertaining.

Herb gardens have been grown for thousands of years: in Egypt, Persia, Greece, and Rome, in many different designs, always trim and geometrical, frequently in elaborate patterns. These classic patterns, like the minuet, are expressions of a slower, more mannered age, not exactly in keeping with the hamburger and the twist.

The usual recommendation to make the herb plot outside the kitchen door seldom fits into the plan of modern houses. Our way of living makes herbs belong with the barbecue and its adjoining terrace, handy for the salads, the marinades, and the drinks, sweetly perfuming the air and even helping to keep away the flies, a feat said to be one of the extraordinary talents of the heady basil.

Herbs yield up their odors in the heat of the sun or in the heat of the cooking process; bruising, too, releases aroma, which is one reason many people like the mint bruised in a julep. Walking on a carpet of thyme was a serene pleasure advocated by Francis Bacon in his essay "Of Gardens": "Therefore you are to set whole alleys of them, to have the pleasure when you walk or tread." Even brushing against the aromatic leaves of herbs releases their warm fragrance.

> As aromatic plants bestow
> No spicy fragrance while they grow,
> But crushed or trodden to the ground
> Diffuse their balmy sweets around.
> —OLIVER GOLDSMITH, *The Captivity*

No flowers that grow give so much pleasure and satisfaction in the outdoor living room as aromatic herbs, delighting the nose as well as the eye.

An herb-scented terrace is the busy housewife's dream garden. Few herbs are prima donnas demanding special soil, light, fertilizer, and sprays in order to produce a few showy blooms, too soon gone. All the herbs ask is a good light soil, some sun, and some shade, and they grow peacefully, needing very little care. Many of the annuals save extra work by seeding themselves, poking up tentative green shoots early in the spring; in fact, herbs tend to come earlier and stay later than most plants. After getting them established, the hardest job comes in holding them back.

There are tall plants and short ones; herbs that like the shade (angelica and nearly all the members of the parsley family will tolerate, even when they do not prefer, the shade); plants for damp spots; plants that keep fresh green foliage all summer and others that are evergreen, accenting the winter scene.

Tender, bushy plants like rosemary, lemon verbena, and lavender do best in their own separate pots, which will carry their fragrance inside in winter. Also into pots go the tender geraniums, scented rose, apple, apricot, lemon, mint, nutmeg; satiny peppermint, crisp and crinkly Prince Rupert; they offer cool greenery all summer long, and lend their scented freshness to finger bowls and punches, to jellies, to scented sugars which will contribute a subtle fragrance to sweets—custards and fruits, ices, sugary candies, crystallized flowers.

At the terrace clambake or lobster party, put out large, sturdy finger bowls scented with herbs. A clambake is a fine lesson in seasoning: each ingredient seasons the other without smothering its flavor and the whole is seasoned by the salty tang of seaweed.

NEW ENGLAND CLAMBAKE

(for people far from the sea)

Those who live far from the seacoast needn't worry about lack of seaweed. Spinach is a very flavorful alternate—in addition to contributing all those vitamins and minerals, though no sea salt.

3 pints water	*6 medium onions, peeled*
2 packages (10 ounces each) fresh spinach (or seaweed)	*6 ears fresh corn*
	4½ dozen small clams
2 ready-to-cook broiler chickens	*6 African rock lobster tails (or 1 whole fresh lobster apiece, if available)*
salt	
ground black pepper	
7 medium or 14 small potatoes	*melted butter*

A clam steamer consists of two parts, a lower and an upper section. Into the lower section, pour 3 pints water. Place the upper section of the steamer on top (the steam enters through perforations). Wet the spinach and cover the perforated bottom of the upper section with half of it. Cut chickens into quarters. Sprinkle with salt and ground black pepper. Tie each quarter in a square of cheesecloth. Place on top of spinach. Wash potatoes and arrange over chicken along with peeled onions. Remove outer husks from corn. Pull back the inner husks and remove silks, keeping the husks intact, then fold them back over the ears. Place the ears over potatoes and onions.

Divide clams into 6 portions and tie each in a square of cheesecloth. Place on top of corn. Wrap African rock lobster tails in the outer husks removed from corn ears and arrange over clams. Top with remaining wet spinach. In the center place one medium-size potato and put on the cover. Place over medium heat and steam 1½ hours or until the potato on top of spinach is tender. Strain the liquid in lower section of the steamer through cheesecloth and season with a little salt and ground black pepper. Serve as clam broth. Always have plenty of melted butter on hand to serve with each of the foods. Makes 6 servings.

Note: If desired, a large can, which has a tight-fitting cover, may be used instead of a clam steamer. A new galvanized garbage can is ideal or an old-fashioned tin lard can, holding about 5 gallons. Place a layer of washed rocks or a wire rack in the bottom, pour in water and put in a layer of wet spinach. Continue as if using the clam steamer.

Damask roses, nasturtiums, violets, marigolds, pansies, and poppies are not out of place in an herb garden, adding a splash of color to the more subdued gray, green, lavender, and soft yellows of the herbs. In salads, the flowers, though rather bland in flavor, are pretty to look at, and really taste quite good if they are well seasoned.

Kitchen herbs are not to be spurned for the flower garden, where many of them—sweet woodruff, sweet cicely, lovage, tansy, and rue, for instance—are more helpful than in the cooking pot. Their feathery greenness carries the flower border through a hot, dull August, when blooms are scarce and when ordinary plants, not especially adapted to hot weather, tend to droop. The herbs have oil sacs in their leaves to protect them against drought.

When herbs are grown primarily to beautify a terrace or rock garden, the most difficult task is disciplining oneself for the sake of the plants. Not only do herbs do best if they are snipped frequently, but if some of them are to be dried for the winter, they must be taken at the right moment: just before they flower. Properly dried herbs have more flavor than fresh ones during the winter; only rosemary, bay, and rue retain a like amount of the oils.

DRYING HERBS: The herbs should be put to dry on a

screen, usually, in an airy, sunless place where they are turned from time to time. If the drying is done out of doors, they must be carried in every night in order to protect the leaves from dampness; actually, it is best to dry them inside the house, probably in a room with a fan. They may be put out in the sun for a couple of hours near the end of the drying process to insure that no mustiness taints them. The process takes about a week or perhaps only five days. The dried herbs are then put into sterile, opaque (light fades them) jars, closed tightly, and kept in a cupboard away from the heat.

LEAVES: Parsley or mint may be quickly dried by the following method:

Strip leaves from stems and plunge into boiling salted water for half a minute, strain off water, spread leaves on a fine wire mesh, and dry in a medium oven, long enough for leaves to get crisply dry.

An Italian method of preserving basil is to pack the leaves in a wide-mouthed crock with a layer of salt between layers of basil. When the salt is shaken from the leaves, they are ready for use as if fresh from the plant.

Fresh herbs may also be frozen. Small packets, a tablespoonful twisted in Saran Wrap or aluminum foil, will be found most useful.

FLOWERS: dried in the same way as the leaves, but will take longer, probably about two weeks.

SEEDS: pods and all, should be snipped off to fall in a cloth-lined basket, then spread out thinly on heavy cloth to finish drying.

ROOTS (*angelica, horseradish, sweet flag, iris*): should be dug in the fall when growth has stopped (after a few dry days is best); only perfect ones should be used. Wash and scrub them, scraping if necessary. Very large roots should be sliced and spread in thin layers on the drying screens. They may be dried out of doors, or in an oven with the door left open, or on racks arranged over the stove.

Harvest time is also the best time to make up interesting herb mixtures, herb vinegars, and even packets of sachet both for the house and as unequaled gifts.

HERB MIXTURE

Gather: ¼ pound parsley, ¼ pound lemon thyme, ¼ pound sweet marjoram, ¼ pound savory, 2 ounces sweet basil. Dry them and powder them. Pound 2 ounces dried lemon peel with ¼ ounce celery seed and 1 teaspoonful salt. Pound 6 bay leaves to a powder. Mix all together, bottle and stopper well.

FRENCH HERB MIXTURE

Take 3 ounces each dried thyme, bay leaves, nutmeg or mace, and paprika; 1½ ounces dried marjoram, rosemary, and ground black pepper. Pound to a powder, pass through a fine sieve if desired, bottle and stopper securely.

SAGE IN CLARET

Two ounces green sage leaves, 1 ounce fresh lemon peel pared thinly, 1 ounce salt, pinch of cayenne, a few drops of citric acid or lemon juice, 1 pint of claret. Allow to steep for 14 days, shaking the bottle every day. Decant the infusion into a clean bottle and cork tightly. This is excellent for gravies and sauces.

TARRAGON VINEGAR

Gather the tarragon leaves as if for drying. Pack a glass jar with the leaves; fill the jar with white wine vinegar, cover and let infuse for two weeks. Strain and pour into bottles. A fresh branch of tarragon put into each bottle not only adds strength to the vinegar, but also looks effective. Lemon verbena or balm freshens and lightens tarragon vinegar. Other herb vinegars, basil vinegar, or lavender vinegar, which adds a pleasantly unidentifiable flavor to salads, may be made in the same way. Burnet vinegar, with a delicate cucumber flavor, is delicious for salads.

Mixed herb vinegars may be concocted in all sorts of combinations of herbs, flowers, and light spices. Flowers should not infuse as long as the leaves. Astute herb growers make quantities of these delicious herb vinegars, bottle them in handsome containers, and give them to lucky people for Christmas gifts.

RASPBERRY VINEGAR OR SHRUB

1 pint vinegar   *2 quarts fresh raspberries*
                              sugar

Pour a pint of vinegar over 1 quart of crushed fresh raspberries in a jar and 24 hours later strain the liquid over another quart of raspberries in another jar and let steep 24 hours more. Measure the juice and add 1 pound sugar for every pint of juice. Put in top of double boiler and cook over boiling water 1 hour. Skim, let cool, and bottle. Use on fruit salads.

For a summer drink: dilute with 3 times as much water and serve well chilled.

MIXTURES

There are many combinations of herbs, or herbs and vegetables, which are used together so often that they have acquired names of their own, usually French: the bouquet garni, fines herbes, and court bouillon, for instance, are now common to nearly all languages.

The *BOUQUET GARNI* is a combination of thyme, parsley, and bay leaf. Escoffier recommends $8/10$ parsley, $1/10$ bay, and $1/10$ thyme. Other herbs may be included or substituted: marjoram, rosemary, or others. In India, a bouquet garni is cinnamon, cardamom, and bay leaves. The true meaning of *FINES HERBES* is finely chopped herbs. They may be only minced parsley, or minced parsley with chopped chives or other mild onion. Or it may include other finely chopped herbs: mint, basil, tarragon, chervil, savory, or any combination of them, depending on the herbs available and the flavor desired.

A *FAGGOT* is an English term usually meaning a bunch of herbs for cooking. I like to use the term as meaning a combination of herbs and other seasonings which are thrown on the coals when grilling meat or fish: a sprig of rosemary, a clove of garlic, and hickory or apple wood for a turkey or steak; sage, thyme, and garlic for liver and spareribs.

RAVIGOTE, from the French *ravigoter,* to cheer or strengthen, is a combination of finely chopped herbs: tarragon, chives, chervil, parsley, burnet to be used in salad, sauce, ravigote butter, etc.

A *MIREPOIX* is the name given to a collection of herbs and vegetables used for seasoning stews and braises. It consists of two carrots, two onions (usually stuck with a clove), two bay leaves, a sprig of thyme, a clove of garlic, and a quarter of a pound of fat bacon or salt pork.

A *BATTUTO* is an Italian combination of chopped-up carrot, parsley, onion, garlic, and salt pork, sometimes a little celery.

A *SOFFRITO,* also Italian (meaning under-frying), is the same group of vegetables and herbs, chopped and sautéed for a few minutes in olive oil, in preparation for nearly all soups, sautées, sauces for pasta, etc.

COURT BOUILLON is a combination of herbs, usually thyme, parsley, bay leaf, onion, garlic, peppercorn, salt, sometimes carrot, a slice of lemon, wine (white or even red for matelote) or vinegar, and water. Add any fish trimmings that are available.

Escoffier recommends that court bouillon be brought to a boil and allowed to simmer for an hour, then strained. He suggests putting in the peppercorns only twelve minutes before the end of the simmering time else they would give a bitterness to the preparation, a precaution which sounds decidedly precious. My cook thinks that salt added in the cooking process tends to toughen delicate fish like sole.

21. *Marinades*

MARINADES, the beauty baths that touch up cheap cuts of meat and leftovers, have become popular now when there are no longer any cheap meats. But the principle works even with expensive meats. Although marinades will make nearly anything tender, they also season foods in a most pleasant way. The most expensive of meats, the fillet of beef, can profit from a marinade, not to tenderize this tender-as-butter cut of beef, but to enhance the flavor of one of the most tasteless.

The marinade was originally a seagoing preparation: a brine for preserving fish. The word still means "to pickle in brine," but, as the marinade is used less to preserve and more to season and to make tender, other condiments have joined the salt in its preparation. Escoffier, out of style in modern America, treats marinades mainly as summer preservatives of meat, and as tenderizers to be used only when essential.

The marinade that is most useful to us is a combination of oil, acid, and spices. As the meat stands, or marinates, in the mixture, the acid breaks down the fibers, the oil enters and smoothly carries with it the savory flavors of the seasoning. Letting food stand for some time in an appropriate marinade is an artful way to accomplish many purposes: to make meats more tender; to flavor tasteless or uninteresting foods; to make excellent new dishes of leftovers; to bring out the flavor of certain foods—fresh fruits, for instance; to blend, make a smooth unified flavor of several ingredients, as in a beef stew; to add interest to the menu by using diverse methods of seasoning.

There is no substitute for good olive oil in a marinade, nor for interesting well-flavored vinegar and fresh-tasting spices and herbs. Wines are frequently used in place of vinegar or in its company. Lemon, lime, and other citrus juices are excellent in marinades. Sour cream or yogurt is frequently included in a marinade, onions and garlic nearly always.

Almost all kinds of foods are appropriate for marinating: meats, fish, poultry, vegetables, and fruits. The type of marinade —light or heavy, cooked or uncooked, the seasoning—is chosen according to the kind of food being used and the delicacy or heartiness wished as seasoning.

A COOKED MARINADE

(for a haunch of venison, for instance)

1 pint oil	3 quarts water
1 cup minced onion	3 or 4 stalks parsley
1 cup minced carrot	2 sprigs rosemary
2 tablespoons minced	2 sprigs thyme
shallots or mild onion	2 bay leaves
1 clove garlic, crushed	2 cloves
10 peppercorns, whole	2 tablespoons salt
1 pint vinegar	4 tablespoons brown sugar
2 bottles dry white wine	

Heat oil, add carrots, onion, shallots, garlic, and herbs; sauté a little; add vinegar, wine, water, salt, peppercorns, and sugar. Cook 20 minutes. Allow to steep about 10 minutes, strain marinade and allow to cool before combining with meat.

More liquid is used in a cooked marinade than in a raw (uncooked) one. Whole spices are used, whereas they must be crushed or ground in order to impart their flavor to a raw marinade. Cooked marinades are seldom used except for large joints of meat.

UNCOOKED MARINADE

For a large leg of mutton Escoffier recommends a marinade exactly like the cooked one above with the addition of 1 tablespoon juniper berries, more rosemary, wild thyme, and basil, 2 more cloves of garlic, and 1 quart less water.

Uncooked marinades are generally more highly spiced than cooked ones as they are not subjected to heat to release flavors.

The Spice Trade Association gives the following general tips on marinades:

1. The larger the exposed surface of the meat, the more easily the marinade may penetrate.
2. Meat should be marinated in a pot approximately the size of the meat. It is a good idea to put a weight on the meat also to keep it completely immersed in the marinade.

3. The larger the piece of meat, the longer the marinating period. A ten-pound roast needs overnight in a cooked marinade. Such dishes as sauerbraten and bœuf à la mode can use two days. Small pieces of meat for shish kebab, for instance, need about four hours.

4. When marinating for periods of more than 24 hours, reduce somewhat the amount of vinegar, as its strength increases with time. Wine is easier to deal with.

5. Generally speaking, either wine or vinegar may be used with oil for meats and fish (the proportions are usually 2 acid to 1 oil) though wine is not appropriate for a vegetable marinade.

6. Any kind of dry wine may be used in a marinade if one bears in mind that red wine will darken light-colored foods.

7. Herbs and spices may be placed in a cheesecloth or muslin bag in order to facilitate their removal.

8. When marinating leftover vegetables, remember that they were seasoned once before. For vegetable marinades, remember the herbs: basil, chervil, tarragon, chives, and fennel.

9. Keep marinades in a cool place, or in the refrigerator.

Bear in mind that the acids in a marinade so break down the fibers of fish that frequently the fish seems to have been cooked, as in Seviche.

S E V I C H E (*Lime-cooked fish*)

Although a South American fish called corbina is usually used for this dish, striped bass, cut on the bias in thin slices, is a good substitute. The slices of raw fish are put in a marinade of lime, lemon, and orange juice. This cooks the fish, or seems to, as the fibers or cell structure is broken down. A little hot pepper, thinly sliced Bermuda onions, and sliced green and red sweet pepper complete this pretty and interesting dish.

The new tenderized beef, injected before slaughtering with the papaya enzyme, presents another problem. This beef is good, flavorsome as well as tender, but it literally disintegrates with long cooking. Tenderized beef is not recommended for stews, bourguignon, or bœuf à la mode. Tenderized meat also cooks so quickly that the seasonings, so important in these dishes, do not have time to do their good work. Recommended: a top or bottom round roast of tenderized beef weighing about five or six pounds, cut the length of the round and about five or six inches in diameter, after being marinated for several hours in an uncooked marinade, needs one hour, no more, in a 400-degree oven.

Certain quite delicate flavors will be found pleasant in a marinade: lime-tarragon for chicken or baby turkey, for example. The meat should be marinated for several hours in oil and lime juice with leaves of tarragon, a few crushed peppercorns, sliced onion, garlic, and, of course, salt. Nothing else.

When marinated meats are to be barbecued or grilled, they may be removed from the marinade directly to the grill, then basted frequently with the marinade during cooking. If the meat is to be browned first, as is preferred for many stews, pot roasts, and braises, the meat must first be dried, then browned, after which process liquid is again added and the cooking proceeds. The strained marinade is frequently used for the cooking.

Marinated cooked vegetables—whole string beans, zucchini cut into strips, asparagus—are unusually delicious, either alone or mixed. A simple herbed French dressing makes a good marinade for vegetables. They absorb more flavor if dressed while hot.

MARINATED CAULIFLOWER

Cook cauliflower lightly; drain well, cut into pieces in serving dish. Dress with 3 tablespoons oil, 1 tablespoon vinegar, 1 teaspoon Dijon mustard, ½ teaspoon salt, ¼ teaspoon pepper, pinch of sugar, 1 shallot, and 1 tablespoon parsley, chopped.

22. *Angelica*

ANGELICA (*Angelica archangelica*) is still of real household use, even for those who no longer make their own gin. In praise of angelica, John Parkinson, eighteenth-century herbalist, wrote: "The whole plant, both leafe, roote and seed is of an excellent comfortable scent, savour and taste."

Perhaps our cynical age can afford to ignore this handsome plant with a comfortable scent, which since pagan times has been associated with hope and the promise of good things to come. "Yet for its virtues, it is of admirable use," as Culpeper wrote in his *Herbal* in 1652.

A tall plant, sometimes as much as six feet high, stylishly modern with "great and long winged leaves, made of many broade green ones . . . and at the tops very large umbels of white flowers," it seems to have been created to set off the simple planes of modern architecture. Indeed its graceful formal lines have always appealed to architects and sculptors in wood.

So in the herb garden or out of it, angelica brings grace and form, combining with a tropical kind of luxuriance a musky aura of the Far East. All this showy Oriental glamor grows and thrives in northern climates, even in Iceland and Greenland, where it is the only scented herb that grows.

The lands of the midnight sun have found many uses for angelica as food and seasoning, medicine and decoration. The tender stems can be cooked and served rather like asparagus. The Finns bake these stems in hot ashes, or boil them with fish. The Norwegians sometimes make a flour of the roots.

The "excellent, comfortable scent" of angelica seems more glamorous than comfortable; unusual, full of character, its muskiness is a valuable part of heady perfumes, such as French chypre, and cosmetics.

Unlike real musk from the musk deer, angelica's musky quality is also a pleasant perfume in the kitchen. Custards and crêmes, puddings and soufflés may be flavored with angelica, with fresh stems and leaves, with the essence, or with candied stems.

SNOW PUDDING WITH ANGELICA

1 cup orange juice	½ cup sugar
1 tablespoon unflavored gelatin combined with ¼ cup cold water	2 tablespoons lemon juice
	¼ teaspoon salt
2 drops oil of angelica	3 egg whites

Scald orange juice but do not boil. Add other ingredients except egg whites and stir constantly over low heat until smooth.

Allow to cool and thicken. Beat egg whites until stiff. Beat in gelatin mixture a little at a time. Pour into lightly oiled mold and chill several hours in the refrigerator until set. Serve with custard sauce.

Fresh angelica adds interest to rhubarb. Use about one-fourth angelica to three-fourths rhubarb or add it to other fresh fruit, jams, or preserved watermelon rind. In the sixteenth century the roots of angelica candied in honey were thought highly of in Denmark.

Candied stems of angelica, for sale in many specialty shops, make a delightful decoration.

Drug companies import most of the angelica needed from Germany. From the time of Culpeper in the seventeenth century until today, angelica has calmed indigestion and bronchial colds. Although modern physicians no longer prescribe angelica to comfort the heart, blood, and spirits, or the bite of a mad dog, still it is an important ingredient in medicines, perfumes, and cosmetics, and many a grandmother has brewed a cup of tea of angelica to aid the digestion or comfort a cold.

The taste of angelica has been described as "sweetish at first, then takes on a bitter quality, and producing a warm effect in the mouth, a general impression of the taste of juniper berries pervading."

Angelica, along with juniper berries, is often an ingredient of gin, and is an important flavor in Benedictine and other liqueurs. Perhaps this "hair-of-the-dog" is the reason that angelica was believed to remove the effects of intoxication.

Oil of angelica should be found in drugstores and the candied stems in specialty shops.

23. *Anise*

ANISE (Pimpinella anisum), with its strong licorice taste, must be one of nature's favorites, she made so many on the same model: fennel and chervil, tarragon, caraway, dill and sweet cicely, even a Japanese shrub and a toadstool all have a licorice quality, not forgetting the licorice root itself.

Some are so lucky as to have plants of anise in their herb gardens, so are able to enjoy the dainty leaves in salads and garnishes, or in refreshing drinks, but it is the fruit of the plant, the seed, that has long been important in medicine, perfumery, and in the kitchen.

Even though the Encyclopaedia Britannica seems to think that the anise mentioned in the Bible (Matthew 23:23) is really dill, nevertheless, aniseed, plain and star (from China), has been with us through all our history, useful and popular.

Because of its medicinal value, laws demanding its culture have been in force from Charlemagne's kingdom to our Virginia Colony. Edward I kept London Bridge in repair with taxes on the aniseed that crossed over it.

Its powerful but pleasant character (it is popular with children and evidently with hounds) has caused anise to be found in strangely assorted company: in perfumes, sachets, and perfumed soaps; in cough mixtures and as a drag for hounds; to coat bitter pills; to sweeten the breath or to sweeten the linens. "Lytill bagges of fustian stuffed with anneys" sweetened all the royal linens of England's Edward IV. It flavors many delicious liqueurs and cordials.

The Roman naturalist Pliny the Elder, writing about anise in the first century A.D., said that the kitchen could not get along without it. More than 1,900 years later anise still finds a place in the kitchen, though not to the extent that Pliny recommended. He thought that aniseed served well for seasoning all meats; in fact he liked using it in all seasoning.

Most of the aniseed imported to the United States comes from Spain and Mexico. The Spanish-speaking countries commonly add a few seeds to soups, stews, and to court bouillon for fish and to sweets as well.

Anise is a Scandinavian favorite, too. There, it flavors applesauce, steps up the flavor of soups, and adds interest to beet salad.

Poultry, fruit compotes, and French dressing also like a delicate licorice accent. It is in sweet things that anise stars the world over: in breads and cakes; cookies, puddings, and candies. The well-known Springerle and many other German Christmas cakes and all the pretty, crisp small cakes of Italy are flavored with anise.

In Holland skaters drink hot Anijs Melk. Here and there on the frozen canals little huts protect the skaters from the cold wind. In the middle of the hut burns a small stove which supports a large pot of cheering anise milk, usually dispensed by an old man wrapped in many shawls.

ANISE MILK

4 cups milk	½ cup sugar
1 tablespoon crushed aniseed	2 tablespoons cornstarch

Scald milk with aniseed, add sugar, and heat 5 minutes. Dissolve the cornstarch in a little water and add to the mixture. Stir over a low fire about 5 minutes more, until the cornstarch is cooked. Makes 4 servings.

Anise is an authoritative spice and should be used with a light hand; it is easy to add too much. For a 6-portion recipe, ¼ teaspoon of anise, whole or ground, gives a delicate flavor.

FIVE FLAVOR BEEF

4 pounds brisket of beef	2 cloves star anise * or
4 tablespoons oil	¼ teaspoon crushed
2 cups soy sauce	aniseed
1-inch stick cinnamon	½ cup sugar
	1 tablespoon salt
	1 cup sherry

Heat oil in a deep, heavy pan. When it is very hot add the meat and brown it on all sides. Mix the soy sauce, water to cover, cinnamon, anise, sugar, and salt in a large bowl and pour slowly

* Star anise was imported from Mainland China and is no longer available in the United States.

over the meat. Cover the pan and when the liquid comes to a
boil, turn down the heat and simmer. Baste from time to time
and turn the meat every half hour. After the meat has cooked for
1½ hours, turn up the heat and add the sherry. When it returns
to a boil, turn down the heat and simmer for an additional ½
hour.

During the last 15 minutes cooking time, turn the heat high
and cook until the gravy is thickened and absorbed into the meat.
The presence of sugar will thicken the liquid, therefore you must
watch this last cooking period very carefully. Cut the meat into
thick slices and pour gravy over it. Serve very hot. Makes 7
servings.

24. Balm

BALM (Melissa officinalis), in the Middle Ages known as a
balm for nearly everything, is a member of the mint family, almost, one might say, a black sheep of this distinguished family.
More accurately, the virtues of lemon balm have gone out of style.
Real lemons are plentiful, and not many of us are sensible enough
to take a soothing tisane at bedtime.

Balm, beloved by bees, is easy to grow, has a strong root system like garden mint, and is equally pleasant to look at. It has a
piercing lemony scent of distinction and character, as well as the
characteristic virtue of the mints: the ability to stimulate the
membranes of taste.

Balm is definitely worth new experiments in the kitchen as
well as in the living room, where its graceful lemon-scented
branches add long-lasting greenery to flower arrangements.

BALM–PINEAPPLE CUSTARD

6 pineapple slices
1 pint milk
3 eggs
1½ tablespoons sugar

1 vanilla bean
1 tablespoon fresh balm
leaves or 2 teaspoons
dried

Place the pineapple slices on the bottom of a well-buttered fireproof dish. Beat the eggs and sugar together, add milk, mix well, and pour over the pineapple. Put in the vanilla bean and sprinkle balm leaves over the top. Place in a shallow pan of cold water and bake slowly in a 325-degree oven until set. Serve with chilled cream or whipped cream.

25. Basil

BASIL (Ocimum basilicum). In the spring a young woman's fancy would do well to turn to thoughts of basil, pronounced bay–zil. In Italy her young man would come calling and wear a sprig of basil as a sign that his intentions were serious.

But basil's history is not only one of springtime love; its heady character stirs deeper passions—passions of power and hate, of bleeding hearts. After her gruesome dance, Salome hid John the Baptist's head in a pot of basil, where she could give it loving care, as did Isabella, in Keats' poem *Isabella, or The Pot of Basil,* with the head of her murdered lover. In Greece basil has always been the royal herb; it was also supposed to be an antidote to the venom of the basilisk, a fabulous reptile that was hatched by a serpent from the egg of a seven-year-old cock, its breath, even its look, allegedly fatal.

Basil to us is more than a symbol of power; it is the power of trapped sunlight, of the clear warmth of Mediterranean sunlight. Basil's royal robes are painted in the red-ripe of tomatoes, green and golden peppers, vermilion chilis, and purple eggplant. A few fresh green leaves of basil, which willingly give away some of their clove-peppery oil even at the touch of a ray of sunlight or a drop of rain, makes anything that grows in the Mediterranean air taste better.

For all that basil seems so strong, as if its power would overwhelm nearly everything else in a dish, it is surprising how many leaves of fresh basil a quite simple eggplant dish—which will be served with grilled or roast lamb—can consume without adding a noticeable basil flavor. It is perhaps misleading that the smooth green leaves are so free with their pungent distinctive perfume.

For that matter, basil is one of the few herbs that is permitted to assert itself, to appear as the prima donna in a dish, as in the inimitable *Pesto alla Genovese*.

The true *Pesto alla Genovese,* according to the recipe in Italian, is not difficult to make, but it takes much diligence and patience. One needs a sturdy chopping board, a strong "half-moon" (*lunetta*) knife, and a mortar and pestle. First take 3 cloves of garlic and begin to chop them with the knife, as finely as possible. Then take a good handful (a *big* one) of clean basil leaves and continue to chop patiently. A pinch of salt added to the basil leaves will keep the pretty green color. When they are minced to perfection, put the garlic and basil in a mortar and add, little by little, and always grinding, the quantity of Parmesan cheese that will reduce the intense green of the first mince to a clear green-pea color. This might be 2 or 3 handfuls (*small* handfuls)—about a cup. When this is done, begin to add about 4 tablespoons of olive oil to the compost, mixing well with a spoon so that it becomes like a paste. Before adding the oil, a piece of butter the size of a walnut might be added to the pesto. While this is not necessary, it communicates a better taste to the whole. Those who like their pesto less strong may mince a well-cleaned walnut with the garlic and also add a little marjoram to the basil. At the moment of seasoning the lasagne dilute the pesto with a few tablespoons of boiling water. This is the pesto with which one seasons the pasta and gnocchi di patate (potato dumpling). If the pesto, instead, is being served for soup, it is necessary to add a few dried mushrooms which have been previously cooked and a little fresh tomato juice or tomato paste. (From Ada Boni, *Il Talismano della Felicità.*)

LASAGNE WITH PESTO ALLA GENOVESE

One of the most noted specialties of the Genovese cuisine is the lasagne. Lasagne is made with egg pasta, rolled like the usual *tagliatelle,* but it is cut in large squares, 4 inches or so on a side, cooked in salted water, and seasoned with the celebrated Pesto alla Genovese.

AMERICAN VERSION PESTO ALLA GENOVESE

6 *cloves garlic*	1 *tablespoon butter*
2 *cups fresh basil leaves*	*(optional)*
¼ *teaspoon salt*	6 *tablespoons grated*
¼ *cup olive oil*	*Parmesan cheese*

Slice garlic into container of electric blender. Add basil and salt, which keeps the basil green, and oil. Blend at high speed until finely minced. Add cheese and blend. Add butter and blend. A little more oil or cheese may be added if desired. The result should be a paste the consistency of mayonnaise. A small amount is used to dress pasta, soup, fish, and some vegetables.

Basil goes well with the vegetables and meats and olive oil of its environment—veal and lamb, chicken and fish. A few leaves of basil add their aromatic oil to Italian soups and broth. Even canned tomatoes and tomato paste—the best varieties—carry a leaf or two of basil to blend and to accent.

This delicate annual seldom survives the first touch of frost. It is stronger in flavor when dried—if the leaves are gathered at the right moment—than when fresh. It is a true mint, a valuable seasoning. Basil's peppery oil alerts the taste receptors, blends flavors, and pleases the palate.

Yet our Mediterranean herb is not European, but a native of India, where it is held in high esteem, of religious significance, and sacred. In India basil, free from the sinister associations it has acquired in Europe, is planted around the house to insure happiness, they say. And doubtless it is an ideal foundation planting. Happy is the house with the fewest flies, and basil keeps the flies away—here as well as in India.

VIRGINIA'S EGGPLANT WITH BASIL

1 eggplant, peeled and cut   6 tablespoons olive oil
  in cubes   3 tablespoons fresh basil
1 large onion, chopped   leaves, chopped
  salt and pepper to taste

Sauté all ingredients in olive oil for 5 or 6 minutes. Cover and cook until eggplant is tender, stirring frequently. Add water if necessary. Makes 4 servings.

It is exciting to have one's own pot of basil because it can be Opal basil, with its large purple leaves. Handsome to look at, nutmeggy and sweetly pungent to taste, it is one of the finest and most distinctive herbs to use for flavoring vinegars.

Basil thyme is mild, small-leaved, and decorative, with minty overtones. A delightful summer herb.

Many people consider the small-leafed dwarf bush basil superior as a seasoning to the large sweet leaves of the most familiar basil. It is true that it has a rather coarse, savage distinction, interesting as a seasoning, but it lacks the sweet pungent charm of king basil.

OPAL BASIL VINEGAR

Fill a wide-mouthed jar with leaves of Opal basil, 1 clove of garlic, and 1 small mild onion (shallot, if possible). For maximum flavor the leaves should be picked the day before, a dry day, just before the plant comes into flower. Cover the leaves with white-wine vinegar, for appearance more than flavor. Let it stand for a few days, or as long as two weeks, testing now and then to make sure it is not becoming bitter. Strain the vinegar through a cloth and bottle it, with a new sprig of purple basil standing upright in the bottle. Cork it tightly.

26. Bay Leaf

A wreath of *BAY LEAVES* (*Laurus nobilis*) has long crowned victors on the fields of sport and battle. It seems a more fitting crown for triumphs in the culinary arts—for laureates of the kitchen.

Remote in the mists of mythology, Apollo, the sun god, pursued a reluctant nymph named Daphne until the gods mercifully turned her into a laurel tree. So the laurel became Apollo's favorite tree, and its pungent aromatic leaves are a favorite of everyone who cooks. Most of the bay leaves used in America come from those Grecian groves of magnificent laurel trees that are Daphne's descendants. Along with the laurel crown goes a fringe benefit. Neither witch nor devil, thunder nor lightning, will hurt a man in the place where a bay tree is. For this reason the Emperor Tiberius always wore a laurel crown during a thunder storm, a graceful habit doubtless giving him more comfort than protection.

A gift of the gods indeed, the bay leaf is indispensable as a seasoning, but its robustness should be handled with care. The bay leaf contains a combination of several aromatic oils, including the stunning one that gives anaesthetic power to the clove, and also some of the oil that imbues parsley with its light woodsy quality.

The bay leaf, as a seasoning, likes to take its time. As an essential part of a bouquet garni, it slowly gives off its oils to flavor and to blend a simmering beef stew or ragout, a sauce for pasta, soup or broth. A bay leaf added to a slow-cooking custard or rice pudding gives a different and pleasant flavor.

Bay blends well with hearty fish dishes; it gives character to stuffing for baked fish. Bay is essential in those most satisfying concoctions, the fish stews, whether bouillabaisse, a matelote, zuppa da pesce, or just good fish stew.

Bay leaf belongs in court bouillon and in marinades. As illustrated by Marcel Boulestin in *The Finer Cooking*, "a marinade in which soak for 6 or 7 days, say, a saddle of hare, this marinade being used afterwards, with the addition of cream, mustard and brandy for making the sauce."

A bay leaf is put in the bottom of the dish when making a liver paté, a terrine of game, duck or other fowl, or a meat loaf. Some people like a bay leaf cooked with potatoes or carrots. Two or three bay leaves tucked in the rice supply or in a box of prunes lend a distinctive aroma to vary their simplicity.

The Italians seldom use bay leaf with tomato and are careful about employing it with delicate veal dishes; it is best with beef, they say. Italians also point out that chestnuts have no taste at all if cooked without bay leaf. This fact serves as a good reminder of the true function of a seasoning: to blend, to accent while still retaining its own anonymity.

Bay leaf is sometimes chopped or pounded; powdered bay leaf is now carried in some stores. These forms are for quicker cooking, frequently when a marked taste of bay leaf is wanted. They are especially useful with oily fish, such as mackerel. Whole bay leaf is put in at the beginning of the cooking; the powdered kind is added a few minutes before the end. For two pounds of meat or two quarts of fish broth, an average serving for six people, one bay leaf is adequate.

DAUBE À L'AVIGNONNAISE

(*Pot roast from Avignon*)

4 pounds of lean lamb, cut in fair-size chunks	salt and pepper, freshly ground
4 ounces bacon	½ teaspoon thyme
4 tablespoons minced parsley	2 bay leaves
4 cloves garlic, 1 minced	½ teaspoon marjoram
4 large onions, sliced	½ bottle dry red wine
3 carrots, sliced	1 ounce brandy
5 tablespoons olive oil	1 piece of orange peel

Insert into each piece of meat a small piece of bacon which

has been rolled in the minced parsley mixed with minced garlic. This will use about 1 ounce of the 4 ounces of bacon. Put the prepared meat, 2 of the onions, carrots, salt and pepper, thyme, bay leaf, and marjoram in a dish approximately the size of the meat. Cover with the red wine and brandy and allow to marinate at least 4 to 5 hours.

Put the rest of the bacon, cut up, and 4 or 5 tablespoons of olive oil into a heavy pot; add the other 2 onions and brown with the lamb, fresh herbs, orange peel, and remaining garlic. Add the liquid marinade and let it bubble until it has reduced about one-third. Just cover meat with boiling water. Simmer, covered, very slowly for 4 to 5 hours.

The daube can be made the day before it is wanted, any fat skimmed off the sauce, and reheated. A daube is always better the second day. A few stoned black olives and a half ounce of dried capers may be added before the water is put in.

VENETIAN BAKED FISH

3 pounds of fish (mackerel, snapper)
⅛ teaspoon cayenne
½ cup olive oil
2 bay leaves, shredded

2 teaspoons each of finely chopped parsley, chives, chervil, fennel
½ teaspoon thyme
1 teaspoon salt
1 lemon

Clean and dry the fish and sprinkle with the cayenne. Lay them on a shallow earthenware baking dish and pour half the oil over them. Make a few long incisions along the top of the fish and lay the herbs in the cuts with a little salt. Squeeze half the lemon over the fish; put the dish in a hot oven near the top to brown, or set under the grill for 1 or 2 minutes. Cook for 25 to 30 minutes, according to size; remove dish and set aside to cool. Before fish are cold, pour the rest of the olive oil and squeeze the rest of the lemon juice over them. Serve cold with potato salad.

27. Bergamot

BERGAMOT (*Monarda didyma*) is familiar to all Americans as scarlet sage, and also as the showy flower with pink, blue, or mauve blossoms that grows at the edges of fields and woods.

It is best known as the principal ingredient of Oswego tea, a beverage of which all have heard and few have tasted.

Bees love bergamot—bee-balm was its name—and some insist that man does also. The addicts recommend the flowers, sweet yet pungent, in a salad. The young leaves are reminiscent of sage crossed with rosemary.

Oil of bergamot, so useful in commerce, does not come from this plant but from the fruit of the bergamot orange (*Citrus bergamia*).

SAUSAGE WITH APPLE AND BERGAMOT

1½ *pounds pork sausage*
2 *large tart apples, cored and sliced*
1 *onion, sliced*
1 *clove garlic, minced*
1 *tablespoon butter*

flour for dredging
1 *tablespoon chopped bergamot leaves*
salt, pepper
cinnamon
1 *cup stock or water*

Sauté the apple, onion, and garlic in butter until soft; remove from pan with a perforated spoon. Dredge sausages with flour and fry until golden brown. Place alternate layers of apple-onion-garlic mixture, sausages, bergamot leaves, salt, pepper, and a light dusting of cinnamon in a casserole. Cover with stock or water. Bake, covered, in a 350-degree oven or simmer on top of the stove for 1 to 1½ hours.

28. *Borage*

BORAGE (*Borago officinalis*), for those who have a garden, is blue and graceful and easy to grow, if only to "comfort the heart and increase the joy of the mind." A sure cure for melancholy and hypochondria, no one can afford not to grow borage.

The rough leaves of this pleasant self-seeding annual have a light cucumber flavor, made famous in the Pimms Cup No. 1, and are good in most punches. Its charming blue-star flower is a favorite with the bees and with those who like to make crystallized flowers to beautify cakes, custards, and ices. In a scented bath, borage was said to strengthen the body, beautify the skin.

JERSEY EEL SOUP

2 *pounds conger eel*	2 *cups shelled peas*
salt and pepper	1 *teaspoon flour*
3 *sprigs parsley*	1 *cup milk*
1 *sprig thyme*	2 *teaspoons vinegar*
1 *head cabbage, shredded*	*butter*
2 *shallots, chopped*	12 *marigold petals*
6 *borage leaves*	*lemon, sliced*

Have fish skinned. Put in saucepan with 1 quart water, 2 teaspoons vinegar, salt and pepper, parsley and thyme. Simmer for 40 minutes. Strain liquid into another saucepan. Bring to a boil and add cabbage, shallots, borage and peas. Cook until tender. Add flour to half the milk and thicken soup with it. Add the rest of the milk and a small piece of butter. Serve soup with marigold petals floating in it. Serve eel with lemon separately.

CRYSTALLIZED FLOWERS

For a bit less than a half cup of borage flowers, 1 pound of sugar and 1 cup of water will be needed. Bring the sugar and water to a boil and heat until the syrup reaches 240 degrees on a candy thermometer. Drop the dry flowers into the syrup about a dozen at a time. Boil at the same temperature for a little more than a minute. Lift them out with a perforated spoon and lay them carefully on a sheet of aluminum foil. Place in a slightly warmed oven to dry and to cool gradually, turning once during the process.

A COSMETIC BATH (*from "The Toilet of Flora" in The Scented Garden by E. S. Rohde*)

Take a pound of barley or bean-meal, 8 pounds of bran and a few handfuls of borage leaves. Boil these ingredients in a sufficient quantity of spring water. Nothing cleanses and softens the skin like this bath.

29. Burnet

BURNET (*Poterium sanguisorba*), the dyspeptic's cucumber, is dainty and pretty with a distinct cucumber taste; it is most useful as an edible decoration.

With thin, deeply serrated leaves, rivaling the ubiquitous mint as a summer decoration for platters and punches, burnet is one of the most beautiful herb plants. Though the older leaves gradually become slightly bitter and tough, there are always young ones for eating. They are delicious and useful with fish salads, hors d'oeuvre, green salads, or with tomato slices. In light punches the mild aromatic oil blends and delicately flavors.

The Italians are so fond of burnet in salads that they have made a little verse about it:

> *L'insalata non è buona, ne bella*
> *Ove non è la Pimpinella.*

meaning that a salad is neither good nor pretty without burnet.

Burnet is pleasant, too, in homemade vinegars, of cider, wine, or malt. And Francis Bacon liked to walk on it. (Essay on gardens.)

30. *Capsicums*

CAPSICUMS (Genus capsicum), a brightly colored string of chili peppers ranging from hot to chilly, do not rightfully belong in the category of aromatic herbs and spices. They have no aromatic oils and depend for their effect on a purely chemical reaction: stinging and irritating the membranes of the mouth and nose.

So potent is the sting of some chili peppers that they must be handled cautiously or they will burn the hands. I am told that no chili that grows in the Western Hemisphere is as hot as some which grow in the East. The seeds are the hottest part of the chili.

This single talent of hot chili peppers, to irritate, has its virtues. It induces perspiration, with subsequent evaporation, giving a pleasant, cooling effect in the tropics or on a hot summer day. It stimulates the flow of saliva and the gastric juices, aiding digestion. It has great value as a seasoning force when combined with other foods and seasonings.

The capsicums do not work best alone. They need to team up with one or more aromatic ingredients, hence chili powder, a blend of red pepper, cumin, oregano, garlic, and sometimes other seasonings. The chili arouses the membranes, increases the flow of saliva; the aromatics carry the flavors to the nose.

There are many mistaken ideas about the hot capsicums, especially among so-called gourmets who think that, because chili gives the impression of such strength, it covers or smothers flavor. Just the opposite is true, of course. For example, raw oysters seasoned with a bit of Tabasco give off more oyster flavor than without it. Elmer Roessner, "Rosy," Bell-McClure's witty columnist and editor, and an individual kind of gourmet, claims that Tabasco is a more potent picker-upper of flavors than is monosodium glutamate.

Here are some of Rosy's notes on hot pepper sauce: the big rule is that, if you can taste the pepper, you've used too much. Hot sauces tingle taste buds, enhancing flavor. Here's a test: beat

3 eggs together and divide in 3 lots. Then add MSG to one lot, one drop of red-hot pepper sauce to the second, and nothing to the third. Cook at once in 3 frypans and taste to see which you like best. Have others who do not know which is which to taste too. Also try a single drop of pepper sauce in a cold glass of milk. Surprisingly, milk tastes more like milk. Also two or three drops in gravies, stews, basting water, etc. But beware of recipes calling for a half teaspoon or a teaspoon of Tabasco. A drop of Tabasco, however, would improve fruits cooked for pies, even home-made ice cream. Though the action on the membranes in the mouth is quite different, Rosy's conclusion shows, nevertheless, that his palate is thinking for itself.

It is interesting that the heat of the hot capsicums seems to hit hardest, to explode, at the back of the tongue underneath the nasal passage, making all the taste organs become extremely sensitive to flavors. The function of even a small amount of cayenne in a delicate sauce becomes evident. Every good chef keeps cayenne, or the not quite so hot, made-in-America red pepper, at his fingertips for seasoning almost anything; just a little does wonders. Crushed red pepper has the same kind of effect, but more so, in heartier foods. The vinegar in which tiny green whole chilis are preserved is an excellent seasoning.

Not all the capsicums are hot. In fact, the bigger the pepper, the milder, until one reaches the plump, meaty bell peppers—green, red, and yellow beauties—which are vegetables with an amiable flavor, but hardly piquant. Many varieties of the numerous piquant chilis, when fresh, have warm, sweet, pleasing flavors which those north of the border seldom taste.

CHILI is so well loved in Texas that one writer describes the state as the place where they put chili powder in everything but ice cream. A decade ago chili con carne was named the official state dish. But regional use of the pungent spice is not limited by the boundaries of the Lone Star State. Chili is the seasoning of tamales, tortillas, frijoles, Aztec pies, and dozens of other dishes that reflect in their flavor the buoyant spirit of the whole area south of the Rio Grande.

Chili powder is not a single spice but a blend of chili pepper, oregano, cumin, garlic, and salt. Some blends also add cloves, allspice, and black pepper.

Legend credits chili's invention to an Englishman who had taken up abode in San Antonio in the early nineteenth century. When the supply of curry ingredients that he had brought with him ran out, the ingenious chap devised an American equivalent of curry powder. He used the chili peppers and oregano that grew wild in nearby Mexico.

PAPRIKA (*Capsicum annum*) is the ground, dried, stemless pod of a mild capsicum. Paprika was first discovered growing in Central America, and plants were taken back to Europe by early explorers. The world's most delicious paprika was developed in Hungary. Sweet, inimitable Hungarian paprika can be bought at Paprikas Weiss, 1546 Second Avenue, New York City. The United States now imports most of its mild paprika from Spain, but the Spanish variety is harsh compared to the Hungarian.

The little sprinkle of paprika here and there that most cooks indulge in, is pleasant enough for a garnish, but a little more, a half or a whole teaspoonful would add enough of paprika's mild sweet flavor to enhance almost any dish.

Professor Albert Szent-Gyorgyi, a Hungarian scientist now in the United States, won a Nobel prize in 1937 for his experiments with paprika. He discovered in paprika a new group of substances called bioflavonoids, which are also present in citrus and other fruits. These have been found valuable in maintaining the health of the capillary system and in treating many other ailments. He discovered also that the capsicums contain a fabulous amount of vitamin C, perhaps more than any other plant.

STUFFED FLOUNDER FILLET

2 *pounds flounder fillets*	1/3 *cup celery, chopped*
4 *slices bread, broken into pieces*	1/3 *cup parsley, chopped*
	1 1/2 *pounds crabmeat*
1/2 *cup milk*	1/8 *teaspoon Tabasco sauce*
3 *tablespoons butter*	1 *teaspoon salt*
1/2 *cup onion, chopped*	1/2 *teaspoon black pepper*
1 *clove garlic, minced*	2 *eggs, lightly beaten*

Soak bread in milk; squeeze dry. Melt butter on medium heat and sauté onion, garlic, and celery. Add bread with remaining ingredients to sauté. Spread mixture between fillets, holding together with wooden toothpicks. Place in fireproof serving dish and bake in a 350-degree oven, basting from time to time for 25 minutes. Serve in the same dish. Makes 6 to 8 servings.

SAUCE FOR BASTING

½ cup melted butter	*2 cloves garlic, minced*
¼ cup lemon juice	*¼ cup parsley, minced*

The Hungarians have a whole category of foods called Paprikas; they are stews; they always contain sour cream, seldom vegetables.

CHICKEN PAPRIKÁS

1 3-pound chicken, cut in	*1½ teaspoons flour*
serving pieces	*1¼ cups stock*
1 teaspoon salt	*1 tablespoon cream*
2 tablespoons butter	*1 cup sour cream*
1 onion, diced	*2 tablespoons chopped*
1 tablespoon paprika	*fresh dill (optional)*

Rinse and dry chicken; season with salt and place (covered) for 30 minutes in the refrigerator. Heat butter in a large, heavy pot. Add onion and cook until transparent; stir in paprika. Add chicken. Cook slowly, being careful not to burn the paprika, until pieces are golden, then cover and cook 30 minutes longer, or until tender. Sprinkle with flour. Add stock and cream; stir, cover, and let simmer for 15 minutes. Remove chicken to warmed serving dish. Stir in sour cream and heat. Pour over chicken. Sprinkle with dill, if desired. Serves 4 or 5.

Paprika as a decoration may be used lavishly. It has a fruity quality which never overpowers, as paprika mayonnaise or paprika sour cream on fruits or salads; in hollandaise; to coat meats before roasting.

31. *Caraway*

CARAWAY (*Carum carvi*) seed, a favorite of the Romans, was carried by those legions to the edge of the Scottish moors where, beside the undulating, now green, wall, the Romans built their forts and their gardens. In Scotland, caraway cakes are still called after the old Latin name, "Carvi cakes."

One of the ancient herbs, it is thought that caraway probably originated in mankind's boyhood home in Asia Minor, from where it quickly spread all over the world. The Egyptians thought highly of it as a medicine, while the Romans enjoyed caraway as a condiment.

A member of the parsley family, caraway is worth growing in the garden if it doesn't crowd out more useful plants. It is pleasant to look at, resembling Queen Anne's lace; its root is edible, rather like a delicate parsnip; the leaves have a similar flavor, but are milder than the seeds. The right soil and careful cultivation have made Holland the best source of caraway seeds, and the United States is their best customer.

Caraway seed is refreshing; it has a clean-cut pungency which lightens and cuts heavy kinds of foods such as pork and mutton, liver, the cabbages (including sauerkraut and cole slaw), gravies, and cheese. The oils of caraway are perfumed and light, almost lemony. They are a delightful and valuable seasoning, worth trying in unexpected places.

Although not really assertive, caraway has a pleasant authority, giving a lift to certain foods which might otherwise be a bit dull, as carrots, spinach, potato salad, eggs, cream cheese. It is best known to us in breads, cakes, and cookies, where its clean-cut tang is most appetizing.

Our ancestors, to promote digestion, it is said, used to serve roast apples with caraway seeds at the end of a meal, a habit that could well be reinstated as a pleasure, not a duty. Caraway and apple do have an affinity and the small seeds are excellent in apple pie or any other apple dish.

When at home, do as the Romans do, munch caraway seeds after dinner.

GOULASH WITH SAUERKRAUT

(SZÉKELY GULYÁS *from Anne Sekely Cooking School in New York City*)

2 pounds veal or beef cut in 1½ inch cubes	1 cup chopped tomatoes
4 tablespoons beef suet	1 cup sour cream
1½ cups sliced onions	2 teaspoons chopped caraway seeds
1 clove garlic, minced	1 teaspoon salt
1 tablespoon Hungarian paprika	4 cups sauerkraut

Heat fat in heavy pan. Sauté onion and garlic. Add paprika and meat and sauté together. The juice of the meat will keep the paprika from burning. Hungarians often mix in the paprika off the flame; it gets bitter if burned. Add salt, tomatoes, and 1 cup water. Cover pan and cook slowly (adding a little water from time to time if needed), until meat is nearly done and the sauce is greatly reduced. Stir frequently. When sauce is cooked down, add sour cream and caraway seeds. Simmer ½ hour longer.

Fresh sauerkraut should be used, if possible. Squeeze it out (it will be too sour otherwise) and cook it ½ to 1 hour. Arrange alternate layers of goulash and sauerkraut in a warmed serving dish, ending with sauerkraut on top. Serve very hot. Serves 8.

RICH SEED CAKE

4 ounces sugar	2 level tablespoons caraway seeds
4 ounces butter	¼ teaspoon ginger
2 eggs	grated rind 1 lemon
4 ounces sifted flour	slice of citron for top
½ teaspoon baking powder	

Cream butter and sugar until light and fluffy. Lightly beat eggs and gradually add to mixture, beating well after each addition. Lightly fold in flour, baking powder, and ginger sifted together. Add caraway seeds and lemon peel. Bake in a lined

8-inch cake pan in a 325-degree oven for 60 to 75 minutes. Place a thin slice of citron on center of cake after first 20 minutes, when top is set.

32. *Celery*

CELERY (*Apium graveolens*) has come a long way in a short time—from the perky green bittersweet herb which is a rather acrid wild plant still used as a seasoning over most of the world, to the luxurious tender sweet vegetable of which the highly bred Pascal is a triumphant example.

A native of Europe's marshy places from Sweden to Ethiopia and eastward to the Caucasus, wild celery—"smallage" is its name —has been valued for centuries as a medicinal herb, represented as a purifier of the blood.

Although it has always been essential to the pot-on-the-fire— which we call a stew—it was not until the seventeenth or eighteenth century in France that any attempt was made to produce a cultivated variety of celery. In the United States the first commercial production was started by a group of Dutch farmers in Kalamazoo, Michigan, in 1874. To stimulate interest in their product, they offered bunches of celery for sale to passengers on the trains that stopped at Kalamazoo.

The attributes of celery are many. It is said that the Greeks, who called it *selinon,* gave this herb as a prize to victorious athletes. Celery juice, mixed with honey of roses and barley water, makes a fine gargle. Being mostly water, celery also is held in high esteem by dieters.

A modern book of etiquette, whose writer frowns on the ostentatious habit of holding up a table napkin while removing from the mouth a bad oyster or while picking the teeth, recommends for this purpose a stalk (or bunch) of celery, obviously feathered.

Celeriac, grown for its sweet mild turnip-shaped root, has the celery flavor intensified. It is excellent as a vegetable—fried or braised or mashed with potatoes; as a seasoning its properties are similar to those of celery.

The aromatic oils of celery are a delightful blending agent in soups, stuffings, sauces, and nearly all long-cooking dishes. The water or broth in which celery has been cooked, if kept in the refrigerator, is a convenience in the kitchen and may be used instead of water in sauces, to heat vegetables, etc.

A "stalk" of celery is the same as a "bunch"—the whole plant. Each stalk is made up of several "ribs."

The celery seed that is sold in the grocery store to be used as a seasoning is not a product of the cultivated celery plant. Most celery seed is imported to the United States from France and India. It has a distinctly celery-like flavor, warm and bitter, is strong in aromatic oil, and as a seasoning contributes also a nutty and crunchy quality which adds interest and contrast to dishes. About a half teaspoon of celery seed added to bland vegetables gives them a lift (braised lettuce, for instance). A sprinkle of celery seed is good in split-pea soup.

Celery is a wonderful accompaniment to cheese.

CELERY AND CHESTNUTS

Astringent celery is an excellent foil for the bland, mealy chestnut.

2½ cups diced celery	½ cup all-purpose cream
3 cups lightly salted	salt and pepper
water	1 cup cooked chestnuts,
4 tablespoons butter	peeled and broken
3 tablespoons flour	pinch of sugar
1 cup celery liquid	paprika

Cook celery in water until tender, about 15 minutes; drain, reserving liquid. Blend butter with flour in the top part of a double boiler; stir in the celery liquid and cream. Taste for seasoning and add salt, if necessary, a pinch of sugar, and ⅛ teaspoon freshly ground pepper. When sauce is thickened and smooth, add celery and chestnuts. Before serving, sprinkle with paprika.

CELERY, CABBAGE, AND APPLE SALAD

2 cups sliced celery
2 cups finely shredded
cabbage
2 cups diced unpeeled
apples
¼ cup Roquefort or bleu
cheese

1 cup sour cream
dash cayenne
⅛ teaspoon ground black
pepper
1 teaspoon salt
head lettuce

Place celery, cabbage, and apples in a salad bowl. Press cheese through a fine sieve and blend with sour cream, cayenne, black pepper, and salt. Add and mix lightly. Serve on lettuce. Makes 6 servings.

33. *Chamomile*

CHAMOMILE (*Anthemis nobilis* and *Matricaria chamomilla*). Healthy, soothing chamomile has as many aliases as an international criminal. First, there is both true and false chamomile. True chamomile is named *Anthemis nobilis,* while the false sounds true with *Matricaria chamomilla*. False, or German or wild chamomile, is best for drinking and walking upon. True chamomile is called the Plant's Physician, and is just what the doctor ordered for humans, too.

True, or Roman—to distinguish it from German, or false—chamomile is grown extensively as a medicinal plant (the English say that the English plants are by far the best) and it was for its healing properties that the ancient Egyptians worshipped it above all other herbs. Dried chamomile is sometimes smoked in a pipe to aid asthma sufferers.

As a plant doctor true chamomile has a spectacular bedside manner. Not only does it keep nearby plants healthy in the garden, but it is said that a dying or drooping plant will recover if chamomile is planted near it.

But for a comforting, soothing tisane, the thing to use is false or German or wild chamomile. My teen-age daughters love chamomile tea. And a path sown with this herb is soft as chenille to walk on. The plants are more fragrant if grown on poor ground; they should be kept well trimmed and the path rolled after each cutting. Even Montezuma had his chamomile maze.

Chamomile tea, I should think, is worth trying in punches and in tall drinks, as the South Americans treat their herb teas.

Here is a cure that is worth trying with either true or false chamomile: "It will restore a man to hys color shortly, yf a man, after the longe use of the bathe, drynke of it after he is come forthe oute of the bath."

34. Chervil

CHERVIL (*Anthriscus cerefolium*) is called by frustrated American and English lovers of good food the "neglected seasoning." Why little bunches of fresh chervil are not found beside parsley and chives in the markets remains a mystery.

Chervil looks like a cross between curly and Italian parsley. It is a decorative, easy-to-grow annual, even liking some shade. It not only has a dainty, fresh yet spicy flavor of its own, rather like a light tarragon, but it delights to combine with other herbs. Its blending qualities are outstanding. In France, where fine food is of first importance, chervil ranks high on the list of seasonings.

Chervil is thought to be a native of southern and western Asia, where Man also began his climb toward civilization, so no doubt it has been always with us, though primitive man was more attached to a spectacular herb like garlic than to the modest chervil.

Pliny writes little about chervil as a seasoning, but recommends it highly as a cure for hiccups—vinegar in which chervil seeds have been soaked.

Chervil is an ingratiating herb, a mix-it-in, throw-it-on, toss-it-with herb. Alone, though more often in combination, chervil is an ideal salad herb—with mixed greens, potato salad, etc.; in fresh-tasting sauces—ravigote, vinaigrette, salad dressings, butter sauces. Throw finely chopped chervil on top of soups as they are served. In scrambled eggs or omelet (fines herbes) it is excellent; fine with fish.

Like parsley, chervil should be picked from the outside, allowing it to go on growing from the center.

SAUCE RAVIGOTE

From the French verb "ravigoter" to revive, to cheer, the sauce is well named, and is especially cheering to leftovers.

COLD VERSION

4 tablespoons olive oil	salt, freshly ground pepper,
2 hard-cooked egg yolks, riced and crushed	pinch of sugar chopped parsley, chervil,
2 teaspoons French mustard	chives, and if desired also
2 tablespoons wine vinegar	tarragon, burnet, and capers

Stir oil into yolks, as for mayonnaise, add remaining ingredients and mix well.

WARM VERSION

2 shallots or 1 small mild onion, minced, put in pan with	salt and plenty of freshly ground black pepper, and
1 tablespoon white wine vinegar. Reduce by half, stirring constantly. Add	1 tablespoon each minced parsley, chervil, capers, and
1 tablespoon tomato paste	½ teaspoon minced
1 cup stock. Simmer gently 10 minutes. Blend in	tarragon and chives
1 teaspoon flour; simmer 5 minutes, stirring occasionally. Add	1 teaspoon prepared mustard

ENDIVE AND BEET SALAD

One of the best winter salads.

¾ pound Belgian endives,
washed and cut across in
2-inch pieces
1 large beet, cut in thin
slices

1 tablespoon fines herbes
(parsley and chervil,
finely chopped)
salt, pepper, pinch of sugar
1 tablespoon wine vinegar
3 tablespoons olive oil

Dress just before serving.

35. Chicory

CHICORY (Cichorium intybus and Cichorium endivia). As one might expect, a venerable plant that has been written about for 6,000 years is steeped in legend and in history. For 6,000 years—that we know of—chicory has beeen in demand. "To refresh myself, give me olives, chicory and light mallows," Homer wrote.

Not only Homer wanted to refresh himself with chicory. Today's descendants of the Romans treat it as a spring tonic; they cook up refreshing, astringent batches of chicory as soon as the new season produces them as "a refresher of the blood," the Italian "sulphur and molasses."

Mankind has had a long time to get used to chicory as a medicine, as several kinds of salad green, as a cooked green, as a root vegetable, and as an interesting seasoning.

Graceful, dainty chicory, a perennial herb which is one of the charms of country roads, is cultivated like other root crops in rich, deep, well-drained soil. Its leaves resemble the dandelion, its blue flowers (though white and pink are not uncommon) turn always toward the sun and close when the sun goes down. So chicory is inevitably the symbol of faithfulness: This time it was a vapid young lady named Elytra who, jilted by the sun god, Apollo, could think of nothing better to do than to follow him always with her eyes.

The old name for chicory is succory, and there is no doubt that it is the household's little helper. Its blanched leaves are highly regarded as a winter salad, *barbe-de-capucin*. Its specially grown blanched root is well known as the incomparable Belgian endive (witloof chicory).

Because of its capacity to heighten flavor, chicory is an excellent potherb. A small amount added to gravies sharpens the flavor. It brightens Spanish, Italian, and Mexican sauces. A small amount of chicory may be mixed into a paste with the vinegar and added to salad dressing. Chicory mixed with water or wine will enhance the flavor of potatoes roasted in the pan with meats. The potatoes should be basted only in the last ten minutes of cooking time. The basting liquid, mixing with the fats in the pan, will give the gravy a different, pleasing flavor. Chicory accents flavor in such things as meat loaf and hamburgers. It makes chocolate more chocolaty. One teaspoonful of chicory added to a chocolate custard pie is delicious.

But it is as an accent for coffee that chicory really comes into its own. Many Americans think that chicory is added to coffee as an adulterant, and, in truth, it sometimes is. But in Europe it is added to sharpen the flavor of coffee, and coffee without chicory to many people, especially to a Frenchman, tastes flat. Many Americans like it, too. According to a test run at the University of Michigan, coffee drinkers liked coffee with chicory better than coffee alone.

Although users of chicory in coffee will soon discover the proportions which are pleasing to them, many people like one teaspoonful of chicory to four teaspoons of ground coffee. They also find that less coffee is necessary. Some may not care for it; some will never be content with ordinary coffee again.

CAFÉ AU LAIT   (Café au lait is the national breakfast drink in France and a favorite in New Orleans.)

1½ cups strong, hot, freshly   1½ cups hot milk
*   brewed coffee with*
*   chicory*

Using two pots, pour simultaneously into cups. Makes 3 servings.

VIENNESE COFFEE

It was a Pole, Franz Kolschitsky, who opened the first coffeehouse in Vienna in 1683. As a reward for helping to save Vienna from invading Turks, he received a building and hundreds of sacks of green coffee which had been left behind by the invader. He used his gifts well.

There are many versions of this renowned coffee. It may be spiced with cinnamon or cloves, but there is always a drift of *schlagober,* or whipped cream in Vienna. Brew extra-strength coffee with chicory, sweeten to taste, top with whipped cream.

TURKISH COFFEE

In Turkey at one time, a husband's refusal to give his wife coffee was legitimate grounds for divorce.

The coffee is served in tiny cups, and each guest gets his share of the foam formed by the brewing of the coffee. In Arabic, this is called "the face of the coffee," and one loses face if coffee is served without it. In Turkish homes it is the job of the daughter of the house to make coffee for the guests who come to call in the evening.

1½ cups of water   4 tablespoons ground coffee
*   4 teaspoons sugar   with chicory*

Measure water into a heavy saucepan; add sugar and bring to a boil. Stir in coffee and bring to a boil. Allow brew to froth up three times and remove from the heat. Add a few drops of cold water. Spoon some of the foam into each tiny cup and then pour in the coffee. Makes 4 demitasse servings.

CAFFE CAPPUCCINO

This Italian specialty is named after an order of Franciscan friars, the Capuchins, whose robes are the color of coffee. Although the very best Cappuccino is made with an espresso machine (when both coffee and milk become one under pressure), it is also good when it is made without any special equipment. Cappuccino is often served in mugs.

Use strong coffee with chicory. Combine steaming coffee with an equal quantity of steaming milk. Pour into cups. Add sugar and sprinkle with cinnamon or nutmeg.

IRISH COFFEE

strong black coffee with   *Irish whisky*
chicory   *soft whipped cream*
fine granulated sugar

Place 2 teaspoons of sugar into a warmed wine glass or Irish Coffee glass and fill glass ⅔ full with hot coffee. Mix. Add 2 tablespoons Irish whisky and top with soft whipped cream. Do not stir; sip hot coffee through the cool cream. Makes 1 serving.

36. Chives

CHIVES (*Allium schoenoprasum*), the benign baby of the onion family, are delicious green shoots called by the Norwegians "grass leeks."

Small as they are, chives pack a mighty punch. Their aromatic oil is the same as in mustard, making it a surprisingly fine seasoner.

Chives are invaluable in hors d'oeuvre and dips, both as decoration and seasoning, in salads, and in herb mixtures for many sauces. They combine well with light cheeses and delicate foods such as fish. In all the hearty summer salads of fish and fruit, chicken, potato or rice, chives make a pleasing contribution.

In the herb garden there is nothing prettier than the lavender drift of chives in bloom, so easily grown that it is even easier to neglect them. The little bulbs must be separated every few years or suddenly they will stop growing for want of breathing space.

The refreshing green pungency of chives adds a most satisfactory touch to winter menus. When potting them for the house, separate the little bulbs in order to be rewarded by healthy, long-lasting plants. The same treatment is good for the little plants of chives now sold in the markets.

WEST INDIAN CRAB GUMBO

6 crabs	1/4 teaspoon red pepper
3 large tomatoes, peeled, seeded, and chopped	1 sprig parsley
	1 sprig thyme
7 okras, sliced	4 tablespoons butter
1 onion, chopped	3/4 teaspoon salt
a few blades chives, minced	

Have fish man clean crabs, remove claws, and cut body into four pieces. Sauté crabs in butter; add seasonings and sauté; add okras and tomatoes and sauté. Add 2 to 2½ pints water. Cover and simmer 1 hour. When cooked, the mixture should be like thick soup, Serve in hot tureen with rice. Makes 6 servings.

37. Sweet Cicely

SWEET CICELY (*Myrrhis odorata*) is an herb which belongs in the flower garden. A feathery, graceful plant resembling Queen Anne's lace, it is charming in bouquets or for decorating platters, and is also useful in the kitchen.

The botanical name of cicely translates to mean "musklike

chervil," with a light musky-anise flavor. Like chervil, too, it combines well with other herbs, synthesizing and blending their flavors. It is pleasant in salads and light sauces; moreover, it adds a different note to apple pie or apple sauce.

According to Gerard's *Herbal* of the late sixteenth century, "it is used very much among the Dutch people in a kind of Loblolly or hotchpotch which they do eat, called Warmus."

38. *Coriander*

CORIANDER (*Coriandrum sativum*), like the modern deep freeze, may have the refreshing accomplishment of conferring immortality, but there are perhaps better reasons for eating its fragrant seeds. The manna of the children of Israel, the Bible says in Numbers 11:7–8, "was as coriander seed. . . . And the people went about, and gathered *it,* and ground *it* in mills, or beat *it* in a mortar, and baked *it* in pans, and made cakes of *it.*"

Delicately perfumed and plentiful, coriander has served man since he first learned to season his foods. On early Egyptian papyruses one can read about it in hieroglyphics; Egypt still produced the finest coriander seed even in Pliny's day in first-century Rome. Described in ancient Sanskrit writings, coriander is still a favorite in modern India, as well as being an essential in most curries.

Ancient Greece, too, one learns from Athenaeus, a scholar of the second and third centuries, liked coriander as a seasoning: fennel, anise, asafoetida, mustard and cabbage, dry coriander. Athenaeus points out that coriander must be completely dry, otherwise it smells unpleasantly of bugs and beetles.

In Hebrew history, it is one of the bitter herbs eaten for the Passover.

Today coriander is grown and used all over the world. The Chinese think it especially good in soups. One of the most common seasonings in Mexico, it is cooked in rice, lentil, and meat dishes. The Arab cuisine leans heavily on coriander.

How have we in America lost track of this mild, inexpensive

way to give spirit to our foods? Although it has a faint licorice taste, the general impression of coriander is pleasantly flowery with a distinct hint of orange.

Coriander combines well with protein: meat and eggs, peas, beans, and lentils. Its sweet aroma gives character to frying batters, biscuits, and pound cake. It is good in gingerbread, apple pie, and game stuffings.

With olive oil and browned onion, a dash of coriander will liven a can of beans. In combination with a bit of ginger root, a clove, a few allspice, mustard seeds, parsley, and bay leaf, coriander helps to season a magnificently hearty dish of thick pea soup for a buffet supper.

In the world of commerce coriander is much used as a seasoning and a scenting agent: in candy making, in several meat products, and as a flavoring in gin and in other distilling processes such as perfumes and liqueurs. Many countries value it as a carminative. Its flowery quality makes it, when chewed and kept in the mouth, an excellent breath sweetener.

As nothing is perfect, even with coriander one is taking a chance; it was thought to induce cupidity—misers were said to have eaten of it.

ALBONDIGAS

1 pound beef	1⅛ teaspoon salt
½ pound pork	raisins
1 clove garlic	pine nuts
2 fresh leaves, or ¼ teaspoon each sage and mint	1 onion, chopped
	2 tablespoons fat
	1 ripe tomato
1 green tomato	1 small, hot chili
1 slice bread, soaked in milk	¼ teaspoon crushed coriander seeds
1 egg, beaten	⅛ teaspoon salt
⅛ teaspoon pepper	

Grind together beef, pork, garlic, mint, sage, and green tomato; mix with bread, egg, pepper, 1 teaspoon salt. Mold into balls the size of a walnut, with a raisin and pine nut in the center. Brown onion and meat balls in fat, add crushed tomato, chili, coriander, ⅛ teaspoon salt and a little water. Simmer slowly until sauce is thick.

CARNE DE MARRANA Y CHILI

(Pork with chili)

1 leg pork	*¼ teaspoon coriander*
pulp of 12 red chilies	*¼ teaspoon sage*
or	*1 clove garlic, minced*
3 tablespoons chili powder	*½ teaspoon salt*

Add seasoning to chili pulp and stir to thick paste. If chili powder is used, dampen with water, wine, or vinegar. Cut 5 or 6 holes in the meat and fill with the mixture (alongside the bone carries seasoning best). Plug holes with the meat again and cook in a 325-degree oven, allowing at least 30 minutes per pound. Half an hour before meat is finished, cover with remaining paste.

GARBANZOS *(Chick-peas)*

These can be bought in cans and also are sold dried in Italian or Spanish groceries.

1 cup garbanzos or dried peas	*salt pork or bacon fat*
	½ cup red chili pulp
1 teaspoon salt	*or*
¼ teaspoon coriander	*1½ tablespoons chili powder*
1 onion, chopped	

If necessary (for dried peas) let stand overnight in cold water to cover. Next day, bring to a boil, drain, and cover with fresh water. Add salt and coriander and simmer 1 hour or until tender. Sauté onion in salt pork or bacon fat. Mash the garbanzos lightly. Add onion and chili and reheat.

39. Costmary

COSTMARY (*Chrysanthemum balsamita*), fresh, minty, lem-ony, is a useful, good-looking, much-neglected plant. It grows and grows, spreading by runners, so that one soon becomes popular giving little pots of costmary to friends. It grows even in the shade; it grows when the weather is cold, and it is evergreen. Costmary's growth shoots up to three feet; it can get straggly and out of hand. Both for beauty's sake and for a good supply of tender small leaves, it is best to keep the plants ruthlessly cut back. In August it produces a charming, daisy-like flower.

It is a great satisfaction to reach under a mulch protected by a plastic cover, even under the snow, to find minty green leaves which will add a fresh taste to dried herb mixtures, or to meats, peas, potatoes, and many other dishes.

And in summer, too, costmary is good in iced drinks and punches, vegetables and fruit salads, stuffings for veal, lamb, pork, and chicken.

According to Boulestin and Hill, "the name 'costmary' is borrowed partly from costus, a violet-scented plant from the Himalayas, whose roots were once of almost fabulous value as a perfume, and refers partly to the Virgin Mary, to whom the plant seems to have been dedicated in most European countries. It is sometimes known as alecost, perhaps because it was used to make one of the many herb beers, which were once commonly brewed by country people."

STUFFED BREAST OF VEAL

2-pound breast of veal; have   *1 or 2 rashers of bacon*
butcher cut a pocket, nicely
trimmed and cleaned

Sprinkle veal with salt, pepper, monosodium glutamate, and lemon juice.

STUFFING

¾ *cup bread crumbs soaked in a little milk*	*1 teaspoon crushed rosemary*
2 eggs, slightly beaten	*1 tablespoon minced parsley*
1 rasher chopped bacon	*1 tablespoon minced*
1 tablespoon melted butter	*costmary, if available*
1 garlic clove, minced	*salt and pepper*
1 teaspoon minced onion	*2 tablespoons Marsala, if desired*

Mix stuffing ingredients well, and fill pocket in the meat. Secure the opening. Roll the meat and arrange in a fairly close-fitting oven casserole; this will help to keep meat from drying out. Spread the bacon over the meat and roast at 350 degrees until tender, about 1½ hours.

40. *Cumin*

CUMIN (*Cuminum cyminum*). All the world loves cumin seed, the same kind that lovers carry in their pockets throughout the wedding ceremony, a messy habit said to insure fidelity.

Like many old superstitions, this one, too, doubtless had its origin in good sense. It meant, of course, that the bride who was clever at using this tantalizing, seductive, spicy herb would surely hold her husband. It follows naturally that he, in turn, should be good at bringing home plenty of cumin seed and the fixings.

A native of the Nile Valley, cumin's heady fragrance has spread in all directions. Welcomed in India, it spices most curries, while in the Arab countries, cumin is perhaps the most used seasoning in a spice-packed cuisine. A salad in Morocco might be made, for instance, of ripe olives, two lemons or oranges sliced, seasoned with a pinch of salt and one of sugar, a sprinkling of hot red pepper, and a sprinkle of ground cumin. The Moors probably carried cumin from Africa to Spain, where it quickly ingratiated itself; cumin, saffron, and cinnamon (or sometimes anise), seasoning together a Spanish dish, remind us of Spain's Oriental heritage. From Spain cumin sailed to Mexico and then to the United States, where great amounts are used commercially by meat packers, and for chili sauce, chili powder, and other foods.

Many countries go along with Pliny, who considered it the best appetizer of all condiments. Northern Europe, as well as the south, likes cumin. The Dutch, the Swiss, and the Scandinavians have their cumin cheese (Kumminost), the Germans their famous liqueur, Kümmel (which also contains caraway seed), and an excellent sauerkraut seasoned with fennel, juniper, and cumin. Latin Americans sprinkle a bit of cumin in salad dressings.

As a flavoring, cumin is appetizing and stimulating; the whole seed toasted on any kind of cheese hors d'oeuvre packs a punch.

As a seasoning, cumin's oils are wonderfully aromatic, but powerful, and must be treated with respect. As with most spicing, it is best to start with a quarter of a teaspoonful for four servings and work up if you like, bearing in mind that, no matter how pleasing the flavor of cumin, the idea is to taste the food.

Cumin seed keeps chickens, as well as husbands, at home.

CARROT SALAD, MOROCCAN

1 *pound large carrots,
scraped and cut in
quarters lengthwise*
1 *pinch each, salt and
sugar*
3 *or 4 cloves garlic*

*wine vinegar, salt, and hot
red pepper*
¼ *teaspoon ground cumin
parsley
a few coriander seeds*

Cook the carrots with salt, sugar, and garlic for 15 minutes. Drain and cover with vinegar, a little more salt and hot red pepper to taste. Perfume with cumin. Decorate with parsley and a little coriander.

M E X I C A N   S T E W

2 *pounds beef*
1 *pound fresh pork*
3 *slices bacon*
1 *apple*
1 *pear*
1 *turnip*
1 *bunch carrots*
2 *onions*
1 *stalk celery*
2 *summer squashes*
1 *underripe banana*

2 *white potatoes*
2 *sweet potatoes*
2 *whole corn on the cob*
1 *cup chick-peas or beans,*
   prepared by recipe under
   Coriander
1 *generous pinch of*
   oregano
1 *teaspoon salt*
½ *teaspoon cumin*

Cut meat in large cubes; wash fruit and vegetables but do not peel. In a large kettle put the meat, then chick-peas (garbanzos), corn broken into 2- or 3-inch lengths, potatoes, onions, and turnips. Cover with water. Add seasonings. Add the other vegetables and fruit for the last hour of cooking. Simmer slowly 3 or 4 hours. Soup and meat are served separately. The following 2 sauces may be offered.

SWEET SAUCE

1 *onion chopped*
2 *tablespoons lard or bacon*
   fat
2 *tomatoes*

2½ *tablespoons sugar*
½ *teaspoon salt*
3 *tablespoons vinegar*

Sauté onion in fat until it begins to brown. Add other ingredients and cook until thickened. Serve hot.

PIQUANT SAUCE

½ *onion, finely chopped*
2 *tomatoes, mashed*
2 *pods red chili pulp*
   or
½ *teaspoon chili powder*

½ *teaspoon salt*
2 *tablespoons vinegar*
1 *tablespoon oil*

Mix all ingredients and beat until smooth. Serve cold.

In most poor countries a stew is the most important dish, meant to last for several meals, and often fried for breakfast. In Beersheba on the edge of the Negev desert I ate leftover couscous fried for breakfast.

41. Dill

DILL (Anethum graveolens), a pungent, peppy, parsley plant, has lulled babies to sleep for hundreds of years. Even the word dill, coming from Old English and Old Norwegian, means to lull, to soothe, to dull. So its amiable oil soothes the savage stomach.

Dill seems to belong to the North Countries: Norway relishes dill-cooked lamb (Dillkott Lamm); dill accents lobster smorbrod in Denmark; Rassolnick, Russia's kidney soup, is laced with great globs of sour cream, pungent with dill; Sweden in August is tipsy with gay kräftor-cooked-in-dill parties—one tot of aquavit goes down with every crayfish.

But dill is not only of the North. It has another name, *anet,* coming from the Latin. Actually, dill is native to Europe and southern Russia and grows wild even in Africa and Asia. Consequently, we import most of our dill from India. The Indians, too, have become very fond of dill and one now finds it in all their bazaars. The Romans, who were always crowning themselves with something, did it with dill *(anethum,* to them), too.

The whole plant is aromatic; the young leaves and the green fruit—the seeds—are used for seasoning and flavoring. The feathery leaves lose their flavor when dry, but the fruiting umbels are ready to dry for winter use when the seeds are fully developed but not yet brown.

The fresh leaves of dill are a delicious seasoning for lobster and shrimp, or when added to the mayonnaise that dresses cold shellfish, or in dill butter to be used in sandwiches, fish, meats, and vegetables. New potatoes cooked and dressed with fresh dill are superb and refreshing.

Dill seeds flavor not only the inimitable pickles, but also suavely season cucumber, cole slaw, and potato salads, fish stuffings and sauces, broiled meats, and chicken fricassee.

KRÄFTOR (*Crayfish which look like tiny lobsters*)

The great end-of-the-summer treat in Sweden and Norway is kräftor (known in Norway as "kreps"). The season for the little lobster begins the first part of August, an occasion for great excitement. The kräftor, which have been caught the night before, are cooked sometime during the day in heavily salted water with lots of fresh dill. Then they are allowed to cool in the water in which they are cooked.

The kräftor, at least twenty-five per person, are beautifully arranged on an enormous platter decorated with fresh dill in the center of the table. Everyone is liberally supplied with paper napkins and finger bowls, hot toast and butter. Although some people like white wine with kräftor, the traditional drink is aquavit and beer.

The drinks and the kräftor are consumed to the accompaniment of old Scandinavian drinking songs. Tradition decrees one glass of aquavit to each kräftor, although I am happy to say that few people actually go along with this. Inevitably, however, every kräftor dinner is the gayest of affairs, looked forward to from year to year.

DILL–COOKED LAMB (*Dillkott Lamm*)

3 pounds lamb shoulder	*a few sprigs fresh dill or*
1 tablespoon salt	*1 teaspoon dill seed*

Bring all ingredients to a boil in 2 quarts water; skim foam from liquid, reduce heat, cover, and simmer slowly for 1½ hours or until lamb is tender. Remove meat to warm serving platter and allow to stand about 20 minutes before carving. Slice lamb thinly; garnish with dill; serve with sauce.

SAUCE

2 tablespoons butter	1 cup lamb broth
2 tablespoons flour	2 tablespoons vinegar
¼ teaspoon salt	2 teaspoons sugar
¼ teaspoon monosodium glutamate	2 tablespoons fresh dill, finely chopped or
⅛ teaspoon pepper, freshly ground	½ teaspoon ground dill seed
	1 egg yolk

Blend butter with flour, salt, monosodium glutamate, and pepper. Heat, stirring constantly, until mixture bubbles. Gradually stir in lamb broth; stir until sauce thickens. Remove from heat and stir in vinegar, sugar, and chopped fresh dill. Blend in slightly beaten egg yolk. Heat over hot water for 3 to 5 minutes, stirring constantly.

KIDNEY SOUP (*Rassolnick*)

1 beef kidney	handful spinach, washed
6 cups stock	2 large dill pickles
1 onion	2 tablespoons dill-pickle liquid
1 rib celery	sour cream
2 teaspoons chopped parsley	salt and pepper
2 tablespoons butter	chopped fresh dill
4 medium potatoes	

Trim and clean kidney and cut in 4 parts. Put in cold water and bring to a quick boil; drain and rinse with cold water. Put in kettle with stock and simmer, covered, for 1½ hours. Brown chopped onions, celery, and parsley in the butter. When kidneys are tender, remove them to a warm platter and put potatoes and browned vegetables in the stock; simmer 25 minutes. Five or ten minutes before vegetables are cooked, add spinach cut in strips, salt and pepper to taste, and add dill-pickle juice. Cut kidneys into small pieces and return to soup. Serve in a tureen or individual bowl with plenty of heavy sour cream sprinkled with chopped fresh dill.

42. Fennel

FENNEL (*Foeniculum vulgare* and *Foeniculum vulgare dulce*) has long since performed its big deed for mankind: knowledge, in the form of a coal of fire, was transmitted in a stalk of fennel to humanity below. After that, though everything concerning fennel is something of an anticlimax, man has continued to enjoy its valuable attributes.

Whether the household of Edward I of England liked the taste of fennel, or whether it came under the category of medicines (our ancestors believed it to be one of the nine sacred herbs which could counteract the nine causes of disease), at any rate, they consumed 8½ pounds of fennel seed a month.

A member of the parsley family (Umbelliferae)—dill, anise, caraway, coriander—many of which store their essential oils in the seeds, fennel's feathery leaves, like those of dill, are to be used fresh, while the season allows. In winter it is the seed that seasons our fish and our borscht.

Although fennel is native to Europe, most of the fennel seed in America is imported from India and Rumania. The seed comes from ordinary fennel, a handsome plant that grows to as much as six feet of fine green feathers, finally producing a pretty yellow flower. If only this sweet and agreeable plant were largely grown here, we could enjoy a long season of its flavorsome stalks, seasoning salads and soups, and most of all, fresh fish.

SNAPPER OR BLUEFISH WITH FENNEL

In the markets of Southern Europe bunches of fennel stalks are sold especially for grilled and baked fish.

Clean and split the fish (about 2 to 4 pounds) and put inside 2 or 3 stalks of fennel. Put them on a bed of dried fennel branches, brush with olive oil or melted butter, and put under (or over) the grill. These are wonderful grilled outdoors, small branches of fennel being thrown on the fire. Remove fish to serving dish and pour over a glass of warm brandy, set alight and serve while still burning. A *few* fennel seeds (they can be overpowering) will season fish pleasantly, also.

Fennel finely chopped into Sauce Mousseline or hollandaise makes a delicious dressing for fish, hot or cold.

Fennel seeds, which resemble microscopic watermelons, are packed with a pleasing aromatic oil of a sweet licorice flavor, and evidently contain nourishment, for they had the reputation of making a meager diet more satisfying. Called "meeting seed," they hold enough for the stomach to work on and stop its rumblings during the long silence of a Quarker meeting. Fennel seed allays hunger pangs enough to make it worthwhile for weight-watchers to give them a try. The Ale Wife in *Piers Plowman* carried in her bag "a farthing's worth of fennel seed for fasting days."

Fennel seed is good with floury things, in bread and rolls, in pastry, under the top crust of an apple pie.

Sweet fennel with its bulbous root is a most excellent vegetable. Its stalks may be used in the same ways as the *vulgare* variety, but the bulb (the bigger, the tenderer) of the delectable fennel (finocchio) is so delicious that one can never get enough of it during its short season. The bulb is good raw, cut into sticks like celery hearts or carrots. Or the bulb can be cut into thin slices, dressed with good olive oil and a fine wine vinegar, and served with a simple veal steak and a glass of Valpolicella—a meal to remember. It is said that finocchio makes even inferior wine taste good.

Cooked finocchio is the most succulent of vegetables.

B R A I S E D   F I N O C C H I O

2 fat bulbs of finocchio   *olive oil and butter*
1 clove garlic chopped (or 2 cloves)

Cut off stem; remove heavy outer leaves; wash and cut, from top to bottom into 6 sections. If bulbs are smaller, cut in 4 pieces and use 3 bulbs. Melt garlic in olive oil and butter, add the finocchio and brown lightly for 10 minutes. Add about ¼ cup of water, cover, and simmer until tender. Serve at once. A dash of vinegar may be added at the last minute.

43. Garlic

GARLIC (*Allium sativum*), is a lily of the field from way way back. This member of the lily family, also has something that even Solomon in all his glory did not have. The unobstrusive, so to speak, little bulb may not be much to look at, but it has an extraordinary capacity to season foods, to cause any kind of dish, except dessert, to taste its best.

Garlic is probably one of Homo Sapiens' oldest friends, oldest and best friends. It is likely that Man and garlic had their origins together in that remote part of southwest Asia that is thought to have seen our beginnings. No doubt the potent little bulb made more palatable primitive man's raw meat and cured his body of the "vapors," as our ancestors called the mysterious small ailments to which we are all subject.

Civilized Marco Polo was quite shocked to find, as late as the thirteenth century, when he made his travels, primitive tribes in Asia whose diet consisted solely of raw meat seasoned with garlic and spices.

Garlic has not set seed for thousands of years; it is propagated by the cumbersome process of bulb separation. Now that garlic powder and garlic salt have become popular, a quicker way to grow garlic is needed, instituting a world-wide search for the original wild garlic with seeds, probably long since buried under the sands of the Gobi desert.

Incense has risen to many gods; dances have been danced and revels reveled; hatfuls of garlic have been happily eaten at festivals celebrating the new garlic harvest. Obviously garlic has something to offer. They tell the story in Provence of a man from

Marseille who died at the age of 104 convinced that it was the
daily consumption of garlic and the weekly lunch with aioli that
had made him so old and kept him so brilliant. His oldest son
died at the age of ninety. "Ha," the father mourned, "I told him
many times he would not live to an old age. The poor little one
did not like garlic well enough."

For the many people who object to the smell of garlic, and
who have an idea that the eating of it leaves one offensive for
days, it is best to put down a few facts about garlic.

Moncrieff in *The Chemical Senses:* "Haggard and Greenberg
investigated breath odors after eating onions and garlic and found
that the odors were due entirely to solid particles which remained
in the mouth. . . . Brushing the teeth and tongue and rinsing the
mouth with a 3 per cent solution of chloramine banished the
odor" (Report in *Journal of American Medical Association*).

Ford Madox Ford, in *Provence,* wrote a now famous story of
the beautiful model who loved garlic:

"I came yesterday at a party upon a young lady who was the type
of young lady I did not think one ever could meet. She was one of those
ravishing and, like the syrens of the Mediterranean and Ulysses, fabulous beings who display new creations to the sound of harps, shawms
and tea-cups. What made it all the more astounding was that she was
introduced to me as being one of the best cooks in London—a real
cordon bleu, and then some. She was, as you might expect, divinely tall
and appeared to appear through such mists as surrounded Venus saving
a warrior. But I found that she really could talk and at last she told me
something that I did not know—about garlic.

"As do—as must—all good cooks, she uses quantities of that bulb.
It occurred to me at once that this was London and her work was social.
Garlic is all very well on the bridge between Beaucaire and Tarascon
or in the arena at Nîmes amongst sixteen thousand civilized beings.
But in an *atelier de couture* in the neighborhood of Hanover Square!
. . . The lady answered mysteriously: NO: there is no objection if only
you take enough and train your organs to the assimilation. The perfume
of *Allium officiniale* attends only on those timorous creatures who have
not the courage as it were to wallow in that vegetable. I used to know
a London literary lady who had that amount of civilization so that when
she ate abroad she carried with her, in a hermetically sealed silver
container, a single clove of the principal ingredient of aioli. With this
she would rub her plate, her knife, her fork and the bread beside her

place at the table. This, she claimed, satisfied her yearnings. But it did not enchant her friends or her neighbors at table.

"My instructress said that that served her right. She herself, at the outset of her professional career, had had the cowardice to adopt exactly that stratagem that, amongst those in London who have seen the light, is not uncommon. But, when she went to her studio the outcry amongst her comrades, attendants, employers, clients and the very conductor of the bus that took her to Oxford Circus, had been something dreadful to hear. Not St. Plothinus nor any martyr had been so miscalled by those vulgarians.

"So she had determined to resign her post and had gone home and cooked for herself a 'Poulet Béarnaise,' the main garniture of which is a kilo—two pounds—of garlic per chicken, you eat the stewed cloves as if they were *haricots blancs*. It had been a Friday before a bank holiday so that the mannequins at that fashionable place would not be required for a whole week.

"Gloomily, but with what rapture internally, she had for that space of time lived on hardly anything else but the usually eschewed bulb. Then she set out gloomily towards the place that she so beautified but that she must leave forever. Whilst she had been buttoning her gloves she had kissed an old aunt whose protests had usually been as clamant as those of her studio-mates. The old lady had merely complimented her on her looks. At the studio there had been no outcry and there too she had been congratulated on the improvement, if possible, of her skin, her hair, her carriage.

"She had solved the great problem; she had schooled her organs to assimilate, not to protest against, the sacred herb."

There are many good dishes in which twenty cloves to a pound or so of garlic appear without overwhelming either the house or its inhabitants with the odor and taste of the notorious bulb; the cooking odors are pleasant, in fact. But one unusual consequence is always noticed by those not accustomed to garlic in quantity: there is a feeling of complete clearness of the respiratory organs, an amazing sensation of liberation in the head, and it is as if one had acquired a completely new sense of smell. And it is so well known to be good for the complexion that in England garlic capsules are sold for that purpose.

Nevertheless, these garlic dishes are extremes; they do not show how to season with one of the most pleasingly potent seasonings that nature has put in man's garden. Mr. Ford himself says: "I will here again take occasion to emphasize that the real function of a condiment is not to be tasted, but to be just merely suspected. . . . A chef whose dishes leave you certain of the ingredients he has used is not a good chef . . . you should be left in the condition of thinking that you catch fleetingly the perfume of garlic, thyme, absinthia officinalis, nutmeg, cloves, or anything but perhaps tarragon or basil of which certain quantities may on special occasions be used. Such regional cooking as the 'Poulet Béarnaise' is suited for the regions in which it is cooked, by reason of climate, occupation, or for other local reasons . . . or of course for Protest Kings who are above the law."

Mr. Ford is right and he is not right. To insist that everyone eat only local dishes except when traveling in another region would be to condemn most people to a spiritless cuisine, to defeat one of the delights of travel, even if the travel is confined to cookbooks. But it is mistaken kindness when one has a visitor to feed him dishes of his own region, or worse yet, like Ford Madox Ford, of his adopted locale.

Misunderstood and maligned, garlic has an extraordinary capacity to insinuate itself into a dish, blending and accenting the other ingredients to a remarkable degree without revealing its own identity. Like onion, garlic's gift as a blending agent, as a conjurer among seasonings, is such that one thinks there must be more undiscovered virtues of the glamorous garlic. It is so fundamentally useful that until the middle of the eighteenth century many Siberian villagers paid taxes in garlic: fifteen bulbs for a man, ten for a woman, and five for a child. Garlic should at least be approached without prejudice.

Though we have learned that sizable amounts of cooked garlic will be easily assimilated, yet as a seasoning, the little cloves should be used with discretion, especially when consumed raw. In order to introduce raw garlic into a salad, it may be rubbed on the bowl, marinated in the dressing, or rubbed on a piece of bread, called a "chapon," which is tossed with the salad, then removed before serving. I usually slice a clove of garlic which is tossed with the salad, and frequently removed before serving. Raw garlic which is to be left in a dish should be mashed or reduced to a molecular state with a knife, blender, or garlic press.

In all the great cuisines garlic is one of the principal season-ings. How could there be a great cuisine without it? The tomato-garlic cooking of Sicily, Naples, and southern France, sunny and hearty as it is, cannot be called great cuisine.

As one might expect, the best Italian cuisine knows how to use garlic discreetly:

PORK CHOPS MODENESE
(*Costolette di Maiale alla Modenese*)

4 or 5 pork chops	*rosemary, 1 teaspoon*
salt and pepper	*fresh, ½ dried*
sage, 1 teaspoon fresh,	*1 clove garlic very finely*
½ dried	*chopped*
	½ cup dry white wine

Put the pork chops side by side in a large, lightly greased fry-ing pan. Sprinkle with salt, pepper, minced herbs, and garlic. Cover with water. Cover the frying pan and cook slowly until the water has evaporated and the chops begin to brown in the pan. When they are nicely browned on both sides, add the wine. Allow the wine to reduce by nearly half. Serve hot.

Delicately seasoned Chinese cooking uses garlic freely:

LOBSTER CANTONESE (*Chow Loong Ha*)

1 large lobster	*peanut oil for sautéing*
1 teaspoon black beans,	*1 cup stock*
soaked (Black-bean sauce	*dash of pepper*
may be bought in Chinese	*1 teaspoon monosodium*
stores)	*glutamate*
2 cloves garlic	*½ teaspoon sugar*
2 scallions	*½ teaspoon salt*
4 ounces chopped raw lean	*3 eggs, well beaten*
pork	*2 teaspoons cornstarch*

Split lobster in half and cut through shell into 1-inch pieces. Wash black beans thoroughly; crush them with garlic. Chop the scallion fine. Put black beans, garlic, chopped pork, and unshelled lobster pieces in a hot well-greased skillet; sauté in oil 2 minutes. Add stock, pepper, glutamate, sugar, and salt. Cover and cook 5 minutes. Add scallions and beaten eggs. Mix thoroughly. Add cornstarch which has been made into a fine, smooth paste; cook 2 minutes. Serve at once. Makes 4 servings.

The French cuisine, too, haute or just plain good, knows the seasoning value of garlic:

CHAMPIGNONS À LA CRÊME
(*Creamed mushrooms*)

1 **pound mushrooms**	1 **teaspoon minced fresh**
1½ **tablespoons olive oil**	**basil or ½ teaspoon**
1½ **tablespoons butter**	**dried basil**
1 **clove garlic, crushed**	½ **teaspoon salt**
1 **teaspoon minced**	1 **pint cream**
parsley	**toasted French bread**
	lemon juice

Wash and remove stems. Always keep mushrooms in acidulated water (lemon juice is best) to keep them white. The stems are better kept for soup if this dish is to be served to guests. Sauté the mushrooms in the olive oil and butter with the garlic, parsley, and basil. Sprinkle with salt. When the mushrooms are nearly cooked through, long enough only to dry the water in which they were soaking, about 5 minutes, pour on the cream. (The proportions should be ¼ pint cream to ¼ pound mushrooms in order to achieve a perfect dish with sufficient sauce.) Cook, stirring, until the cream thickens. Squeeze lemon juice over the cream at the last moment. On a serving dish put slices, about ½ inch thick, of toasted French bread; divide the mushrooms over the bread and serve at once. Makes 4 servings.

All the onion family, from onion and garlic, and to a progressively lesser degree, shallots, leeks and chives, possesses in abundance the qualities it takes to make a great seasoner: the capacity to irritate the membranes of the mouth and nose to alert them to taste; one or more of the basic sweetness, saltiness, acidity, or bitterness which will appeal to one set at least of the taste buds; an oil which melds and blends flavors and is strongly aromatic, able to carry the final blended flavor to the seat of taste—the nose.

The following eulogy to garlic shows how garlic fanciers in southern France feel about it:

Garlic all powerful; marvelous seasoning; you are the essence, the incense which revives and exhilarates; you are the spur that excites, stimulates. Garlic! You stir up, you impel, you cheer; you are the only condiment, you are the glorious one, the sovereign extract of the earth.

—GUSTAVE COQUIOT

44. Horseradish

HORSERADISH (*Armoracia rusticana*) is a mustard, but it is piquant in its own way.

The important part of the horseradish plant is its root, which is "long and thick, white of colour, taste sharp, and very much biting the tongue like mustard," according to Gerard's *Herbal*.

Between boughten horseradish and freshly grated root there is no comparison in flavor. As a seasoning it is of the mustard school; as a condiment it is excellent.

Horseradish seems to have a special affinity for seafood, but perhaps this is only habit. Once having tasted a sauce for broccoli made with sour cream and horseradish, the usual hollandaise is a disappointment. Just add a tablespoon of horseradish and a good teaspoonful of paprika to a regular sour-cream sauce.

ROAST PHEASANT

3 pheasant	2 cups chicken stock
4 tablespoons butter	1 teaspoon salt
1 cup green onions, chopped fine	½ teaspoon pepper
	2 cups cream
6 slices bacon	¼ cup freshly grated or
½ cup brandy	prepared horseradish

Melt butter in an iron frying pan, add the pheasant and onions and brown well. Transfer birds with juices to smallish roasting pan. Cover the breasts with bacon slices and secure with kitchen string. Pour warmed brandy (this is a good way to swish the juices out of the frying pan) over the birds, and flame. When flame dies, add stock, salt, and pepper. Roast uncovered in a 375-degree oven for 30 minutes, basting frequently. Add cream and horseradish to sauce and continue roasting for 15 minutes longer, basting frequently. Serve birds on heated platter. Makes 3 or 6 servings. Increase roasting time if birds are large.

45. Hyssop

HYSSOP (*Hyssopus officinalis*) is a hardy little plant, a shrub really, with spiky leaves rather like winter savory. Its odor is somewhat uncouth and camphorous, though not unpleasant.

As a small garden shrub—it grows to about two feet—it is handsome and useful, being covered throughout the summer with spikes of violet flowers. Although for cooking hyssop should be used with the greatest care, when thrown on the coals of the barbecue it gives off a wonderfully aromatic smoke.

46. Juniper

JUNIPER berries (*Juniperus communis*), to be had for the picking, have all but disappeared from our kitchens. Yet Escoffier considered them, along with cinnamon, ginger, nutmeg, cloves, mace, and vanilla bean, to be part of the permanent kitchen stock.

Juniper's oil is strongly aromatic, cleanly astringent. The

crushed berries, in moderation, are an unusually fine seasoning for strong foods such as game or the cabbages or for fatty meats such as pork. Gin owes most of its pleasant perfume to juniper berries.

Juniper's low spreading branches and handsome blue-green needles do double-duty as background planting near the barbecue. The little berries burning on the coals purify the air and perfume the grilling meats. Sir Thomas Browne, seventeenth-century physican and author, went so far as to say that the coals of juniper raked up will keep a glowing fire for the space of a year.

According to Boulestin and Hill, the berries take two or more years to ripen and to acquire the blue-black color of maturity. In order to save them from the birds, it is best to pick them when they are large enough, dry them slowly, and bottle them for future use.

S A U C I S S E   A U X   C H O U
(Sausage with cabbage)

> 1 *pound or so well-*
> *seasoned pork sausages*
> ¼ *pound salt pork, cut*
> *rather fine*
> *bouquet garni*
> *a few crushed pepper-*
> *corns*
>
> 1 *medium-size head of*
> *cabbage, shredded*
> *salt and pepper*
> *pinch of nutmeg*
> 3 *crushed juniper berries*
> 1 *cup stock*

Cook the salt pork in boiling water with the bouquet garni and crushed peppercorns. Take out the salt pork and cook the shredded cabbage in the same water for 10 minutes. Drain well. Mix with salt and pepper, nutmeg and juniper berries. Grill or fry the sausages to remove much of the fat. In a fireproof casserole place half the cabbage, lay the sausages on it, cover them with remaining cabbage, pour stock over the whole. Cover and cook in a 350-degree oven for about ½ hour. Makes 4 servings.

47. Lavender

LAVENDER (Lavandula vera)

> Here's flowers for you;
> Hot lavender, mints, savory, marjoram;
> The marigold, that goes to bed wi' the sun,
> And with him rises weeping . . .

So Shakespeare in *The Winter's Tale* tells us that lavender is one of the *hot* mints.

About three centuries ago, lavender was widely used as a seasoning not only for confections but in all sorts of food. And why not? It is a hot mint; it has everything. The plant looks like a blue-gray rosemary; it is lavishly endowed with a strongly perfumed aromatic oil, made up of a most pleasing synthesis of sweet lemony aromatics; its hot mint power arouses the taste sensations. Can it be that lavender is so deeply associated with sachet and soap that we can no longer think of it in the cooking pot?

Lavender grows best in a well-limed plot. Let some experimental cook start with lavender sugar, putting two or three stalks in a smallish canister of sugar for use in sweets, casseroles, vegetables, and French dressing.

48. Leek

LEEK (Allium porrum), the Welsh national emblem, a popular seasoning with the French, is practically ignored by Americans.

This mild, sweet, ingratiating member of the onion family is most pleasant and useful both as a vegetable and as a seasoning, but it is now hard to come by; it has run afoul of mass production —"there isn't enough demand."

In soups and stews (What is lamb stew without leeks?) it makes a contribution to the whole flavor that no other member of the onion family can equal. Leek and potato soup is one of the best.

There is a big movement afoot, the National Society for the Elevation and Propagation of the Leek, to bring back the leek.

LAMB STEW

2 **pounds boned shoulder of lamb**	**bouquet garni**
2 **tablespoons bacon fat or butter**	1 **cup carrots, diced**
salt and pepper	1 **cup turnips, diced**
pinch of sugar	10 **leeks**
2 **tablespoons flour**	1 **clove garlic, mashed**
	12 **small new potatoes**
	1 **cup cooked peas**

Have meat cut into good-size chunks. Brown meat well on all sides in bacon fat. Season with salt, pepper, and sugar. Add flour, stirring well until it is lightly browned. Add warm water slowly, stirring, until meat is covered. Add bouquet garni. Cover and simmer for 1 hour. Remove meat and bouquet and skim off as much fat as possible. Return the meat to the liquid, add all vegetables except peas. Simmer 30 minutes; add the peas and simmer 15 minutes longer. Makes 4 or 5 servings.

49. *Lemon Verbena*

LEMON VERBENA (*Lippia citriodora*), a native of South America, is not hardy above Virginia. It makes a luxuriant potted plant, however, growing sometimes to a height of ten feet, to be carried indoors for the winter.

While the Chinese, and in the course of time, also the Europeans, enjoyed the fruity lemon, Americans contented themselves with lemon verbena. The early Americans didn't fare too badly, because the lemon verbena is one of the most satisfactory of flavors. At the slightest touch the leaves of lemon verbena release floods of pure lemon scent and, unlike lemon, they do not become bitter when boiled. Lemon juice has no aromatic oil, lemon verbena has enough for two. They make a good team, worth trying in many dishes.

Dried, lemon verbena's aromatic leaves are a delightful addition both to the kitchen and to the linen closet.

50. Lovage

LOVAGE (*Levisticum officinale*) is another pleasing flower garden herb, a perennial, displaying fern-like foliage and pretty yellow flowers.

The whole plant is useful; leaves, seeds, stems, and roots all contain an aromatic oil resembling in taste a nutty sort of celery. But the celery taste is much stronger and harsher than our well-bred modern celery, so that any sizable amount of it cut up in a salad, for instance as we use celery, would be overpowering and quite unpalatable. Raw, it should be used sparingly.

Nevertheless, it does have a rightful place in the garden, if only for its name. It is much easier to grow than celery, prettier, too, as well as economical. Any part of the plant gives its celery-like attributes to soups, stews, and stuffings.

The stem, like angelica, may be blanched and candied.

51. Marjoram

MARJORAM (*Origanum Majorana*). Feminine marjoram, sympathetic and adaptable, is a proper descendant of the graceful nymph Menthe, who unwillingly founded the mint family. Venus, goddess of love, liked sweet marjoram, grew it on Mount

Olympus, and named it "Joy of the Mountain." In fact, Venus liked it so much that she encouraged young married couples to wear wreaths of the stuff around their brows. Shakespeare echoed the old stories in *All's Well That Ends Well:*

Indeed, Sir, she was the sweet marjoram of the Salad, or rather the herb of grace.

"It forms neat, gray-leafed little bushes about 3 or 4 inches high," we learn from Boulestin and Hill, "and towards mid-summer produces curious little flower-heads in which the small flowers are obscured by tightly packed bracts, so that they look rather like hops. It is these flower-heads which have given the plant its name of 'Knotted Marjoram,' for the 'knots' here (like the 'nuts' in 'Here we go gathering nuts in May') were almost certainly 'knops,' that is, buds or buttons."

Marjoram is an amiable seasoning, giving willingly its pleasant oils. It may be used quite freely, though in keeping with the delicacy of the dish. With veal and liver it is especially good, as well as giving a welcome bit of sweetness to spinach—a few of the chopped leaves added with the butter or olive oil just before serving, for instance, or when making eggs or other dishes à la Florentine.

Marjoram is usually a welcome addition to the bouquet garni and most herb mixes. It goes well in casseroles and braises, stews, stuffings, meat loaf—all the aromatic long-cooking dishes. Like the rest of the mint family, it is good with the legumes, especially the dried ones: beans, peas, and garbanzos. Its sweetness with a slightly bitter finish gives character to these bland, floury foods.

Though not quite so free with its scent as some of its family, it releases its engaging perfume when heated or bruised. It was much used in baths before they gave them up during the Middle Ages. During the Middle Ages it was more valued, and needed, as a sweet strewing herb, the medieval air-sweetener. Stephen, king of England in the early twelfth century, is said to have created the post of "Strewer of Herbs in Ordinary to His Majesty," a post finally abolished by Edward VII in the twentieth century.

The coronation of James II in the middle of the fifteenth century smelled lovely; the Strewer of Herbs in Ordinary was assisted by six women who scattered eighteen bushels of marjoram and other sweet herbs.

Although there is a certain amount of confusion about marjoram and oregano, there are evidently three varieties of marjoram in rather general use, not counting oregano: sweet marjoram (*Majorana hortensis*), and wild or pot marjoram (*Origanum vulgare*) often found in Italy, and pot marjoram (*onites*). Both pot and wild marjoram are much stronger in flavor than sweet marjoram and should be used with more caution. All are perennials, but so tender that they winter-kill in the northern United States, and are treated as annuals.

Boulestin and Hill introduce another variety, *Origanum microphyllum,* sometimes known as the eau-de-cologne plant, which has an intriguing lemon-cedar aroma. They think it superior even to sweet marjoram for use in the kitchen.

RED SNAPPER TURBAN

4 red snapper steaks, ¾ inch thick
1 teaspoon lemon rind
¼ cup lemon juice
¼ cup green onions, chopped
¼ teaspoon marjoram
1 teaspoon salt
¼ teaspoon white pepper
4 teaspoons butter
4 tablespoons minced parsley
4 9 × 12 pieces aluminum foil
lemon wedges

Mix together in a bowl lemon rind, lemon juice, onions, marjoram, salt, and pepper. Turn up edges of a piece of foil large enough to envelop steaks. In center of foil put a teaspoon or two of the sauce and ½ teaspoon of the butter. Lay fish on sauce. Pour remaining sauce over fish. Dot with remaining butter. Sprinkle with parsley. Fold foil over fish and place on baking dish. Bake in 350-degree oven for 30 to 35 minutes. When serving, garnish with lemon wedges. Makes 4 servings.

DUCKLING WITH FRUITS AND CURAÇAO

3 ducklings, cleaned	*marjoram*
salt, pepper	*¾ cup melted butter*
powdered thyme	

Wipe ducklings with damp cloth, and rub inside and out with mixed salt, pepper, powdered thyme, and marjoram, then with melted butter. Truss by tying legs together, and braise in a covered pan or roaster in ¼ cup of the butter. Cover, and set the pan in a 350-degree oven for 40 to 45 minutes, shaking the pan occasionally. No basting necessary. From time to time, however, add a little more butter. When ducklings are done, remove them from the pan; drain thoroughly and reserve the butter for other uses.

SAUCE FOR THE DUCKLINGS

¼ cup orange curaçao	*3 tablespoons English bitter*
2 tablespoons orange peel,	*orange marmalade*
parboiled	*1 large bay leaf*
1 cup orange juice	*7 or 8 sprigs parsley*
	2 whole cloves

Put the braising kettle on the stove and pour in Curaçao, orange peel cut into strips and drained, orange juice, and marmalade. Deglaze the pan by scraping and rubbing the bottom and sides with a wooden spoon. Then add 1 bay leaf, parsley, and cloves and bring the mixture to a boil, stirring occasionally. Allow to boil for 2 or 3 minutes; remove bay leaf, parsley, and cloves, and season to taste with salt and pepper. Place the breasts, or fillets of the ducklings, or the ducklings cut in halves on a hot platter. Beside them arrange 2 mounds of a macédoine of fruits (similar to a fruit salad) thoroughly heated but not boiled. Over all this pour the orange-curaçao sauce and serve at once and very hot.

Note: A roast of pork is improved by being sprinkled 5 minutes before it is taken from the oven either with half a teaspoon of dried marjoram or with a chopped fresh mint.

52. Mint

MINT (*Mentha spicata*) was not created solely for juleps and cool green refreshment on a hot summer day. Mint gives her name to a sturdy, prolific herb family of strong, pungent aromatics—basil, sage, thyme, marjoram, savory, balm, rosemary; quite a family for the dainty nymph Menthe, who was turned into a slim green herb by a jealous Proserpine, when Menthe's charms became too attractive to husband Pluto.

The cool sweetness of garden mint misleads the cook; mint is a powerful seasoner of foods, of meats and stews and vegetables. Like all the members of its family, it is an herb of character, beloved and respected by all the great cuisines that have ever existed.

Invaluable Pliny tells us that mint whets the appetite for meat. The ancient and modern Persian cuisine—and its descendants in the Middle East, Greek, old and new, Arabian, Spanish, Indian, and Chinese cuisines—all use mint as an aromatic stimulant, a stinging irritant that opens the taste buds, blends and carries the flavors with its powerful, aromatic oil. All of the mint family are unusually lively seasoners. In Mexico it is called the good herb, Yerba Buena.

Mint's origins are considered by Boulestin and Hill to be somewhat mysterious. "It is known only in gardens, of which it is a very ancient inhabitant, and it has never been found indubitably wild. . . . It may be that the parent of our garden mint awaits rediscovery by some remote stream in ancient Europe." They forget mint's mythological origins, forget that mint has no parent. Mint is a dainty nymph, Menthe.

Culpeper, the ever-ready sixteenth-century physician, warns that mint is a powerful aphrodisiac—generally full of virtue, helpful indeed for many of those loathsome diseases to which everyone in the Middle Ages was prone, but never to be eaten by a wounded person, for thereafter there can be no cure.

Not only the French still keep the comfortable habit of a tisane, a soothing cup of herb tea—mint or chamomile, anise, vervain, linden or orange—flavored with a drop of sugar and a piece of lemon or orange, as a nightcap. The South Americans drink their pleasant yerba maté, beloved by reducers because it stays hunger. Peppermint, the clean, sharp mint that flavors candy and liqueurs and medicines, is even better than garden spearmint as an evening tisane, as are the lesser-known fruity-flavored mints: apple mint, pineapple or orange mint, even little crème de menthe are winning additions to the herb garden or to the teapot.

Apple mint deserves a prominent spot in the herb garden or in the vegetable garden for cutting; it tends to run rather too wild for the flower border. Its handsome, graceful, woolly leaves, growing close to the stem, make it useful in cut flower arrangements, but mostly it is grown for the pleasant delicate smell of apples and mint, so desirable in many dishes, in mint tea, with fresh fruit and salads. If concocted with care, the very best mint sauce is made with apple mint, as illustrated here in Constance Spry's own recipe:

The best mint sauce is: "Take half a cup of crushed apple mint and the same quantity each of orange juice and vinegar and 2 tablespoons sugar. Make the vinegar hot, pour over the other ingredients, stir till cool, and adjust sweetening."

Red currant jelly is another variant. It is melted and added to the sauce. Two or three tablespoons of jelly will suffice.

Crème de menthe (*Mentha requieni*) is not a cordial, but an enchanting cress-like plant, its tiny leaves forming a miniature green bush so compact as to look almost like a mound of moss. It smells strongly and cleanly of peppermint.

It seems a shame to cook such a pretty thing, but no doubt the pretty leaves infused in a tea soothe an upset stomach. Folded into homemade ice cream, plain sugar candy, or chocolate fudge, they impart a pleasantly unsynthetic peppermint flavor.

FRIED EGGPLANT WITH YOGURT
(*Beyt-in-jan 'Mfas-sakh*)

1 *large eggplant*	2 *cups yogurt*
¼ *cup olive oil*	1 *tablespoon dried mint,*
½ *clove garlic*	*or 2 of fresh*
1 *teaspoon salt*	

Peel eggplant; cut in half lengthwise; cut each half into 4 pieces lengthwise, making 8 long wedges. Fry in olive oil until crisp and brown, remove, and drain well. Cool and then refrigerate. Mash garlic with salt and mix in bowl with the yogurt. Add mint. Place eggplant slices on serving dish and pour sauce over them. Serve cold.

COMBINATION DOLMA (from Armenia)

1½ pounds ground lamb shoulder	3 medium onions, minced
3 green peppers	3 tablespoons parsley, minced
3 zucchini or summer squash	1 teaspoon chopped fresh mint leaves or ½ teaspoon dried
3 long-type eggplants	1 teaspoon salt
3 firm tomatoes	¼ teaspoon black pepper
½ cup rice	

Wash all the vegetables. Scoop out the centers of the green peppers; cut the eggplant and squash in halves, lengthwise, and scoop out centers. Cut off tops of tomatoes and scoop out some of the pulp, which is added to the meat mixture. Knead the meat with rice, onions, parsley, mint, salt, and pepper. Fill the hollows of the vegetables, not too full, with the meat mixture. Arrange side by side in a baking pan, add a little water, cover, and bake in a 350-degree oven for 1½ hours.

53. Mustard

MUSTARD (Sinapis alba and Brassica juncea). Mustard seed, like the little acorn, packs a powerful potential; but a great oak is just a big tree while mustard is a medicine and food, a cooking oil, and one of the finest seasonings, and will overcome lassitude in females.

Mustard seed comes from an ancient plant originating in southwest Asia. Two varieties are commonly used: the dark-colored *Brassica* and the yellowish white one called *Sinapis alba.* The Italian word for mustard, *senape,* comes from the Latin word for the white variety. The whole seeds are used in pickles, with boiled beets, cabbage and sauerkraut.

Mustard mixed with turmeric is a magnificent, flamboyant color and it tastes quite pleasant with cold meats, sandwiches, and frankfurters. Mustards which are mixed with seasoned vinegar, horseradish and other condiments are also excellent.

It is plain mustard in plain mustard color, in powdered form, which accenting in its own way innumerable dishes, will overcome lassitude in anyone. It is perhaps possible to get some idea of the seasoning qualities of mustard when one knows that the aromatic oil of mustard is closely related to the aromatic oils of the greatest seasoners in the plant kingdom: the onion family—onions, garlic, leeks, and chives. No wonder a large section of India prefers to prepare its food with an oil which contributes such potential flavor. I regret to say, however, that these same people have come to prefer rancid mustard seed oil to fresh, after so many years of poverty and making do with the worst.

Mustard itself has a clean, sharp, green kind of flavor plus the strength and character of its oniony oil. It combines the capacity to awake the taste with a powerful aromatic oil which blends and carries flavors. Mustard as a piquant condiment is enormously pleasant and useful, but as the power-behind-the-flavor, it is exceptional.

The name of mustard goes back to its origins when it was made from the seeds pressed and mixed with must, which is the newly pressed juice of grapes, or the new wine, or one beginning the fermentation. Dry mustard must still be mixed with liquid—wine, wine vinegar, or water; the chemical reaction which liberates mustard's essential oil requires water. Dry mustard, or mustard flour, was first made in the early eighteenth century by a Mrs. Clements of Durham, England.

Dainty, decorative little mustard cress contains the same aromatic oil as the mustard seed itself.

LAPIN À LA MOUTARDE

3 tablespoons French   1 rabbit, cut in serving-size
  mustard   pieces
2 tablespoons bread crumbs   1 cup dry white wine
1 tablespoon olive oil   1 cup fresh cream
                              ¼ teaspoon salt

With a fork mix the mustard, crumbs, and oil. Spread it on all
sides of the rabbit. Put the rabbit in a roasting pan; pour white
wine in the pan. Roast in 400-degree oven for ¾ hour or until
rabbit is tender but not dry. It is not necessary to salt the rabbit;
the mustard is sufficient. Remove rabbit from oven onto warmed
serving platter. Pour cream and salt into roasting pan. Boil 2 or
3 minutes, stirring constantly with a wooden spoon. Pour over
the rabbit. Makes 4 to 5 servings.

54. Onion

ONIONS (Allium cepa) are so obviously potent—the skin
smarts, the eyes stream—"Onions can make even heirs and widows
weep" (B. Franklin)—that our ancestors attributed no end of
virtue to them, even that they could cure baldness. Although
there is no evidence of the onion's power as a pilatory (surely
the opposite of depilatory), our ancestors were wiser than they
knew. The onion is possibly more necessary in the kitchen than
the cook.

It is thought that onions are native to that region in west
Asia where Man first showed signs of becoming civilized. They
have accompanied Man on the long road toward civilization,
giving him always pleasure, and health.

The ancient Greeks took their oaths with one hand on an
onion, its sphere being considered a symbol of eternity.

The Israelites on their slow trek back to Canaan complained to

Moses about the comforts they had left behind in Egypt: ". . . the fish, which we did eat in Egypt freely; the cucumbers and the melons, and the leeks, and the onions, and the garlic." Egypt's civilization leaned heavily on slaves—and onions, quantities of onions, radishes, and garlic were consumed by the slaves who built the great pyramids. The Egyptians made the onion a god.

Scientists have recently discovered, according to chef Louis de Gouy, a "mysterious bacteria-destroying substance" in the onion, the same mysterious substance which has been helping mankind for thousands of years. It was because onions are so effective in the treatment of intestinal disorders that General Ulysses S. Grant informed the Government in 1864: "I will not move my army without onions." Three carloads were shipped off to him at once.

In Germany in 1947 green onions cured a persistent scurvy epidemic which had not responded to man-made ascorbic acid. Onions contain many minerals and vitamins, as well as other nourishing factors, yet are low in calorie count. It is satisfactory to know that anything so good is also good for you. Some people even consider onions a nerve sedative, perhaps because they keep the madding crowd at bay.

Robert Louis Stevenson called the onion "the poetic soul of the capacious salad bowl"; it might be called the soul of the kitchen, for it is the onion family that gives life and zest to nearly all our foods except dessert. Without onion, discreetly used, or its other relatives in the lily family—leeks, shallots, chives, garlic—foods taste flat. Soups, stews, sauces; salads and hors d'oeuvre; meat, fish, poultry and egg dishes; vegetables; sandwiches and dips, and even bread and rolls all are starving for a bit of onion or its milder relatives. Not only is onion a great seasoner, it is also a great vegetable for sturdy dishes like onion soup, onion pies and tarts, fried onions, baked onions, stuffed onions, and buttered onions.

Three-quarters of the nearly 2 billion pounds of dry onions consumed every year in the United States are the familiar yellow onions. These are the onions generally used in soups, stews, and casserole dishes, in hamburgers, meat loaf, and for frying. Frequently they are finely chopped and browned lightly in butter or oil before incorporating with other ingredients.

Small white onions are often used to flavor more delicate foods: eggs and omelets, peas, carrots, or sauces, for instance. They are the best onion for blanquette de veau or bœuf Bourguignon and for boiling or baking.

The big, sweet, juicy Spanish onions and the sweet red Italian onions are excellent raw in salads and sandwiches.

Large Bermuda onions are the best for stuffing and roasting.

Green onions, which are yellow onions harvested when the bulbs are very small—or scallions—which are shoots of white onions—are excellent uncooked in salads, hors d'oeuvre, and sauces such as tartar sauce. They are good as a vegetable or to season other vegetables, fish stuffings, and spring lamb roast.

Instant minced onion and onion flakes are useful additions to the kitchen shelf. Minced onion is rehydrated in an equal amount of water; onion flakes, being larger, require a little less water.

Dried onion may be made at home, to use up an already cut onion, for example. Slice or mince the onion and toast it to a golden color in the oven. Store in tightly covered jars in the refrigerator.

I don't know how people peel and cut up onions while holding them under water. While dealing with onions, I try to breathe through the mouth—a piece of bread held between the teeth is a help—and wear glasses.

To take away the smell of onions from the hands or from utensils, rub with lemon juice or rind, or vinegar, then wash with soap and water. Leftover cuts of lemon kept in the kitchen soap dish are handy for removing strong odors from hands and utensils.

When buying onions, make sure that they are of good quality —bright, clean, hard, mature onions with dry skins and no sprouts. Green onions should have fresh green tops, medium-size necks which are well-blanched two or three inches from the root. Bear in mind that supermarket chains make millions of dollars a year by selling vegetables already packed in bags, concealing the bad with the good. It is economical to take time to buy fresh healthy produce.

Onions and apples are a surprisingly good combination, either raw in salads—thin slices of apple and thin slices of sweet Spanish or Italian onions, lettuce leaves, and French dressing—or cooked, as in the following pie, an excellent dish for a Sunday-night buffet.

O N I O N   A P P L E   P I E
(from the early eighteenth century)

pastry for 2-crust pie	MIXED:
3 medium-size potatoes (1 pound)	*¼ teaspoon mace*
	½ teaspoon nutmeg
3 medium-size apples (1 pound)	*1 teaspoon freshly ground pepper*
6 medium-size onions (1 pound)	*3 teaspoons salt*
	¼ pound butter or margarine
8 hard-cooked eggs	*6 tablespoons stock or water*

Line a 9-inch pie or cake pan with pastry. Peel and slice the potatoes, onions, apples, and eggs. Spread a layer of potatoes on the crust, then a layer of onions, then a layer of apples, then hard-cooked eggs. Sprinkle with seasoning and dot with butter. Repeat layers until ingredients are used. Sprinkle with stock or water. Put on top crust, prick it, and bake 1 to 1¼ hours in a 375-degree oven.

O N I O N   R A G O U T

2 pounds white onions, peeled	*1 cup stock (made with 2 bouillon cubes)*
¼ cup butter	*3 medium-size tomatoes, peeled and seeded*
2 tablespoons dry white wine	*½ teaspoon salt*
3 cloves, 1 large bay leaf, ½ stick cinnamon, tied in a cheesecloth bag	*½ teaspoon sugar*

Cook onions with the butter in a heavy pan until they are golden brown. Add the other ingredients, cover and simmer for about 1 hour. Serve hot. Makes 6 servings.

CHICKEN STUFFED WITH GREEN ONIONS

1 2½-pound broiler
  oil and tarragon
1 cup chopped green
  onions, tops included
  salt and pepper
1 teaspoon savory
1 teaspoon melted butter
  or bacon fat
2 cups broth
½ cup dry white wine
½ cup light cream
3 tablespoons cornstarch

BROTH:
  neck, wing tips, gizzard,
  and feet
1 carrot, chopped
1 onion, chopped
1 beef bouillon cube
1 teaspoon basil
1 teaspoon salt
  a few peppercorns

Rub chicken with olive oil and tarragon and keep overnight in the refrigerator. In the morning mix the onion, salt, pepper, savory, and melted butter, and stuff chicken. Do not sew. Simmer the ingredients for the broth in 2 cups of water for 1 hour or more. Cool and strain, mashing some of the vegetables through a sieve. Simmer chicken and broth, covered, for 50 minutes, turning two or three times. Fifteen minutes before it is done, add wine. Blend cornstarch with cream. Add slowly to chicken broth and cook until thickened. Serve with hot brown rice. Makes 4 servings.

55. Oregano

OREGANO (Origanum veredis), masculine marjoram, is a savage herb that belongs to wild high hills and hot sun—goat's marjoram. It grows in the ghostly craters of the Canary Islands, near Sicily's smoldering volcanoes, and on the benign slopes of Popocatepetl in Mexico.

Oregano makes one think of grills and out-of-doors, of Southern foods—tomatoes and olives, piquant peppers and beans.

GRILLED STEAK OR LAMB CHOPS

Rub meat with a cut clove of garlic; brush on olive oil or melted butter with a branch of dried oregano (many Italian markets sell large bunches of oregano branches). Some of the leaves adhere to the meat. Grill; turn meat and repeat the process.

GRILLED TOMATOES

There is no better vegetable nor one quicker to prepare than tomato halves sprinkled with a little salt, sugar, a good pinch of oregano, grated Parmesan cheese, and about ¼ teaspoon olive oil. Grill slowly until just cooked through.

Old herbals recommended cheerful oregano in a drink for people "that are given to over-much sighing." In a drink, perhaps; better give them crisp pizza, piquant with oregano.

A Mediterranean native, oregano traveled early to Latin America where it is often known, because of its cross-between-marjoram-and-sage flavor, as Mexican sage. In Mexico, as in Italy and Spain, oregano's strong aromatic oil gives interest to floury beans and potatoes.

FRIJOLES

2 cups frijoles—black beans are best	⅓ pound salt pork
	½ teaspoon oregano

Soak beans in water overnight. Next day add salt pork and oregano and boil slowly until tender, 4 to 6 hours. If possible simmer all day. As water boils away, add boiling water to the beans. Frijoles may also be served the next day, mashed and fried or refried. Makes approximately 10 servings.

The island of Crete, where, nearly 2,000 years ago, everything was perfect, has a lovely little gray-green bush called dittany of Crete, which is an excellent oregano, as well as an exquisite plant for garden or house. Stillwater Gardens in Salisbury, Connecticut, carries this unusual herb.

PIZZA (see also page 259 for more pizza)

DOUGH

1 pound flour	*1 tablespoon each, butter*
1 package yeast	*and lard mixed*
1 cup water (about)	*1 teaspoon salt*

Melt yeast in ¼ cup of tepid water. Pour ¾ cup boiling water over the butter and lard in a large bowl. When cooled to body temperature mix in yeast and flour. Knead on a board. Add flour to make a consistency which does not stick to the hands. Set dough in a warm place to rise. When risen to double in bulk, knead again and stretch as thinly as possible on the pizza pan.

TOPPING

salt and pepper	*tomatoes*
¼ cup olive oil	*¼ to ½ cup Parmesan*
mozzarella cheese, cubed	*cheese*
anchovies, chopped	*2 teaspoons oregano*

Sprinkle dough with salt and pepper. Rub over about 2½ tablespoons of the olive oil. Dot with small cubes of mozzarella about every ¾ inch. Dot with pieces of fillet of anchovy—a few here and there. Use either canned or fresh Italian tomatoes, chopped and peeled; spread over pizza about ¼ inch thick. Sprinkle with grated Parmesan cheese. Sprinkle again with salt and freshly ground pepper and also a sprinkling of olive oil. Lastly, sprinkle with dried oregano. (Dried oregano is far stronger than fresh.) Bake 10 minutes in a 400-degree oven or until the pizza bubbles.

Add a little oregano and mustard to cheese sauce for deviled eggs and to stuffing for fish.

56. *Parsley*

PARSLEY (*Petroselinum crispum*). When Parsley Pies were popular in England, in Good Queen Bess's time, then Britain really ruled the waves. None other than whole pastures of parsley were good enough for the horses of the Greek gods, who evidently knew the dietary secrets of keeping their steeds swift and spirited, for parsley is nature's own vitamin pill. One pound of deep-green-colored parsley contains 225 calories; protein, 16.8 grams; fat, 4.5 grams; carbohydrate, 40.9 grams; calcium, 876 milligrams; phosphorus, 381 milligrams; iron, 19.5 milligrams; vitamin A, 37,360 international units; thiamine, .49 milligrams; riboflavin, 1.25 milligrams; niacin, 6.5 milligrams, and vitamin C, 877 milligrams. No wonder the ancients considered parsley a symbol of joy and festivity; "I'm feeling full of parsley today," they probably said.

For thousands of years parsley has been nourishing man as well as horses. Like many valuable plants, it originated in that ideal breeding ground east of the Mediterranean, from whence it has spread all over the world until it is so common that we hardly appreciate its superiority as a food, a seasoning, and a decoration.

Parsley doubling as a flower, or mixed with flowers—Homer is said to have been fond of a parsley-and-rose motif decorating his banquets—has gone out of style, or perhaps only out of mind, as have the parsley crowns such as Hercules wore after conquering the Nemean lion. But no one doubts that dainty bouquets of parsley make many a plain dish feel wanted.

There is no easier and prettier garnish than parsley, especially the curly kind, when fresh, crisp, and green. Limp, tired, faded parsley is not for garnishing; it will also have lost some of its vitamins.

The garnish is good to eat. The taste of parsley is hard to describe: one of my children says there is a faint taste of onion, the other suspects a hint of licorice. We all agree, however, that there is a light piney characteristic in parsley; but mostly they say that it tastes fresh, "like parsley." There is no doubt that the flat-leaf (Italian) parsley is vastly superior in flavor, more full-bodied, yet lighter, sweeter, and more delicate than the more decorative curly kind.

Parsley stems have far more flavor than the leaves; the French often use only the stems where taste is more important than appearance. Full-of-chlorophyll parsley stems, when crushed, tint mayonnaise and other sauces a lovely shade of green. The root, too, is full of flavor, excellent in soups and stews.

Parsley blends well with other seasonings, or it stands well alone. It is essential in every herb combination: bouquet garni, ravigote, mirepoix, etc., and at times becomes the only herb in "fines herbes."

According to the Roman naturalist Pliny, who always has something appropriate to say, generous amounts of parsley give a peculiar palatability to seasoned foods. The Italians, who have an unusually sensible diet—varied, interesting, and well-balanced, yet not too rich—eat parsley in generous amounts. Most Italian recipes say, "Take a handful of parsley . . ."

In spite of the discouraging old Shropshire saying that "parsley must be sowed nine times, for the devil takes all but the last," almost every home can have its own parsley pasture, be it a pot of parsley in the kitchen window or a large parsley bed outdoors, big enough to hold a large potential family. In England the reply to "Where did I come from, Mommy?" is not "The stork brought you," but "From the parsley-bed, my dear."

Modern dehydrated parsley flakes are also immensely useful in the kitchen. They, too, should be used generously and frequently; old parsley flakes which have lost their savor are useless. Though most foods like their share of parsley, pale foods especially are made much more attractive with minced fresh parsley or parsley flakes. For mashed potatoes, add the parsley to the hot milk before it is mixed with potatoes. It is also good with any kind of potatoes, buttered noodles, cream soups and sauces, cottage or cream cheese, and cauliflower.

Even though the fragrance of parsley was said to excite the brain to agreeable imaginations, in actual fact the essential oil in parsley is less volatile than that of many other herbs. It does not have a strong scent, though its fragrance, of course, increases when the herb is heated.

Each person has his own pet way of keeping parsley in the refrigerator:

1. With the stems kept in a glass of water
2. Washed; water shaken off; sealed in glass jar or plastic bag
3. Unwashed in plastic bag
4. Washed and folded into a cloth; the cloth absorbs the dampness

CHILLED TOMATO SOUP

10½-ounce can tomato soup	*¼ teaspoon salt*
	pinch garlic powder
10½ ounces buttermilk	*¼ teaspoon onion powder*
1 tablespoon fresh lemon juice	*2 teaspoons parsley flakes*

Combine ingredients and mix well. Chill and serve. This soup may also be served hot. Makes 3 to 4 servings.

STUFFED MUSHROOMS AU GRATIN

12 large mushrooms	*½ cup minced parsley*
2 cloves garlic, minced	*4 anchovies, minced*
1 tablespoon olive oil	*⅛ teaspoon ground black pepper*
3 tablespoons butter	*fine dry bread crumbs*
1 tablespoon beef or chicken broth	*Parmesan cheese*
	½ cup white wine

Clean mushrooms, remove and chop stems finely. Leave mushroom caps whole and set aside for later use. Sauté chopped mushroom stems and garlic in olive oil and 1 tablespoon butter about 7 minutes. Add broth, parsley, anchovies, and black pepper. Mix well. Spoon the mixture into mushroom caps. Sprinkle each with bread crumbs and Parmesan cheese and dot with remaining butter. Place in a buttered baking pan. Add wine to pan. Bake in a 350-degree oven for 30 minutes or until mushrooms are browned on top, basting twice with the wine. Makes 6 servings.

57. Poppy Seed

POPPY SEEDS (*Papaver somniferum*) will not give you wild, exhilarating dreams, nor will they put you to sleep. The pretty blue poppy seeds you buy in the stores are not only good to eat, they are legal, too—not a trace of opium in them. But poppy seeds do have a kick; they are considered a stimulant for the appetite, and in that role can be recommended for use in hors d'oeuvre.

According to Boulestin and Hill, poppy seeds, a world-wide builder-upper, have been nourishing mankind since the Stone Age. "Mixed with wine and honey, they formed a regular part of the training diet of the competitors in the Olympic games."

The Dutch have made an art of growing and harvesting poppy seed. The finest blue seeds come from the province of Zeeland in Holland, where the secrets of cultivating the seed are passed on from generation to generation. Each pound contains approximately 900,000 seeds, they say.

Poppy seed, whole or ground, mixed with honey is good as a filling in cakes, especially coffee cakes. Poppy seeds which have been soaked in water can be mashed with a fork for fillings, or ground in a poppy seed grinder which is quite common in Europe.

In order to bring out the flavor when mixing with vegetables or noodles, heat poppy seeds first in butter, then pour the mixture over the other ingredients. Toasting the seed, in a heavy frying pan in the oven or on a low fire, improves the flavor; heat brings out the essential oils in all seeds, nuts, coffee beans and the like. The toasted seeds are a delicious addition to fruit or vegetable salads, to sandwich fillings, to cheese canapés, and other appetizers.

As always, they are tops as topping for breads, rolls, and cookies.

POPPY-SEED TORTE

¾ cup raisins	½ teaspoon ground cloves
½ cup rum	1 teaspoon ground
10 eggs, separated	cinnamon
1 cup sugar	butter
grated rind of ½ lemon	fine bread crumbs
¼ cup ground poppy seeds	sweetened whipped
1 cup flour	cream

Plump raisins in the rum. Beat egg yolks with sugar until creamy. Add raisins, lemon rind, and poppy seed. Gradually add flour sifted with cloves and cinnamon. Fold in egg whites, beaten but not too stiff. Grease with butter two 9-inch springform cake tins and sprinkle with fine bread crumbs. Put half the mixture in each pan. Bake in 350-degree oven for 1 hour. Turn out cakes; brush with rum. Allow cakes to cool. Serve with whipped cream piled on top, and between layers, too, if desired.

58. Rosemary

ROSEMARY (*Rosmarinus officinalis*), one of the most fragrant of herbs, is for remembrance, doubtless because no one can forget its spicy bouquet.

There is a charming legend explaining how rosemary got its name and the little blossom its pale blue color. The story is that back in Biblical times rosemary had a white flower. At the time of the flight into Egypt, the Virgin Mary one night hung her garment on a rosemary bush; the next morning the flower had become as blue as Mary's gown, so inevitably the herb was thenceforth known as the rose of Mary.

Rosemary will grow only in the gardens of the righteous, it is said. As one might expect, it is an amulet against the evil eye. Also, if given to the right person, it insures faithfulness.

To turn to more mundane, if less practical uses, as a seasoning, rosemary is strongly individual. From the Mediterranean region, which is its home, word of its talents had spread to England, where Izaak Walton advised fishermen to dress their catches with "a handful of sliced horseradish root, with a handsome faggot of rosemary."

Rosemary is a powerful herb, pungent and piney, sort of a cross between sage and lavender, with a touch of ginger and camphor. Used with caution, it is one of the finest seasonings—a true *hot* mint.

In warm countries where it is hardy, rosemary is a little tree or bush. In cool climates it is interesting as well as useful as a house plant, trained in odd shapes like Japanese dwarf trees.

Once having eaten roast chicken or roast lamb or roast veal cooked with rosemary, no one is interested again in the insipid without-rosemary kind.

BAKED BEANS, ITALIANO

2 cups (1 pound) pea beans or navy beans
5 cups water
1 cup tomatoes
3 teaspoons salt
¾ teaspoon rosemary leaves
½ teaspoon ground black pepper
½ cup minced onion or 2 tablespoons instant minced onion
¼ teaspoon instant minced garlic or 1 clove chopped garlic
¼ pound Italian sausage

Wash and pick over beans. Rinse well. Add water, bring to boil for 2 minutes. Remove from heat and let stand 1 hour. Cook slowly 1 hour or until beans are tender. Drain off water and add to it tomatoes, salt, rosemary, pepper, minced onion, and garlic. Brown sausage, slice, and add to beans. Turn into a 2-quart bean pot or casserole. Add seasoned bean liquid. Cover and bake in a 350-degree oven for 2 hours. Remove cover and bake 30 minutes longer or until browned. Makes 6 servings.

In some European countries rosemary, pungent and piney, is used to stuff pillows, inscribed, I imagine, in the language of the country, "Rosemary for Remembrance."

ROAST VEAL

Five pounds lean veal, cut from leg or rump, rolled so that it is long and not more than 4 or 5 inches in diameter.

Use a pan just a little larger than the roast; a bread pan is often a good pan for a veal roast. Sprinkle the meat with chopped garlic and rosemary, salt and pepper, monosodium glutamate, and olive oil; dot with butter. Roast in a 350-degree oven 30 minutes to the pound.

Roast veal is delicious with a lemon sauce. Lemon juice and beaten egg yolks and a little water or stock are added to the gravy in the pan on the same principle as in making hollandaise, stirring constantly; make sure the gravy never boils or the yolks will curdle.

Rosemary, like the other pungent hot mints, is a good seasoning for beans.

59. *Rue*

RUE (*Ruta graveolens*). Working on the theory that the more bitter the medicine, the more effective it is, rue was once alleged to cure some eighty-four ills.

> . . . here in this place
> I'll set a bank of rue, sour herb of grace.

Shakespeare in *Richard II* was not the only one to use rue as a symbol for the bitterness of life, often in contrast to the good

things, as "her wine is pressed from rue" and "for one shall . . .
drink life's rue, and one its wine."

It is an herb with a strong aromatic oil of decidedly bitter
overtones which the pretty leaves release at the slightest touch.
Bitterness frequently adds interest and cleannesss when combined
with other seasonings. Perhaps rue has possibilities.

Rue is pleasant in small quantities in salads; Boulestin and
Hill think that a sandwich made with whole-wheat bread and
butter and chopped rue is appetizing.

There is no qualification about its beauty; a handsome evergreen plant with charmingly arranged blue-green leaves, it bears
little yellow flowers all summer long. There is no doubt about its
welcome in the flower garden.

60. Sage

SAGE (*Salvia officinalis*) is the fountain of youth:

> Who eats sage in May
> Will live for aye.

Its healing properties have given sage its name, *Salvia,* from
the Latin *salvere,* to heal.

In Provence, where anyone who dies under the age of ninety
must have died for love or in the bullring, sage and garlic are
given credit for the longevity of the population. In the soft language of Provence, the saying is:

> *Qu'a de' sauvi dins soun jardin*
> *A pas besourn de medecin.*

> Who has sage in his garden
> Has no need of a doctor.

SAGE AND GARLIC SOUP
OF PROVENCE

L'Aigo-boulido
Sauvo la vidao

The garlic soup
Saves the life.

1 quart of water	½ bay leaf
6 or 7 cloves garlic, peeled and cut in quarters	1 egg yolk
a branch of sage	a few tablespoons olive oil
a sprig of thyme	slices of French bread

Add the garlic to the water, season with salt and pepper; add the sage, thyme, and bay leaf. Cook for 15 to 20 minutes. Remove the sage, thyme, and bay leaf. In a soup tureen, beat the egg yolk slightly. Pour, a very little at a time, the soup onto the egg, beating constantly. Put slices of French bread which have been dampened with olive oil into each soup plate. Serve the soup on the bread.

Among its other virtues, sage oil contains "Salviol," which aids in the digestion of rich foods, probably the reason sage is said to be so good for the liver.

Whether or not it is good for the health, sage is certainly the most popular herb in the United States, most of it, I imagine, going into stuffings for poultry.

The flavor of sage is so strong that it is capable of covering the taste of the onions in the famous sage and onion stuffing.

SAGE AND ONION STUFFING

(*From Mrs. Beeton's* Poultry and Game)

Take 4 large onions, 10 sage leaves, ¼ pound of bread crumbs, 1½ ounces of butter, salt and pepper to taste, and 1 egg. Peel the onions, put them into boiling water, let them simmer for 5 minutes or rather longer, and just before they are taken out, put in the sage leaves for a minute or two to take off their rawness. Chop both these very fine, add the bread, seasoning and butter, and work the whole together with the yolk of an egg, when the stuffing will be ready for use. It should be rather highly seasoned, and the sage leaves should be very finely chopped.

Many cooks do not parboil the onions in the manner just stated, but merely use them raw, but the stuffing then is not nearly so mild, and to many tastes, its strong flavor would be objectionable.

When made for a goose, a portion of the liver of the bird, simmered for a few minutes, and very finely minced, is frequently added to this stuffing; and where economy is studied, the egg and butter may be omitted.

This should be sufficient for one goose, or a pair of ducks.

The Italians add ham and olives, as well as herbs, to several of their stuffings. Grapes make a good addition to stuffings for duck.

In small amounts, sage's powerful and aromatic oil and its bite make sage an outstanding blender of flavors; it liberates pleasant, appetizing aromas. Here are two Italian dishes which illustrate the excellent seasoning abilities of sage-in-moderation.

SALTIMBOCCA (*Jump-in-the-mouth*)

1 *pound veal scaloppini pounded well with a mallet*	1 *thin slice ham (about ⅛ pound all together) for each scaloppini*
1 *leaf sage for each scaloppini*	*about ¼ cup butter flour, salt and pepper*
	¼ *cup Marsala (optional)*

Place 1 leaf of sage and 1 slice of ham on each scaloppini and fasten with a wooden toothpick. Mix flour with salt and pepper and coat lightly each scaloppini. Heat butter in a large frying pan.

Put in the scaloppini, ham side down, and brown quickly. Turn carefully and brown the other side. Add a little water to the pan and cook a few minutes until the water is gone. Remove saltimbocca to serving plate. Add Marsala to pan. Boil briskly, scraping up the pan juices. When wine is reduced by half, pour the sauce over the saltimbocca. Serve at once. Makes about 5 servings.

FEGATO DA VITELLO CON SALVIA

(Calves liver with sage)

1 pound calves liver, sliced	*2 tablespoons butter*
¼ inch thick and cut in	*5 leaves fresh sage or*
3-inch pieces	*1 teaspoon dried*
2 tablespoons olive oil	*salt and pepper*

Heat oil and butter in a frying pan. Put in the liver and the sage and cook quickly on both sides. Sprinkle with salt and pepper. The cooking should take only about 3 minutes, until liver is just cooked but remains light and tender. Serve at once.

Not only is Vermont sage cheese excellent—good in hors d'oeuvre—but sage goes well in cheese dishes, especially those made with a good nippy Cheddar or coon cheese. A little sage added to biscuits which are to be served with meat is pleasant.

The lesser-known varieties of sage make handsome and most useful additions to the garden. Purple sage and pineapple sage have the well-loved sage character, but are milder and a bit fruity. Variegated sage, although a good-looking plant, is extremely pungent in a good sagey way.

LEEK TART WITH SAGE

PASTRY FOR 8-INCH TART

1 cup flour	*3 ounces butter*
¼ teaspoon salt	*¼ cup cold water with a*
	little lemon juice

Sift dry ingredients. Rub butter in lightly with fingertips or pastry knife. Mix water in gradually with a knife. Roll lightly and place on pie pan.

FILLING

1 dozen leeks
1 tablespoon chopped parsley
1 tablespoon minced sage leaves or
½ tablespoon dried sage

1 egg, beaten
½ cup light cream or whole milk
½ cup grated cheese—Swiss or Cheddar
salt and pepper

Wash and cut leeks into thin circles. Simmer gently in a little water until soft. Drain, add herbs, egg, cream and cheese. Add salt and pepper. Pour leek mixture into pastry shell. Arrange bacon on top of tart. Bake in 400-degree oven for 20 to 25 minutes.

61. Savory

SAVORY (Satureia hortensis and S. montana). The savory twins, summer and winter, though they look quite alike, are by no means identical. In fact, they might be called masculine and feminine, the characteristics of winter being heavy and strong, while summer is lighter, daintier, more subtle.

Both savories are warm and pungent. Piney winter savory makes one think of roasts and grills, the smoke of outdoor fires, of hearty meats such as pork pie and sausages, of country cooking. Several of the French country provinces favor the easy perennial winter savory, which grows well in rocky places and in rock gardens, too.

Lighter summer savory, an annual plant, is the savory usually found commercially, sold dried in leaf form or powdered, as well as an ingredient of poultry seasoning.

Summer savory is pleasant, alone or with parsley, sprinkled on vegetables, especially peas, beans, or carrots, or on a vegetable cocktail. It goes well with cheese, omelets, scrambled eggs, rabbit; with fish and fish sauces; with lamb. It is good in cream soups and chowders and as an ingredient in salad dressings.

A native of southern Europe, savory is a member of the invaluable mint family, stinging the taste buds just enough to bring out flavors in the dishes it seasons.

Like basil with tomato, savory and beans always go together. Although a sprinkling of savory and parsley is indeed nice on string beans, it is with the long-cooking kind of beans that this combination has become famous.

It is hard to imagine why savory was once credited with the power to cure "blastings by lightning, planets or gunpowder," but it really is true that a poultice made of savory leaves makes bee and wasp stings feel better.

PLYMOUTH COLONY STUFFING

9 cups toasted bread crumbs (whole or cracked wheat)	½ teaspoon grated orange or lemon peel
1 teaspoon each summer savory, marjoram, thyme, celery leaves, parsley	2 teaspoons salt
	¼ teaspoon pepper
	2 large onions, minced
	2 tablespoons butter
	1 egg, slightly beaten

Clean the bird, rub the inside with 1 teaspoon salt. Toast day-old bread and crush into crumbs. Toasting not only prevents bread from becoming soggy, but gives a delightful, nutty flavor. Mix dry seasoning and crumbs well. Cook the minced onion in butter until golden brown and mix with other ingredients. Stir in the egg. If a moist stuffing is desired, add about ¾ cup hot milk or water. When the stuffing is cold, fill the bird, but do not over-stuff; leave room for the bread to swell. If possible the bird should be stuffed the night before so the flavor will infuse through the whole. This stuffing is also good with pork chops.

BRAISED DUCK (Shropshire)

1 4½- to 5-pound dressed duck
2 tablespoons chopped bacon
1 large onion, chopped
2 carrots, chopped
1 white turnip, chopped
grated rind of 1 orange
1 large bay leaf

1 sprig winter savory
½ teaspoon sage
salt and pepper to taste
stock
½ cup red wine
1 piece fried bread per person
sliced orange } for
parsley } garnish

Fry bacon in large heavy pan and sauté vegetables. Add grated orange rind, bay leaf, sage, savory, salt and pepper. Just cover with stock. Place trussed duck on bed of vegetables, cover tightly, and simmer or bake in a 350-degree oven for 1½ hours. Add wine and cook in 350-degree oven for another 30 minutes. Cut duck into serving-size pieces. Skim fat off stock, thicken if desired. Serve duck on fried bread with sauce poured over. Garnish with slices of orange and parsley.

62. Sesame

SESAME (Sesamum indicum). "In this province they make an oil from sesame, as they have no olive oil," Marco Polo relates in the thirteenth century of Badakshan, then a part of northeast Persia. Second only to olive oil in flavor, sesame oil is now, as in Marco Polo's time, highly prized throughout Asia. And highly prized here, too, by a diet-conscious generation as a leading source of polyunsaturated fats.

The excellent oil of sesame is worthy of attention by discriminating cooks who realize that the oils they use are more than a vehicle for frying; they are also an important part of the seasoning. For their most delicate dishes, Chinese cooks always use sesame-seed oil.

Sesame seeds are part of the beginning of time. We are given to understand that the gods of Mount Olympus were fond of them. Ali Baba's "Open Sesame" has brought them into every child's life. But the adult seldom thinks to bring home from the store a package of these excellent little seeds.

Sesame seeds are a valuable addition to the kitchen; they ask little in work to give much in nourishment, texture, accent, and interest to every kind of food, and their delicately flavored oil is a seasoning of high quality.

Toasting enhances the crisp nut-like flavor of sesame seeds and liberates the oil, making them an economical substitute for expensive nuts in an infinite variety of dishes from appetizer to cake. About twenty minutes in a moderate oven, thinly scattered on a baking sheet, toasts them pale brown, ready to be mixed with buttered noodles, showered on a salad, stirred into a stuffing. If untoasted seeds are sprinkled onto unbaked breads, rolls, or cookies, they will turn golden as the dough bakes.

Today the world produces about 3.4 billion pounds of sesame seed, most of which is turned into oil. Sesame seeds are grown in Texas and Louisiana, where they are widely used in cookery, especially in New Orleans, which knows them as bene seeds. But, except for golden loaves of sesame-topped Italian bread and tempting, fattening Turkish halvah, the rest of the country has known little about them until recently. Almost overnight, sesame seed has taken over the biscuit and cracker shelf in the supermarket. At home, sesame seed can be toasted in butter to dress vegetables, fish, and pasta; take the place of chestnuts in poultry stuffing, and dress up leftovers, not counting all the breads and pastries they so enhance.

The people of the Middle East know the value of sesame; it is an integral part of their cuisine. Sesame paste, called tahini, is the basis of sesame cooking. It can be bought in gourmet stores, health-food stores, or at groceries selling Armenian, Egyptian, Greek, Lebanese, or Syrian products.

SESAME SAUCE

¾ *cup tahini*	*1 clove garlic, mashed*
1½ *cups water*	½ *teaspoon salt*
juice of 3 lemons	

Stir tahini in the can and then put ¾ cup of the paste in a bowl. Add twice as much water as paste. (A peculiarity of sesame paste is that water stiffens it and lemon juice thins it.) Add lemon juice, a little at a time, until a smooth, thick sauce is formed. Mix mashed garlic with salt and stir into the mixture. Makes 2½ cups.

Good as a dip with Syrian unleavened bread or Euphrates bread. Blend with canned chick-peas. Serve with pomegranate seeds on top. Very good on baked fish.

Sesame sauce is good in hors d'oeuvre, on hot and cold vegetables, fish, hard-cooked eggs.

BARASAK (Crisp, flat, thin cookies)

1 pound sweet butter,
    clarified (Lebanese cooks
    clarify a big pot of butter
    once a month; it never
    gets rancid)
6 cups flour, sifted
1 cup sugar

¾ cup milk with 1 table-
    spoon water in it
    syrup of ½ sugar,
    ½ water
    sesame seeds, toasted
    (see above)

Sift flour and sugar together. Add a little milk; knead; more milk; knead, etc. Add melted butter the same way. Knead 10 to 15 minutes. Allow to rest 10 minutes.

Make a simple syrup by boiling together 1 cup sugar with 1 cup water. (Lebanese cooks have this on hand all the time.) Cool syrup. Roll out cookies on a floured board. Roll very thin. Cut out with large cookie cutter, cup, or water glass. Have at hand the syrup and a flat plate with toasted sesame seeds, and a baking sheet lightly greased with olive oil. Take a cut-out cookie in the palm of the hand. Pat syrup on it with a knife, spoon, or fingers. With a quick movement turn hand holding cookie onto seeds, then place the cookie on the baking sheet. Bake in a 350-degree oven for 10 to 15 minutes, until brown. Take a fresh baking sheet for every batch of cookies; they do not like a hot pan. Makes about 35 cookies.

63. Shallots

SHALLOT (*Allium ascalonicum*) is said to be simply the old-fashioned bunching onion. It is sweetly mild in flavor and is much appreciated by the French.

It is a pity that we have let this pleasant little onion leave our markets. It is easy to grow and keeps well all winter.

Shallots are used in place of onion wherever a milder onion flavor is preferred. Their seasoning qualities are equally effective.

MUSHROOMS HOHENOF

1 pound mushrooms, well washed	1/4 teaspoon salt
1 cup sour cream	1/4 teaspoon pepper
1 tablespoon chopped parsley	1 tablespoon lemon or lime juice
3 shallots, minced	1 tablespoon Parmesan cheese
1 tablespoon butter	

Butter a covered, fireproof dish. Place mushrooms, stem side down, in dish. Mix other ingredients and pour over mushrooms. Cover tightly and bake in 350-degree oven for 30 minutes. Makes 4 servings.

SEA BASS AU GRATIN

2 small bass	2 cups dry white wine
1/2 cup butter	salt and pepper
1/2 cup shallots, chopped	2 tablespoons bread crumbs

Place 6 tablespoons of the butter in warm fireproof dish and place shallots on it. Place the fish on the shallots. Score them lightly on either side. Warm the white wine and pour over the fish. Sprinkle with salt and pepper. Bake, uncovered, in a 350-degree oven for about 25 minutes, basting frequently. Five minutes before serving, sprinkle with bread crumbs, dot with the remaining butter, and place under grill until crumbs are lightly browned. Makes 4 servings.

64. Tarragon

TARRAGON (Artemisia Dracunculus). Say "tarragon"; think "estragon," in French. It is the French tarragon (born, they think, in southern Russia) which is the only true tarragon, the sturdy spear-like green leaves, so pregnant with the sweet-bitter, licorice-scented oil which makes its indescribable characteristic contribution to vinegars and sauces, fish and chicken dishes.

There is an inferior plant, *Artemesia dracunculoides,* a native of North America, which is *not* a substitute for French estragon. The true tarragon does not set seeds and can be propagated only by division.

The most temperamental of the herbs, not only has it not set seed in the past 200 years, but neither does it like cold damp feet, nor does it care to associate over much with other herbs; it prefers to appear alone, or perhaps with a little parsley. It is too individual to do its best when subdued to the qualities of other herbs.

Possibly, however, it is for quite the opposite reason that tarragon does not combine too well with other herbs: it deadens or subdues the taste of the others. In the thirteenth century when the Arabs led the world in science, a well-known Arabian botanist, Iban Baithar, wrote that tarragon (in Arabic *tarkhum,* meaning dragon) was a soporific, and that if it were chewed before taking medicine, it dulled the taste. It is unlikely that the dragon chose to overcome only medicines, it probably subdues pretty tastes also.

Tarragon vinegar is indeed a joy, giving its distinctive flavor to mixed green or potato salads and to marinated vegetables.

Tarragon is much used with chicken and with fish; eggs and

all light foods appreciate its definite quality. Tarragon flavors pickles and mustard and bottled capers, and tarragon butter is used with shellfish, grilled fish, and grilled chicken.

SAUCE TARTARE

1 egg yolk
⅛ teaspoon each of salt, mustard, and freshly ground pepper
½ cup olive oil
1 tablespoon tarragon vinegar

2 teaspoons chopped green olives
2 teaspoons chopped tarragon
1 teaspoon chopped capers

Stir the egg yolk in a bowl with the mustard, salt, and pepper. Add the oil, drop by drop, beating well all the time until the mixture is smooth and thick. Beat in vinegar carefully. This may be done in a minute or two in a blender. Add the olives, tarragon, and capers. Serve with fish.

CRAB AND AVOCADO MOLD

2 cups crabmeat
2 avocados, peeled and diced
1 tablespoon chopped tarragon or 1½ teaspoons dried
1 cup diced celery

1 teaspoon salt
¼ teaspoon freshly ground pepper
2 envelopes gelatin
1 cup tomato juice
½ bunch watercress
1 melon

Mix crabmeat, avocado, tarragon, and celery together with the salt and pepper. Sprinkle gelatin over ½ cup of the tomato juice, heat remaining juice to boiling, then stir it into softened gelatin until it is dissolved. Mix with crabmeat mixture; set in a rinsed mold. When set, turn out on a bed of watercress or shredded lettuce surrounded by slices of melon.

BABY LAMB CHOPS À L'ESTRAGON

8 to 12 baby lamb chops	*1 teaspoon dried tarragon*
3 tablespoons butter	*2 tablespoons chopped*
¼ to ½ cup dry vermouth	*parsley*
or white wine	

Sauté lamb chops in butter until they are cooked to the desired doneness. Remove to a hot platter. Pour off excess fat from the pan. Add the vermouth or wine, tarragon, and parsley. Boil briskly, stirring frequently until reduced by one-half. Pour over chops and serve at once. Serves 4.

65. *Thyme*

THYME (*Thymus Serpyllum*) is the mother-of-thyme, the wild matriarch of some fifty refined progeny. Her hearty, astringent warmth cheers the melancholy and cures a cough. Escoffier always recommended one part wild thyme in his herb blends.

Thymus vulgarus, however, is the ordinary English and French thyme which is commonly sold, packaged, in the stores. It is a sturdy low-growing perennial, a member of the mint family, whose tiny leaves and pretty lavender flowers give off more scent when grown in poor limy soil than in the heavier rich ones.

An herb of faultless charm, yet not insipid, thyme seems to belong everywhere, giving a cheering lift to almost every kind of dish—meat, fish and cheese, eggs, stuffings and bland, creamy foods. It is a charter member of the bouquet garni. A handful of thyme thrown on the coals when barbecuing, a sprig or two resting on lamb chops or steaks as they are grilling, tones up the taste delightfully. The "sprig of thyme" often called for in recipes is about a half teaspoonful dried thyme.

Of the medicinal properties attributed by the ancients to this doughty herb, many have stood up to modern science. It acts on the circulatory and nerve centers; its essential oil, thymol, is a strong bactericide; thyme is a stimulant—one hears that the Persians nibbled the leaves as an appetizer.

The Romans, who thought thyme a sure cure for melancholy spirits, recommended stuffing beds and pillows with the lovely stuff. It works, too.

There are several soft, creeping and trailing varieties of thyme which contribute notes of interest both to planting and to the cooking pot. Although these trailing thymes are seldom recommended for cooking, there is no reason not to use them in the kitchen. A strawberry jar with a different variety of thyme trailing from each lip would be a charming object either for the house or terrace.

Here are some of the best varieties of thyme for double work—looks and utility:

WHITE MOSS (*albus*): A beautiful dainty variety with a pretty white flower.

CLEAR GOLD: Good looking with a pungent thyme-like odor.

GOLDEN LEMON (*aureus*): Very pretty and lemony.

MOTHER-OF-THYME (*serpyllum*): Unusually satisfactory. Strongly scented.

NUTMEG: Dainty. Flavor more like cardamom than nutmeg—sweet, spicy, and fruity.

SILVER THYME AND VARIEGATED GOLD: Two upright varieties have handsome foliage and pleasant perfume.

Here is a fine recipe showing off thyme's aromatic quality:

SEAFOOD AND TOMATO SOUP

2 pints mussels or clams or 1 pound shrimp
2 cups diced onions
2 cloves garlic, crushed
4 large tomatoes, skinned and seeded
2/3 cup olive oil
1 bay leaf
1 teaspoon thyme (lemon thyme is good here)
2 to 3 tablespoons chopped parsley
salt and pepper

Clean mussels and clams; let them steam over 2 cups boiling water until they open. Let juice drip into the water. The liquid must be strained afterward through a cheesecloth to remove sand. If shrimp are used, they should be cooked, unpeeled, for 5 minutes in a well-seasoned court bouillon and allowed to cool in the liquid. Peel the shrimp and use the strained broth for the soup. A mixture of shellfish may be used.

Cook onions, garlic, and tomatoes in olive oil until just tender; add fish liquid plus enough water to make 6 cups. Add bay leaf and thyme and let simmer 15 minutes. Strain through a coarse sieve; add the seafood and parsley.

POLLO ALLA ROMANA

2 *2-pound broilers, split*	1 *tablespoon tomato paste*
3 *or 4 tablespoons olive oil*	3 *tablespoons Madeira*
1 *teaspoon salt*	1/4 *pound mushrooms*
1 *or 2 cloves garlic*	*butter*
1 *bay leaf*	*juice of 1 lemon*
1/2 *teaspoon dried, or*	1/2 *cup strong stock*
1 *teaspoon fresh, thyme*	

Sauté the chickens in a covered pan with the olive oil, salt, garlic, bay leaf, and thyme. Turn them until they are well browned. Take out the chickens, pour off excess oil, add butter and mushrooms and sauté for 3 or 4 minutes. Stir in tomato paste, Madeira, lemon juice, and stock, and return the chickens to the pan. If the chickens are young and tender they will need only about 15 minutes to simmer in the sauce. Serve with buttered noodles.

Thyme is always planted near beehives; the bees love it— "Where the bee sucks, there suck I."

66. Sweet Woodruff

SWEET WOODRUFF (*Asperula odorata*), which will grow in shady places, deserves a spot of earth somewhere, if only on the unlikely chance that it might be needed; it is used to flavor May wine.

Sweet woodruff is pleasant in flower arrangements; it is hard to think of an odor more to be desired in the house on a hot summer day—new mown hay with lemon.

WALDMEISTER BOWL (*May wine*)

This is a famous old German drink which depends for its flavor on the herb Waldmeister (sweet woodruff), which can be gathered green in the spring.

6 bunches sweet woodruff	½ pint cognac
½ to ¾ pound powdered sugar	4 bottles Moselle
	2 bottles champagne

Place sweet woodruff in a glass bowl and sprinkle with sugar. Add the cognac and 1 bottle of Moselle. Cover and let stand overnight. Stir and strain. Pour over ice into a punch bowl. Add 3 bottles of Moselle and the champagne.

EEL SOUP (*from Luchow's Restaurant, New York City*)

2-pound eel, skinned and cleaned	sprig of parsley
1 pint May wine	1 bay leaf
1 quart light beer	½ teaspoon thyme
2 slices pumpernickel, grated	4 tablespoons butter

Cut eel in small pieces. Place in kettle with other ingredients except butter. Bring to a boil and simmer for 30 minutes. Remove eel to soup tureen; add butter; pour on soup. Makes 4 servings.

Walnut Tree.

SPECIAL SEASONINGS

Purple Violets.

Cherry Tree   *67. Anchovy*

Primitive people who lived near the sea soon found out that salt was a good thing, both as a seasoning and as a preservative. It is reasonable to suppose that these early sea dwellers also knew about the little anchovy—one of the oldest known seasonings as well as one of the most interesting. Apicius in his old Roman cookery book and even Shakespeare seem to have been aware of the seasoning qualities of anchovies; for it is as seasoning, rather than as food, that they are most admired. The principal season·ing of the Romans, liquamen or garum, was little else but a concoction made with salt and anchovies or sardines. It is still made in Provence, which is as old as its stones, where it is called Le Melet.

There is hardly any type of food except sweets that cannot be made more tasty by a bit of anchovy. But it is as an added flavoring in delicate, bland dishes, such as poached fish, eggs, chicken, or veal, that it is most useful. This is not to say that heartier fare does not also profit; steaks and roasts, vegetables such as artichokes, eggplant and broccoli like a touch of anchovy. In fact, what doesn't? The clever cook can lift many an ordinary dish into the gourmet class with anchovy, carefully and unobtrusively used. Care must be taken, of course, not to be heavy-handed with anchovy, but this is true with any seasoning.

Although anchovy imparts its own elusive goodness to a dish, its action on other foods as a seasoning is not so mysterious as it is often made out to be. Its salt and its oils accent, blend, and permeate the other ingredients. Its piquant quality stimulates the taste receptors and prepares them to receive flavors. Other salt fish, such as the bummalo, known as Bombay duck in India, have long been used as condiments. The Chinese use abalone juice as a seasoning. But none can compare to the fine flavored anchovy.

Most of the standard basic sauces, including French dressing, profit from a dash of this incomparable seasoning. An anchovy sauce is excellent with oysters, fish, and cold meats. Louis P. de Gouy says: "The confirmed anchovy addict . . . draws thin strips of anchovy through roasts of meat or game, fowl and wild birds to impart a tang of salt and a mysterious flavor."

No seasoning is easier to keep available at home, and in perfect condition. Small tins of flat fillets of anchovy in oil are most useful. Tubes or jars of good, thick anchovy paste are handy, especially for little knife points of seasoning. In every cluttered, pungent Italian grocery a wooden tub of salted anchovies is prominent on the counter. These are very good, but they must be washed, split, and the backbones taken out before using.

Although strips or small pieces of anchovy garnish many dishes, it is in paste form that anchovy is incorporated into most foods. Fillets of anchovy in oil or the washed, boned kind are mashed in a mortar, or chopped, then mashed with a wooden spoon. One fillet in oil is about equal in flavor to one of the washed and boned anchovies. Four fillets equal one scant tablespoon of good thick anchovy paste.

The anchovy is most familiar when garnishing hors d'oeuvre; it prepares the taste sense for drinks or other foods. It is present where we don't see it, too, as in anchovy butter on toast or melted in with other seasonings or dressing.

ANCHOVY DRESSING

Mash two anchovies. Mix with: ½ cup olive oil and 2 tablespoons tarragon wine vinegar; a dash of English mustard; 1 fresh egg yolk; minced parsley, chives, and chervil; a few capers; very little salt and freshly ground pepper.

EGGS WITH ANCHOVY BUTTER

Butter well an oven casserole; break the eggs into it. Season with freshly ground pepper. Put on top of each egg two thin strips of anchovy and a very thin slice of mozzarella cheese. Put the eggs in a preheated 350-degree oven and when they are set, take them out of the oven and pour over the eggs anchovy butter, which has been made by mashing 2 or 3 anchovy fillets (½ tablespoon paste) with 4 tablespoons of butter.

68. Beer

Nuns in the fifteenth century were rationed one gallon of beer each day. Whether or not they voluntarily gave up some of this liquid for use in the cooking pot, we are not told. Certainly beer or ale was one of the commonest seasonings.

Although races have been found so ignorant of the facts of life that they never knew the relationship of father to child, anthropologists say that no tribe has ever been discovered that did not know how to make some fermented and intoxicating beverage, usually beer. Eight thousand years ago the Babylonians in their hanging gardens drank beer. In ancient Egypt, men and women of all classes drank beer, for nourishment as well as for refreshment. The wine-drinking countries tended to look down on the beery ones, although Xenophon, around 400 B.C., admitted that beer could be "agreeable to those accustomed to it."

Beer, which is cereal fermented with yeast, and bread, a close relative, have been associated since Egyptian times. In ancient monasteries the brewery and the bakery were side by side, and beer yeast was doubtless used to make the bread.

Ewers of milk, too, sat on the board beside pitchers of beer or ale, and fifteenth-century writers never let one forget that beer is food as well as drink and warmth. "In ale is all included . . .

meat, drink and cloth." Sometimes milk and ale were used together in a dish, in soups or even with meats and eggs.

To our Pilgrim ancestors, who for many years had no cows, beer was a life saver. Even on the Mayflower there was more beer than water. No doubt Governor William Bradford's famous plum pudding was seasoned with beer, as was venison pie, baked fish, and squirrel and rabbit stew.

Although beer is mostly water, it also contains protein, an appreciable amount of B-complex vitamins, and sufficient mineral salts to be useful body replacements on a hot day. Some authorities tell us that the hops resin is a pleasant aid to digestion.

Bittersweet hops has not always been the flavoring herb for beer; the ancients used spices and other herbs. When "hopped" beer first appeared in the thirteenth century, the monopoly which sold beer herbs (at that time generally myrtle, wild rosemary, yarrow, and sometimes heather) tried all the usual bans and prohibitions against hops, but the flavor of hops soon won out over the seasonings of the previous centuries.

Possibly because we are accustomed to thinking of beer as a liquid, foaming and cold, we have rather lost sight of its interest as an ingredient in cooking. The herbal quality of the hops combined with the grainy flavor of the malt make a unique seasoning, heartily good in a surprising variety of dishes with cheese, in ragouts and stews of beef and game, with ham, with fish, and in several sauces.

I include here one recipe from the fifteenth century. For those who can figure it out, it should open a sizable field for experiment.

A POTAGE ON FYSSHDAY

Take an Make a styf Poshote of Milke an Ale; than take & draw the croddys thorw a straynoure wyth whyte Swete Wyne, or ellys Rochelle Wyne, & make it sum-what renning an sum-what stondyng, & put Sugre a gode quantyte ther-to, or hony, but nowt to moche; than hete it a lytil, & serue it forth al a-brode in the dysshys; an straw on Canel & Gyngere.

In the following modern dishes, the cooking drives off the alcohol in the beer. These recipes were developed by the Schaefer Brewing Company.

BEER–PINEAPPLE CHEESE CAKE

*¼ cup butter or
margarine
1½ cups graham-cracker
crumbs
½ cup pineapple
preserves
2 pounds cream cheese*

*½ cup grated Cheddar
cheese
1½ cups sugar
1 teaspoon vanilla
4 whole eggs
2 egg yolks
¼ cup heavy cream
¼ cup beer*

Melt butter or margarine; stir in graham-cracker crumbs. Blend well. Press mixture on bottom and sides of a well-buttered, 9-inch springform pan. Spoon pineapple preserves evenly over crumb-lined bottom of pan. Beat cream cheese until soft. Add Cheddar cheese and gradually blend in sugar. Stir in vanilla. Beat in eggs and yolks one at a time. Beat mixture until smooth and satiny. Fold in heavy cream and then fold in beer. Pour cheese mixture into crumb-lined pan. Bake at 300 degrees for 1½ hours. Remove from oven. Let cool. Chill well before serving. Serve with whipped sour cream or whipped cream. Makes 6 to 8 servings.

ROULADE OF BEEF IN BEER SAUCE

*6 ¼-inch slices of beef
round
3 carrots, peeled
3 leeks
3 dill pickles
3½ cups beer*

*⅓ cup butter or
margarine
1½ cups beef stock
1 tablespoon cornstarch
1 cup sour cream*

Cut each beef slice into two pieces about 3 by 6 inches. Cut carrots, leeks, and pickles into quarters. Trim to a 3-inch length. Place one strip carrot, one strip leek, and one strip pickle on each piece of meat. Roll meat like a jelly roll and fasten with a wooden toothpick. Place beef rolls in a bowl. Cover with 2 cups beer. After 2 hours drain.

Melt butter or margarine in a skillet. Brown beef rolls on all sides. Remove from skillet and place in a 2-quart casserole. Cover with a mixture of beef stock and remaining beer. Cover and simmer on top of range until meat is tender (approximately 1½ hours).

Remove rolls and place in serving dish. Blend cornstarch with ¼ cup cold water. Add mixture to sour cream. Gradually add sour cream mixture to the hot meat stock remaining in the casserole. Cook, stirring constantly, over a low flame until sauce thickens. Do not boil. Pour sauce over meat, glazing entire surface. Makes 6 servings.

JUMBO SHRIMP IN BEER SAUCE

3 pounds jumbo shrimp, peeled and cleaned
1 large red onion, coarsely chopped
1 clove garlic, mashed
3 tablespoons olive oil
1 teaspoon salt
sprinkle cayenne pepper
2 cups beer
⅓ cup lemon juice
½ teaspoon crumbled oregano
2 tablespoons minute tapioca
¼ cup chopped parsley

Add chopped onion and garlic to hot oil and sauté until transparent. Then add shrimp, salt, cayenne pepper, beer, lemon juice, and oregano. Stirring constantly, bring to a boil and simmer until shrimp are firm and pink (about 5 minutes). Drain liquid off shrimp and pour it over tapioca, stirring constantly. Simmer to consistency of good sauce. Return shrimp. Garnish with parsley before serving. Makes 6 servings.

69. Cheese

Cheese: the word spins one off on a world tour of different shapes and flavors. Each country makes its special types of cheeses and uses them in its cooking. America uses Cheddar; Holland employs Gouda; in Norway bittersweet *gjietost* seasons the gravy for roast reindeer.

Cheese seasons after the manner of fats, carrying its own and other flavors through a dish. Cheese has an extra seasoning dimension, however, in its own piquant, aromatic quality that has a wonderful capacity to jack up flavors. What is a bowl of soup without grated cheese to give it a fillip?

To my mind the greatest cheeses for seasoning are Swiss Gruyère, Emmenthaler (called the "King of Cheeses"), and Italian Parmagiano. The Swiss cheeses have a smooth, nutlike flavor, with excellent melting and combining qualities. The French use it on and in everything, including soup.

Parmesan cheese has amazing power to accent and blend flavors. Parmesan cheese mixed into almost any dip or spread will smooth and meld flavors and give surprising zip to the taste without revealing its own identity. This is the happy duty it performs when sprinkled on soup or pasta.

Gruyère and Parmesan are often used together—the one mild and rich, the other piquant.

TARTLETS MARIA

CRUST

2 *cups flour*	$\frac{1}{8}$ *teaspoon pepper*
1 *tablespoon grated*	*grated rind of* $\frac{1}{2}$ *lemon*
Parmesan cheese	1 *cup butter, slightly*
$\frac{1}{2}$ *teaspoon salt*	*softened*
	1 *egg, beaten*

Mix flour, cheese, salt, pepper, and lemon rind. Turn out on a floured board; make a well in the center; put in egg and butter and mix lightly until amalgamated. Form into a ball; wrap in waxed paper and place in refrigerator for $\frac{1}{2}$ hour. When it is cool, divide in 8 pieces and roll out each to make a small tart, using large muffin tins. Prick the crust on the bottom; cover with a piece of waxed paper; fill with dried beans, rice, or heavy salt and cook in a 425-degree oven for about 15 minutes.

Meanwhile, prepare this filling:

1 *pound mushrooms,* *cleaned and sliced*	2 *tablespoons butter*
2 *tablespoons Marsala* *butter*	1 *tablespoon flour*
	1 *cup milk*
¼ *pound cooked ham,* *diced*	*salt and pepper*
	¼ *pound Gruyère cheese,* *grated*
1 *cooked chicken breast,* *diced*	2 *egg yolks*
	bread crumbs

Sauté the mushrooms in butter, dampening them from time to time with a little Marsala, until cooked. Put aside to cool. In a saucepan melt 2 tablespoons of butter and stir in flour. Gradually add milk, stirring constantly with a wooden spoon until it begins to thicken. Add a little salt and pepper. Stir in half the Gruyère and mix until it is well incorporated. Remove from fire and beat in 2 egg yolks. Stir in the diced ham and chicken.

Sprinkle the bottoms of the tart shells with bread crumbs. Divide the ham-chicken mixture into the shells. Sprinkle with the rest of the Gruyère. Return to 425-degree oven until they are lightly browned. Serve hot.

70. Fats

Meat itself has no appeal to the taste buds, except to give a satisfactory sense of a good mouthful; the flavor is only in the fats. "Without the fats," Moncrieff says in *The Chemical Senses,* "all meats taste alike."

"Fat" is now almost a naughty word in our diet-conscious vocabulary. Although the sight and smell of too much fat in one's food is neither esthetic nor wholesome, nevertheless, as seasonings —and for our bodily health, too, for that matter—fats in moderation and in variety are indispensable.

Fats, of course, have many uses in cooking; it is both difficult and depressing to try to get along without them, as the people of many countries discovered during the war. Although these same people found themselves to be healthier on the reduced amount of fats, there is no doubt that foods do not taste so good without them.

But if fats are used with care and thoughtfulness, with due consideration for the special flavor and quality each fat adds to a dish, it is possible to enjoy your fats and good lines, too. This means using fat of good quality and flavor, and it means, most importantly, removing all excess fat from a dish before it is served.

Certainly dishes should be appetizingly dressed with good butter—but not swimming in it. Some restaurants, hard as it is to believe, keep on the stove pots of melted suet which is spooned over steaks and other meats as they are served to the customers!

Not only is each fat adding its own unique flavor to a dish, it is helping to bind and to blend the other ingredients. The melting fat carries all the seasonings with it as it melts and permeates, distributing the flavors evenly throughout. Many good cooks, therefore, mix all the seasoning together with the fat before adding to the rest of the ingredients.

Everyone who cooks soon learns that fats are necessary to keep things from sticking to the pan, to fry foods, and to make tender pastry and cakes. Unfortunately, there has been a growing tendency to forget flavor and beauty, and to think that one quite tasteless all-purpose fat will take care of everything. This is a quick and easy way to make dull and uninteresting foods.

Butter, for instance, is one of the greatest of seasonings. There is absolutely no substitute for good butter, whether its golden form is to be carved into magnificent sculptures and designs by the monks of Tibet, or whether it is contributing its pleasant, sweet flavor to a delicate sauce. What a pity that so few of our children have ever known the unforgettable pleasure of biting into good crunchy bread spread with lovely butter! How the flavor of good fresh butter enhances the taste of fresh vegetables, or a melting coffee cake, delicate fish, or a smooth sauce!

Butter may be blended with flour (*beurre manie*) or seasonings, formed into balls or not, and kept in a covered jar in the refrigerator for several days, if necessary. It is useful and attractive, ready to add to gravy, sauces, and vegetables or to dress steaks and chops. There are many combinations; here are some suggestions:

KNEADED BUTTER (*beurre manie*): Cream approximately 1 tablespoon of butter with 2 teaspoons of flour. It is employed for quick blending and thickening of soups, stews, gravies, and sauces.

ANCHOVY BUTTER: Cream 2 tablespoons sweet butter with 1 teaspoon anchovy paste.

BERCY BUTTER: Reduce by half, 1 cup of dry white wine. Let cool. Cream with ½ teaspoon finely chopped parsley and ⅓ cup salt butter.

CHIVRY BUTTER: Cream together ½ teaspoon each of minced parsley, chervil, tarragon, mild onion or shallot, and 2 tablespoons salt butter.

GARLIC BUTTER: Cream 1 clove crushed garlic with salt butter, more or less depending on the strength of flavor desired.

HORSERADISH BUTTER: Cream 1 teaspoon grated horseradish with 1 tablespoon salt butter.

MUSTARD BUTTER: Cream 1 teaspoon prepared mustard with 1 tablespoon sweet butter.

PAPRIKA BUTTER: Cream 1 teaspoon paprika, 1 tablespoon salt butter, and ½ teaspoon grated onion (optional).

RUSSIAN NUTMEG BUTTER: Cream 2 tablespoons salt butter with ⅙ teaspoon grated nutmeg, ¼ teaspoon lemon juice, dash of freshly ground pepper (preferably white), and 1 teaspoon finely chopped chives.

SHRIMP BUTTER: Pound, or grind finely, 6 large, peeled and cooked shrimp. Cream with an equal weight of salt butter.

TARRAGON BUTTER: Cream 1 teaspoon pulverized dry tarragon or minced fresh leaves with 2 tablespoons salt butter. Blend very thoroughly.

TOMATO BUTTER: Cream 1 tablespoon tomato paste, a pinch granulated sugar, a dash of salt, a sprinkling of cayenne, and 2 tablespoons salt butter.

Fresh sweet cream is a magnificent seasoning on the same principle as butter, but with its own inimitable flavor.

Chicken fat and duck fat add an unusually delicate flavor and texture to many foods, especially to pastry. The best chopped liver is made with chicken fat.

Lard is excellent for pastry if combined with butter (1 part lard to 2 of butter). Butter donates its flavor and lard gives a special tenderness.

Suet is good not only in old-fashioned plum pudding, but in many country-style meat and vegetable dishes. Beef suet is best, the most desirable coming from around the kidney. When using suet in cooking, all excess fat should always be removed from a dish before serving.

Grandmother's stand-bys, bacon and salt pork, are outstanding seasonings that accentuate the flavors in almost any meat dish. Several vegetables, especially the legumes and leafy greens, are lifted out of the ordinary by the addition of even a little bacon, salt pork, or ham. A combination of bacon and butter is pleasant with vegetables. Bacon and salt pork are favorites for basting and larding meats; butter is best for delicate poultry and fish.

Meat fats are generally saturated fats; poultry contains a good percentage of polyunsaturated fats. Fish fats are polyunsaturated. Butter, although saturated fat, is high in valuable vitamin A.

Fats coming from vegetables and fruits, nuts, seeds and flowers vary greatly in flavor and composition, though most of them tend to contain some polyunsaturated fat in their natural state.

As a seasoning, pure unadulterated olive oil of good quality is unsurpassed among the vegetable oils. Olive oil is superior for frying, for looks as well as for flavor; it colors fried food a light golden brown. The flavor of olive oil is harmed, however, if the oil is heated too high.

The light sweet quality of butter together with good olive oil makes a delicious combination for braising, sautéing, and dressing meats and vegetables. Olive oil produces light batters, and here again the combination of olive oil and butter is excellent.

For those who take the trouble to taste and who care much about the flavor of salad dressing, there is no substitute for pure olive oil. For those who are willing to compromise with flavor for the positive qualities given by a completely polyunsaturated oil, a creditable dressing can be made with safflower oil, wine vinegar, and salad herbs. Next to olive oil, sesame seed oil has the finest flavor for salad dressings and delicate foods.

Margarines are made from a variety of vegetables, nuts and seed oils and differ greatly in flavor. In Norway, excellent margarine is made from whale oil. Each person must choose the margarine he prefers based on flavor, color, quality, and type of fat content. Although margarine cannot be considered a substitute for butter where flavor is paramount, it is a useful and economical fat. Margarine, especially combined with butter, makes good cakes and pastry.

Margarine is a combination of many ingredients, including milk and salt, which leave a residue in the pan when heated to the boiling point. Margarine, therefore, is not recommended for braising, sautéing, or frying.

There are many vegetable and nut oils on the market (some are solidified, hydrogenated) which are tasteless and odorless. They keep well without refrigeration and some are quite cheap. These oils, being odorless and tasteless, have their usefulness. They are easy to use: the smell of frying is less objectionable and they are favored by some good cuisines. The great Chinese cuisine recommends peanut oil for the quick sauté of delicately flavored Chinese vegetables and fish.

71. Flowers and Fruits

Don't throw away your old roses; save them for dinner. In Persia and in Africa, in China, in England, and in young America, the dainty essences of flowers have perfumed foods for centuries. Teas, cooling drinks, candies, cakes, and puddings smell sweetly of roses and jasmine, quinces and orange flowers, pussy-willow blossoms, violets, or hollyhocks.

The exquisite Persian cuisine teaches that flowers and fruits, both fresh and dried, are good not only in sweets, but also in soups and meat dishes. Persian physicians believed that eating fruits and sour juices with a meal would neutralize fat.

A Persian stew called Khoreshe, for instance, is mildly spiced and flavored with fruit.

APPLE KHORESHE

1 pound round steak or *1 pound sour cherries,*
 veal, minced   *pitted*
4 tablespoons cooking oil *½ cup lemon juice*
1 pound apples, peeled and *brown sugar to taste*
 chopped

Sauté the meat in 2 tablespoons of the oil until browned. Add ½ cup water, cover and simmer about 30 minutes. Sauté apples in the remaining oil until partially soft and add to the meat with the cherries. Continue simmering, partially covered, for about 30 minutes longer or until meat is tender. When nearly done, add lemon juice and, if too sour, as much brown sugar as desired. Khoreshes are served with Chelou, a simply cooked buttered rice which is baked in the oven in such a way as to form a crunchy crust on the bottom of the pan. Makes 6 servings.

Acid fruits, when incorporated into a dish, or when served as a salad or a relish, such as cranberry sauce, are not only an interesting texture contributing enlivening contrasts, but they also serve to add an extra seasoning dimension by appealing to the acid taste buds. Grapes, for instance, are much used in this way, as a seasoning, as illustrated in Sole Véronique.

SOLE VÉRONIQUE

1 pound sole fillets *2 cups fish bouillon (boil*
2 egg yolks   *together for about 15*
¼ cup dry white wine *minutes, fish trimmings,*
4 tablespoons butter *½ jigger orange curaçao*
½ pound white grapes *or ¼ cup white wine, a*
         little chopped onion, a
         pinch of salt, 1 bay leaf
         and water)

Poach the fish in the bouillon, barely simmering, for 10 minutes. Remove to a fireproof serving dish. For the sauce, mix the egg yolks with the white wine in the top of a double boiler; add 3 tablespoons butter; gradually add strained fish bouillon, stirring constantly. Sauté the grapes for a few minutes in the remaining butter. Spread on the sole. Cover with the sauce. Place under the grill for a few minutes until lightly browned. Makes 3 or 4 servings.

Nero, he who watched Rome burn, seasoned everything he ate with roses. His drink, of course, was rose wine. Perhaps this is the reason he tired so soon of a wife named Poppaea.

Children are fond of desserts and drinks that are lightly scented with orange flower water or rose water. Constance Spry suggests that children are delighted with sugared currants: the bunches of currants are dipped first in beaten egg white to which 2 or 3 spoonfuls of orange flower water has been added, then dipped in sugar and allowed to dry on a wire tray. Thin custards seasoned with orange flower or rose water are pleasant over fresh berries.

Cooked apples taste good when they are cooked with sweet geranium leaf, a leaf of lemon verbena, or with elder flowers.

Elder flowers, and their bittersweet little fruits which follow, are delicious. The flat pretty bunches of either flower or fruit make excellent pancakes; just dip them in pancake batter and cook as usual on a griddle. Serve them with cinnamon and sugar.

Apple and crab-apple jellies may be scented with rose leaves (if scented ones any longer exist), verbena, thyme, or angelica stems. Constance Spry used the following method:

Make the apple jelly in the usual way. Pound a quantity of strongly perfumed rose petals with sugar so that the sugar absorbs the juice from the crushed petals. Cover with the smallest quantity of water, and stew gently in a covered dish in the oven till the sugar is dissolved. Add this to the jelly and boil it up.

Herb jellies such as mint and scented geranium are best when the herbs are added at the last minute and for 1 minute only. Tie up a bunch of mint or geranium leaves leaving a long end of string for pulling it out. As the jelly is boiling and just about ready, drop the bunch of leaves in the boiling liquid for 1 minute, then remove. A few drops of vegetable coloring of the appropriate tint may be added before pouring the jelly into glasses.

There are mysterious Oriental ways to perfume sweets. One way is to put the vanilla bean or orange peel or bay leaf or flowers in with the sugar. The Persians perfume the nuts that will go into the sweets. Blanch almonds, dry them well in the oven and perfume them by putting them in a deep jar or bowl filled with flower blossoms. Cover tightly and add flowers daily for ten to twelve days, stirring the nuts each time. When the almonds are well perfumed, remove the flowers and keep almonds covered until ready for use.

72. *Mushrooms*

Where fairies hold their dances, a magic circle of mushrooms will grow, showing plain as moonlight that there is magic in mushrooms. This magic is glutamate.

Mushrooms are therefore unique among vegetables for their subtle, individual bouquet and seasoning quality. As a garnish or ingredient of sauces, a delicate hors d'oeuvre, salad or hearty entree—mushrooms are an endlessly versatile seasoning and food. Even if they don't grow overnight as is popularly supposed, the culture of these wonderfully edible fungi can truly be said to be mushrooming.

Mushrooms have long found favor among many peoples, civilized and savage. The Pharaohs of Egypt knew them. The Emperors of Rome prized the mushroom so highly that they passed stringent laws regulating its sale in order to keep plenty for their private banquets.

The French take credit for being the first to cultivate mushrooms. Mushroom culture was begun in France in the seventeenth century in the extensive caves on the outskirts of Paris. The Italians also understand the seasoning value of mushrooms, as is shown in the following recipes translated from the Italian.

MUSHROOM STUFFED TOMATOES

8 medium-size tomatoes
  salt
¾ pound fresh mushrooms,
  washed and sliced
1 clove garlic, minced
1 tablespoon olive oil
1 tablespoon minced
  parsley

Béchamel Sauce (see
page 260)
32 cubes (each ½ inch)
  Gruyère cheese
  fine dry bread crumbs
2 teaspoons butter

Wash tomatoes, cut a slice from the top of each and carefully scoop out some of the pulp and seeds. Sprinkle inside with salt. Invert on plate to drain while preparing stuffing. Sauté mushrooms with garlic in olive oil for 10 minutes. Add parsley just before removing from heat. Add Béchamel Sauce and mix well. Put 4 cubes cheese in each tomato and fill with mushroom mixture. Sprinkle with bread crumbs. Dot each with ¼ teaspoon butter. Bake in a 400-degree oven for 30 minutes or until done. Makes 8 servings.

FRESH MUSHROOM CRÊPES

¾ pound fresh mushrooms
¼ cup chopped onion
1 clove garlic, chopped
1 tablespoon olive oil
2 medium-size fresh
  tomatoes
1¼ teaspoon salt
½ teaspoon sugar

⅛ teaspoon ground black
  pepper
⅛ teaspoon ground thyme
½ cup grated Parmesan
  cheese
2 tablespoons butter or
  margarine

Wash and slice mushrooms. Sauté with onion and garlic in olive oil about 10 minutes. Peel and seed tomatoes, dice and add. Stir in salt, sugar, black pepper, and thyme. Cook until liquid is evaporated. Top each crêpe (see next page) with a heaping tablespoon mushroom mixture. Roll and place in a buttered baking dish, sprinkling each layer with ¼ cup grated Parmesan cheese. Dot with butter. Cook in a 400-degree oven for 10 to 15 minutes. Makes 6 servings.

CRÊPES

2 *whole eggs*	¼ *teaspoon salt*
2 *egg yolks*	1¾ *cups milk*
1 *cup sifted all-purpose flour*	2 *tablespoons butter or margarine*
1 *teaspoon sugar*	

Beat eggs in a mixing bowl. Sift together flour, sugar, and salt, and gradually add to eggs. Stir in milk and melted butter. Beat batter until smooth. Let stand 1 hour before using. Heat a 5- or 6-inch frying pan. Rub pan with a buttered paper after cooking each crêpe to prevent sticking. Pour in 2 tablespoons batter or just enough to cover bottom of pan. Rotate pan quickly to spread batter uniformly over the surface. Cook on one side 1 to 2 minutes or until brown underneath. Turn and cook other side. Turn out onto a clean, warm towel. When all pancakes are completed, fill, roll, and heat as in above directions. Makes 18 crêpes.

73. *Nuts*

Perhaps nuts should have been included in the "fats" category, because it is there that their greatest value as a seasoning lies, though in fine flavors and crunchy contrasts, nuts contribute extra dividends as seasoning.

Walnuts, almonds and hazelnuts, cashews, pecans and delicious (but expensive) macadamia nuts, little pine nuts and ubiquitous peanuts—all are high in calories, but in cooking, pack a lot of seasoning power in a relatively small amount of fat.

Nuts are also a valuable source of protein, vitamins, and minerals. When heated, the fat content permeates the other ingredients with delicious nutty flavors, and tenderizes also, in the manner of all fats.

The almond, a brave tree whose bright rosy blossoms often spread their delicate perfume before the last ice has melted in the spring, produces many varieties of tender meaty fruits for the table, for cooking, for extracts, oils, and cosmetics. The bitter almonds (hard-shelled) are used to produce oil of almonds for cosmetics. Two or three of these bitter almonds mixed in with the sweet give a bit of a lift to many dishes.

To remove the brown peel from the seed of almonds, immerse for a few seconds in boiling water; the peel will then slide off easily. Cool the almonds immediately in cold water and dry them well in a sieve over heat.

The hazelnut grows on a bushy shrub possessing mysterious legendary qualities. Medieval necromancers were never without their hazel wands; Moses used one to smite the rocks from which came forth water to quench the thirst of the people of Israel; the caduceus, a hazel branch entwined with two serpents, emblem of the doctor of medicine, was also carried in the hand of Mercury, messenger of the gods. And, of course, the very best dowsers use a hazel branch to divine hidden springs of water.

There is nothing mysterious about the wonderful flavor of these excellent little nuts. Hazelnuts are more easily digested than either almonds or walnuts, an optimum source of energy and precious nutritive qualities. Dr. Giuseppi Gallo of Milan recommends them highly for adolescents. The versatility of hazelnuts, sliced, chopped, or ground, is a challenge to the ingenuity of the cook.

In Germany, unripe hazelnuts are eaten in salads, or they are pickled in brine spiced with vinegar and bay leaf for use in various sauces.

Preferred in the markets are large hazelnuts, well filled, round in shape, with a hard shell and good color.

When gathering walnuts, it is well to remember that it is considered dangerous to stand in the shadow of a walnut tree. Even worse, the base of walnut trees is a well-known gathering place for witches.

In the less hazardous aisles of the supermarket, look for walnuts of medium size. The very large ones are likely to be less well filled and often contain meat less tender and flavorsome.

Walnuts not only invite thirst, they also have the capacity to refine the taste qualities of the palate, enhancing the appreciation of wines which follow.

In parts of Italy and Sicily an interesting liqueur is made from walnuts which makes an especially desirable flavoring for ice cream.

Pine nuts, standbys in the cuisines of countries in the southern temperate zone, are small and handy, don't have to be shelled, add delicate seasoning and pleasing contrast to meats, vegetables, and sweets.

Pistachio is prominent in the best Italian cooking. Its pungent, almost almondy flavor is a very fine seasoning, and the gay green coloring is decorative, especially in desserts.

For those who can afford it, Hawaii's macadamia nuts, unexcelled in flavor and crispness, deserve experimentation.

Peanuts, plentiful and cheap, have long been valued here as a feed for prize hogs. In Indonesia and Malaya they are valued for their flavor and nourishment. Delicious sauces and dressings made of peanuts are staples of their cuisines.

MIXED VEGETABLES WITH PEANUT SAUCE (*Petjel*)

SAUCE

3 tablespoons peanut butter	1 clove garlic, minced
salt to taste	1 tablespoon brown sugar
1½ cups water	1 tablespoon ground hot red pepper
1 teaspoon shrimp paste (available in specialty stores)	1 tablespoon lemon juice

VEGETABLES

1 cup sliced cabbage	1 pound spinach
1 cup diced green beans	1 cup bean sprouts

Make a thick sauce by mixing peanut butter, salt, water, shrimp paste, garlic, sugar, red pepper, and lemon juice. Bring to a boil, reduce heat and simmer 2 minutes. Cool.

Boil cabbage and beans in water to cover for 20 minutes. Add spinach and simmer 5 minutes longer. Add bean sprouts and stir 1 minute. Drain. Put vegetables on a large serving plate, pour sauce over, and serve immediately. Makes 6 servings.

74. *Wines*

In France in the shadow of the yellow and black tiled roofs of the most ancient of hospitals, l'Hospice de Beaune, a dollop of some robust wine of the district goes into nearly everything cooking on the stove. Or, in the houses perched on the edge of a canyon near California's San Joaquin River, a cup or so of wine is poured into every simmering pot of soup. In the 7,000-mile zone between France and California, the preconceived misconceptions about the usefulness of wine in cooking are so deep that it is hard to root them out.

A faint air of moral superiority frequently goes along with the "We don't like the taste of wine in food," or "Of course the children don't care for wine in the things they eat."

Cooks who always keep in their kitchens lemon extract (85 per cent alcohol), almond extract (85 per cent alcohol), and vanilla extract (35 per cent alcohol), and who use heavily starched and spiced canned soups, vinegars, or catsup to flavor their stews, gravies, and sauces, for some reason are reluctant to try wine as a seasoning.

Although it is doubtful if children appreciate the delicate flavors that wine adds to a dish, it most certainly will not lead them into alcoholism, as one horrified man suggested when I asked him if his wife used wine in her cooking.

Wine is cooked; the extracts are cooked; in the cooking process they lose completely all their alcohol, leaving the flavorsome aromatic residue which seasons the dish.

Learning a little about what wine is; what happens to it during cooking; and why it makes things taste so good should help to overcome some of the old prejudices concerning its place in the kitchen.

"Wine is the most ancient dietary beverage and the most important medicinal agent in continuous use throughout the history of mankind," Dr. Salvatore Lucia, Professor of Medicine at the University of California, wrote in his book, *Wine as Food and Medicine:*

"As a food and medicine, wine . . . is significant not only because of the intricate chemistry of the grape (a botanical and biological phenomenon) but also because of the complex nature of the finished product."

Wine is the product of the naturally fermented juice of the grape. "The constituents responsible for its distinctive characteristics are alcohols, aldehydes, fixed and volatile acids, carbon dioxide, tannins, esters, sugars, pectin, vitamins, and aroma-producing substances."

All this from a few grapes that have been left out in the rain and sun. And all this goes into the pot when you add a half cup of wine to the beef stew.

In adding wine to the stew, one is putting in salts, sugars, and other compounds which have the ability to accent and blend many different kinds of food: meats and fish, poultry and game, vegetables and eggs. Vitamins (especially B_1) and minerals are going in, as are substances which help digestion and add color and, finally, the delicious flavor which emerges from cooking the aromatic medley that is wine.

Too many books pompously insist that "the better the wine, the better the dish." This is nonsense, of course, though it is true that wines which are too new contain a high percentage of acetic acid, which imparts a harsh, vinegary taste. Inferior wines which have been cut with water cannot be recommended. But any natural, mature wine will contain enough of what is called "ash," the residue of inorganic material that is left after the liquids have been evaporated, to give excellent flavor, accent, and bouquet to food. An old fine wine, when reduced, contains more ash than lesser wines and the finer the quality of the wine, the greater the quantity of ash. So this is no doubt the basis of "the better the wine, the better the dish."

Red wine always contains somewhat more ash than white. The difference in amount of ash from best to good wines is so small after mixing with other ingredients, however, that only a highly trained taste, savoring an unusually delicate dish, would be able to distinguish between them.

Seasoning with wine is far more than adding raw wine to a dish, heating it, and serving forth food flavored with hot wine. No doubt many well-liked foods are prepared in this way, including several of the popular California dishes. But to get the greatest good from wine, to exploit its unique powers as a seasoning, it is best to cook the wine down to its ash or extract; in other words, reduce it well. For dishes that will cook a long time (beef stew), first brown the meat in fat, add and cook a few minutes the onions, herbs, and spices in order to liberate their flavorsome oils. Then add wine, turn up the heat and let boil until the wine is syrupy. The epicure Apicius described the ancient Romans as seasoning with wine in exactly this way. Water or other liquids are then added and the stew is ready to simmer slowly to its tender, aromatic conclusion.

Foster and Ingle, writing a century ago, *What Is Wine?*, insist that the English and the Americans are the world's greatest dyspeptics and need the nutritive and gentle stimulation of wine in order to digest their meals. It is the most universal, best, and least hazardous cure, according to the authors.

As all wines, even the dry ones, contain sufficient sugar to act as an accent, it is with the dry wines that one gets the best results in cooking. The aim is to bring out natural flavors, not to add sweetness. Nevertheless, taste and inventiveness should decide whether red or white wine is preferred in a dish; there is no rule.

Although red wines are usually cooked with meats, and white wines with delicate fish dishes, red wines add body and gusto to the sunny robust fish stews and matelotes that bring the heady air of the Southland into your dining room.

Here is a delicious matelote of river fish, as made on the banks of the Seine, using carp, eel, and tench. Trout should do well, too.

MATELOTE OF RIVER FISH

The fish should be cleaned and cut in thick slices. The eel may be skinned or not, and cut in sections. Roll each slice in flour, or shake them up with flour, salt, and pepper in a paper bag. In a large pan brown about 24 small white onions in butter, then add 1 tablespoon of flour and ½ cup of stock. Add a pint of ordinary red wine and a bouquet garni composed of thyme, parsley, bay leaf, and a clove of garlic tied together. When the onions begin to soften, add the pieces of fish, pour in a small glass of cognac and light it. Cook another 20 minutes over a brisk fire.

Serve the matelote on slices of toasted French bread and garnished with quarters of hard-cooked egg. The sauce should be creamy but not thick.

All meats, even beef on occasion, take kindly to white wine, as in this economical, hearty Bœuf Provençale.

BOEUF PROVENÇALE

Have 3 pounds of lean beef (round or chuck) cut into large slices or cubes and marinate them for 24 hours in the following marinade: Heat in a pan ½ cup of olive oil; in it brown lightly 1 sliced carrot, 1 sliced onion, and a few ribs of celery cut in 1-inch lengths. Add to this ½ to ¾ cup of white wine and the juice and rind of 1 lemon, 4 or so sprigs of parsley, 4 shallots or leeks, 2 cloves of garlic, thyme, bay leaf, a sprig of rosemary, 6 peppercorns, 1 teaspoon salt, and 1 teaspoon monosodium glutamate. Simmer this for 30 minutes, cool, then pour over the meat.

Take the meat out of the marinade and brown the pieces in bacon fat in a fireproof casserole; pour the strained marinade over it, adding a little more wine, fresh herbs, 2 or 3 crushed cloves of garlic, 2 or 3 thick slices of bacon, cut in pieces, 3 carrots, a cup of stoned olives, green and black mixed.

If the olives are salty, as they probably will be, add no more salt to the meat. Cover the casserole tightly and cook in a slow oven for 3 hours. During last 15 minutes of cooking, skim the fat from the sauce and add 3 or 4 chopped tomatoes.

Serve with noodles dressed with a little olive oil, grated Parmesan cheese, and a ladle of sauce from the beef.

Two French chefs, Brunet and Pellaprat, give us some of the fine points of "wine cuisine":

"In associating so intelligently our wines in their art, our chefs have created a cuisine which knowing people have made their own, because the impressions given by food as well as drink are of the same origin. One obtains a majestic orchestration which leads the 'good-liver' towards a magnificent exaltation. According to old Burgundian proverbs: 'With good wine, good bread, good meat/One can send the doctor in retreat' or 'Good wine revives the heart of man' or 'In a country without wine, the meat is without character.' "

The Frenchmen write that wine to be used in sauces must be reduced by boiling before being added to a sauce.

SAUCE FINES HERBES

Infuse for 10 minutes in a cup of boiling white wine, 4 or 5 sprigs of chervil and parsley (1 teaspoon each of dried) and a chopped mild onion or leek. Strain this and add to the liquid ¾ cup of juice from a roast or 2 good bouillon cubes. Let this simmer another 10 minutes, adding near the end of cooking 1 tablespoon each of the herbs. Take from the fire and add a little lemon juice and butter. Tarragon alone may be used in this sauce. Excellent with fish, eggs, and poultry.

French chefs say: "It is principally with the fish that wine flirts most willingly; one can say that all fish accommodate themselves to wine."

When cooking fine fish such as trout and salmon, they advise adding a bottle or a half bottle of white wine to the court bouillon. Although they know this is not the custom, they say they are judging by the number of compliments they receive on the dish every time they replace the vinegar with white wine.

HALIBUT À LA MIRABEAU

1 pound fillet of halibut (or swordfish)	about four fillets of anchovies, finely cut
1½ tablespoon butter or margarine	1 cup red wine stock or a bouillon cube
1 chopped onion or leek	salt and pepper

Melt butter in a pan not much larger than the fish and simmer the onion or leek until golden. Add fish, wine, and enough stock to bring the level of the liquids just even with the top of the fish. Add salt and pepper to taste. Simmer halibut for 15 minutes; swordfish for 18 minutes. Remove fish to warm serving platter. Reduce sauce to ½ cup. Add anchovies. Pour over fish. Makes 4 servings.

The color of wine sauces, most often those made with red wine, is sometimes not too pleasing. To make a rich and well-colored appearance, add a bit of gravy coloring or a small amount of caramelized sugar. A teaspoon of tomato paste also does wonders, adding richness and body, to a dark-colored sauce or gravy.

POACHED EGGS À LA BOURGUIGNON

1 half bottle red wine	1 scant tablespoon flour,
salt	mixed with 1½ table-
6 eggs	spoons butter
½ pound mushrooms	1 dozen small white onions
3 tablespoons butter or	
margarine	

Boil the red wine, lightly salted, until reduced to half; drop in the eggs and poach them 2½ to 3 minutes. Take them out with a slotted spoon and arrange them on a warm plate. Sauté mushrooms in butter, cook onions slowly in lightly salted water. Add onions to the sauce. Stir in flour mixed with butter and sprinkle with salt and pepper; color the sauce with a teaspoon of caramel or gravy coloring. Arrange mushroom in center of eggs and pour sauce over eggs.

Wine is such an excellent addition to meats, either cooked with them, or in an accompanying sauce, that it is false economy to omit it; even a small amount adds greatly to the flavor.

SMOTHERED RUMPSTEAK

2–3	pounds rump or round steak	½	cup white wine
1	ounce salt pork cut up	1	cup stock
4–5	carrots cut in large pieces		a bouquet (thyme, parsley, bay leaf, peppercorns)
2–3	onions cut in large pieces		salt and a pinch of mixed spices to taste

Brown the steak with the salt pork. Remove it and brown the carrots and onions lightly. Add wine and let it boil 2 to 3 minutes. Add the stock, salt, a pinch of spices, and the bouquet. Seal and cover the pan well (a piece of brown paper under the lid will do) and simmer slowly for 3 hours. Skim off the fat before serving.

Ham takes kindly to certain wines, especially Madeira, port, white wine, or champagne. The ham may be cooked and basted with the wine, then served with a sauce made with the same wine.

"Poultry is almost as much a lover of wine as is fish," French chefs say, "and if one does not always add wine to all foods based on poultry, one may at least be sure that the two elements would not harm each other."

COQ AU VIN À LA MODE DIJONNAISE

1	3 to 4-pound frying chicken cut into serving pieces butter or margarine	1	teaspoon flour
		1	bottle Burgundy
1	or 2 slices of lean bacon cut into pieces		salt and pepper
			bouquet garni (rosemary, parsley, bay leaf)
12	or so small white onions	⅛	teaspoon of mixed spices minced parsley

A little of the blood of the chicken added to the gravy will give it body and character. Before washing the chicken inside, save what blood there is and add a little vinegar to it to keep it until ready for use.

Brown pieces of chicken in the mixture of butter and bacon; add the onions and brown them. Sprinkle with the flour, and let it brown also. Add Burgundy, salt, pepper, bouquet garni, and a little spice. Cover and let cook slowly for 35 to 45 minutes. Skim off the fat, and at the moment of serving, stir in the blood. Sprinkle with minced parsley before serving.

Wine is worth keeping in the house if only for gravies. Many American husbands say that gravy, which they love, is the only thing they can't digest. They eat it anyway, of course.

Instead of the usual heavy, floury gravy, try this: skim off all possible fat from the juice in the pan; add a cup or so of wine, red or white, and let it boil, scraping all the good things that are stuck to the pan into the gravy; a tablespoonful of cream added during the boiling and scraping process gives flavor as it binds and thickens.

Delicious results quite different from ordinary gravy come when small amounts of the heavier, sweeter fortified wines are incorporated into the juices. Marsala is especially good with veal; Madeira is much used with ham; port with fish.

Marinades, usually a mixture of wine and oil, onions, spices, and herbs, are invaluable for tenderizing and flavoring meat, fish, poultry, and game. The toughest piece of meat, after as much as several days in a marinade, becomes tender and succulent. The marinade is usually cooked down to make a sauce for the meat.

Never throw away odds and ends of any kind of wine; they will be useful in the kitchen.

75. *Liqueurs*

Different liqueurs and other beverages which will impart special flavors may be carefully used with all meats and fish in endless variety. Orange or ginger liqueur with duck; cider (preferably hard) with fish, ham, and poultry. Applejack, brandy, rum, or other liqueurs which contain sufficient alcohol to burn give a delicious flavor when poured over the contents of the pan and set alight—to flame. Some excess fat is consumed by the flames.

CHICKEN SAUTÉ ARMAGNAC

(as served on board the S.S. Nieuw Amsterdam)

4 *boned chicken breasts*	2 *tablespoons shrimp*
butter	*butter (see page 202)*
½ *cup Armagnac*	3 *tablespoons Triple Sec*
lemon juice	*or Maraschino*
⅓ *cup cream*	3½ *ounces truffle or*
	mushroom

Cook pieces of chicken in butter without browning. Remove chicken to a fireproof dish. Swish Armagnac around the pan in which chicken has been cooked. Add a few drops of lemon juice and cream. Remove from heat and stir in shrimp butter, adding Triple Sec or Maraschino if desired, then pour over chicken. Garnish with truffles or mushrooms.

Not only meats and poultry, but also omelets, fruits and other desserts profit from this treatment. A row of small bottles containing different liqueurs, especially useful for flavoring desserts, is a great addition to the kitchen.

Here is the sort of things they do with Calvados and apples in Normandy. Why not with applejack?

FLAMING APPLES

Have some good eating apples all the same size and rather small. Peel and core them carefully, leaving a rim of peel around the bottom to keep them from breaking. Cook them slowly in sugared water until just tender.

Remove and drain. Add a little more sugar to the water and let it boil until it is reduced to a syrup. Arrange apples on a crêpe suzette pan, or on any fireproof serving dish that will look

well on the table. Pour a little hot syrup over each apple. Warm
a half cup or so of applejack in a small saucepan. Set it alight and
pour it over the apples. Serve while still burning.

POMMES NORMANDES

apples   *cinnamon and sugar*
butter   *Calvados*

Eating apples should be peeled, cut in any shape you wish as
long as they will lie flat in the pan to cook evenly. Cook them in
butter over a slow fire. They may be cooked in a crêpe suzette pan,
if you wish, which will be brought to the table later. When soft,
but golden brown, sprinkle with cinnamon and sugar. Bring to
the table, pour over warm Calvados (or applejack), and set
alight.

POMMES BALBECS

Peel and quarter some good eating apples. Melt butter in a
fireproof dish and cook the apples carefully until soft, turning on
all sides. When just tender, bring the dish to the table; sprinkle
the apples with sugar; pour over the apples a glass of warm applejack. Set it alight and serve at once. Serve at the same time ice
cold whipped cream, or ice cream.

In the European cuisine, which is part of American heritage,
the most highly prized seasoning for desserts is a cordial or a
liqueur. And with good reason. These highly priced liquids are
composed and blended with the greatest care until the very essence
of the desired flavor is achieved. In place of liqueurs, simple
flavors such as coffee, chocolate, lemon, orange, or mint may be
used to achieve a fine and pleasant dessert, but these will lack a
delicacy of aroma and the interest of subtle blended flavor that is
imparted by a choice liqueur.

The Kahlua Mousse Lafayette was invented by Joseph Amen-
dola of The Culinary Institute of America for former First Lady

Mrs. John F. Kennedy on the occasion of the launching of the submarine U.S.S. *Lafayette*. It is a feathery concoction, its creamy richness topped with a patriotic macadamia nut from Hawaii.

MOUSSE LAFAYETTE

MERINGUE SHELLS

4 egg whites
pinch of salt
½ teaspoon lemon juice or vinegar

1 teaspoon vanilla
1¼ cups fine granulated sugar

Beat egg whites with salt, lemon juice or vinegar, and vanilla. Beat stiff, but not dry. Gradually add ½ cup sugar. Beat constantly until meringue is thick and heavy. Fold in another ½ cup sugar. Scoop meringue into a pastry bag equipped with a small round tube. Pipe ovals of meringue onto a baking sheet lined with wax paper (or parchment paper). Sprinkle the shells with fine granulated sugar and bake in a 250-degree oven for approximately 30 minutes without allowing them to brown. When cool, remove from paper.

FILLING

1½ cups sugar
8 egg yolks
½ teaspoon vanilla
1 quart heavy cream
½ cup cold coffee or coffee extract, to taste

¼ cup Kahlua Sauce
¼ cup macadamia nuts, chopped
whole macadamia nuts

Bring sugar in 1 cup of water to a boil and cook rapidly for 5 minutes. Cool. Beat egg yolks and vanilla in top of double boiler and whip in the syrup gradually. Cook over very hot, but not boiling, water, stirring constantly until custard becomes creamy and thick. Cool quickly over cracked ice. Whip heavy cream until stiff and fold in the cooled custard, strong cold coffee, or coffee extract to taste, Kahlua Sauce, and chopped macadamia nuts. Press out onto meringue shells, place whole macadamia nuts on top, and freeze until ready to serve. Before serving, pour sauce over top.

KAHLUA SAUCE

1 *cup heavy cream*	½ *cup sugar*
1 *cup milk*	½ *cup Kahlua liqueur*
½ *teaspoon vanilla*	1 *ounce brandy*
4 *egg yolks*	

In top of double boiler, heat heavy cream, milk, and vanilla. Whip egg yolks with sugar until the mixture is very light. Add the hot milk and cream slowly, stirring vigorously, and return custard to the top of double boiler. Cook custard over simmering water, stirring constantly, until mixture is thick enough to coat the back of a spoon. Cool, stirring occasionally. When mixture is cool, add Kahlua liqueur and brandy.

PROFITEROLES CRÈME DE CACAO

PUFFS

½ *cup (¼ pound) butter*	1 *cup sifted flour*
or margarine	4 *eggs*
⅛ *teaspoon salt*	

In a saucepan heat 1 cup water, butter, and salt until mixture boils. Add flour all at once to boiling liquid. Stir briskly over low heat until dough leaves sides of pan but sticks very slightly to the bottom of the pan, forming a mixture that does not separate. Take from heat and cool a few minutes. Add eggs, one at a time, beating thoroughly after each addition until mixture is smooth and satiny. Chill batter. On a well-greased and lightly floured baking sheet drop batter a teaspoonful at a time, 2 inches apart, or use a pastry tube. Bake in a 450-degree oven until points are light brown; reduce heat to 325 degrees and continue to bake until profiteroles are dry and crisp.

When puffs are cool, cut a gash in the side of each and fill with custard. Arrange three or more puffs on each serving plate and cover with chocolate sauce.

CUSTARD

1½ cups milk	5 tablespoons sugar
1½ tablespoons cornstarch	2 egg yolks, slightly beaten
¼ teaspoon salt	1 tablespoon coffee liqueur

Scald milk; add dry ingredients; in a double boiler, add mixture to the beaten egg yolks and cook over hot—but not too hot—water until thick. Stir in coffee liqueur.

CHOCOLATE SAUCE

1½ cups sugar	2 tablespoons butter or margarine
½ cup strong, unsweetened cocoa	¼ teaspoon salt
2 tablespoons cornstarch	1 tablespoon crème de cacao

Mix sugar, cocoa, and cornstarch in saucepan; add butter, salt and 1 cup boiling water. Bring to boiling point and cook 4 minutes, stirring constantly. Add liqueur. Serve hot or cold.

76. Oddments

New seasoners lie waiting to be found, old ones to be rediscovered. In the garden or in the field chance will one day release an unexpected scent, an herb of the future.

It happens. A new-old seasoning has recently traveled from Africa into the laboratory of American scientists. This is a strange berry called "miracle fruit" from an African word "Agbayun." Its real name is Synsepalum dulcificum, and it fools the taste buds into thinking that lemons are sweet. The quality of sweetness induced by eating the miracle berry is "so wonderful that it defies adequate description," according to Dr. George Inglett, a scientist who is studying this puzzling berry.

Here is something completely new. "The mechanism of the physiological taste response [induced by the miracle fruit] is completely unknown, as well as the chemical character of the active principle responsible," Dr. Inglett says.

Once upon a time, the following seasonings were all new.

CAPERS

"The erbe caperis shall be scatered," it says in Ecclesiastes, written many centuries ago. Sometimes called "mountain pepper," capers are the flower buds of a trailing, nasturtium-like plant which rambles along walls and rocky places in the south of Europe. Dried and pickled in vinegar, they are used in salads, sauces, and garnishes. Their saltiness, acidity, and pungent quality make them a fine flavor accent. Capers also are very useful to lighten, to cleanse flavor, to cut fattiness. Pickled nasturtium seeds are sometimes substituted for capers, but they are much inferior to the real thing.

T R O U T   W I T H   O L I V E S

4 trout	*2 tablespoons minced*
1 cup green olives	*parsley*
1 tablespoon capers	*1 clove garlic, crushed*
½ cup olive oil	*oregano*
3 anchovy fillets	*1 lemon*
½ cup dry white wine	
salt and pepper	

Wash and prepare trout. Chop olives, capers, and anchovies. In a fireproof casserole, which will be brought to the table, heat the olive oil, put in the anchovies and capers and sauté lightly, mashing the anchovies to a paste with a wooden spoon. Add the olives and simmer 1 minute. Arrange the fish on top of the condiments. Put in a 375-degree oven and bake for ½ hour, basting from time to time with the white wine. When the wine has evaporated, salt and pepper the fish. Mix the minced parsley with the crushed garlic, and 5 minutes before the fish is done sprinkle this over the fish along with a good pinch of oregano. Finish cooking. As soon as the fish is removed from the oven, sprinkle it well with lemon juice and serve at once in the same dish.

CHOCOLATE

Chocolate, pure and unsweetened, is an interesting and subtle seasoner for some meat dishes which want a dark, rich sauce. The fat in the chocolate seasons after the manner of fats. Mexico's well-known Mole Sauce is an outstanding example.

I once made this sauce to serve on leftover Thanksgiving turkey. The whole day was spent in the kitchen, soaking and scraping the different varieties of sweet-tasting chili peppers, grinding almonds to a paste in the mortar, then the peanuts. Finally the bit of chocolate was added, making a smooth dark sauce. It was served with a great flourish. It was chocolate sauce. Turkey with chocolate sauce is a combination which, I promise, is not palatable.

Mexican mole sauce, mild or hot, can now be bought in many specialty shops. Rather than spend all day in the kitchen, now one needs only to add the powder to three times its volume of broth, some tomato puree to taste, and simmer.

PARTRIDGE NAVARRE

(Perdiz en Chocolate a la Navarra)

6 *partridges*
1 *large onion, minced*
4 *bay leaves*
1 *branch thyme*
    about 10 peppercorns
1 *branch fresh (about 1*
    tablespoon) or ¾ tea-
    spoon dried green
    tarragon
2 *tablespoons olive oil*
1 *cup stock*
1 *cup red wine*
1 *cup white wine*

2 *tablespoons slightly*
    sweetened chocolate
    (semisweet chocolate
    bits or regular cooking
    chocolate and a bit of
    sugar)
    sufficient Madeira wine
    to melt chocolate
¼ *pound mushrooms,*
    lightly braised in butter
    or olive oil
3½ *ounces bacon, diced*

Lightly brown the patridges, onion, bay leaf, thyme, tarragon, and peppercorns in olive oil. Add stock and wine and braise until partridges are tender and liquid is reduced to half. Stir in chocolate, which has been melted in Madeira. Dry out the bacon. Serve partridges on a heated platter covered with the sauce and surrounded by bacon and mushrooms. Makes 6 servings.

COFFEE

Coffee is an unusually fine seasoner, one which is always available, yet forgotten except for desserts, when it goes into a delicious mocha sauce or perks up the taste of bland chocolate.

Coffee is another of nature's complicated products; the important thing for the cook to remember is that it is rich in aromatic oil (or should be if it is fresh) and other herbal qualities. In gravies and dark sauces it adds a pleasant and mysterious flavor. Instant coffee is handy for this purpose.

CHILI MEAT BALLS WITH RICE

1½ pounds ground beef
½ cup fine dry bread
  crumbs
¼ cup milk or tomato
  juice
1 egg, lightly beaten
1½ teaspoons salt
1 teaspoon chili powder
½ teaspoon caraway seed
¼ teaspoon ground black
  pepper
  shortening
⅔ cup chopped onion

½ cup chopped green
  pepper
3 teaspoons salt
1 teaspoon whole oregano
3 to 5 teaspoons chili
  powder
½ teaspoon ground black
  pepper
¼ teaspoon garlic powder
  No. 2 can tomatoes
1 pound can red kidney
  beans
¼ cup coffee
4 cups cooked fluffy rice

Thoroughly blend first 8 ingredients. Shape into 1-inch balls. Brown well in hot shortening. Remove meat balls. Add onion and green pepper and cook until limp. Add remaining ingredients, except rice, and heat to boiling point. Add meat balls. Simmer, uncovered, 1 hour or until thickened. Serve over hot fluffy rice. Makes 8 to 10 servings.

TEA

Though a wonder herb, tea is not especially interesting as a seasoning. Perhaps someone will find the way. The exception is that tea is a fine seasoning for punches, where it smooths the whole and gives it character and punch.

BOURBON PUNCH

1 *quart strong cold tea mixed with 4 tablespoons sugar*	2 *quarts orange juice or mixed juices*
	2 *quarts bourbon*
	2 *quarts ginger ale*

Mix and pour over large chunk of ice. Decorate with mint.

OLIVES

Olives, heavy with oil and salt and a piquant bitterness, are a magnificent seasoning.

STEAK WITH OLIVES

4 *medium-size club steaks olive oil*	3 *tablespoons stock or gravy*
½ *cup white wine*	¾ *cup olives, either green or black*

Heat an iron frying pan, add the oil and fry the steaks on both sides to the desired doneness. Put the steaks on a warmed serving plate and keep them warm. Add the wine to the same frying pan and scrape all the juices from the edges of the pan.

Reduce it well. Add the stock and the olives and let them simmer a minute or so. Pour the sauce over the steaks and serve at once.

PÂTÉ DE FOIE

Pâté de foie is used as a seasoning with grilled meats, as in Steak Rossini, braised chicken, or game. Its high fat content and its pleasant flavor are its contribution to seasoning.

VEAL SCALLOPS WITH FRENCH PÂTÉ AND ONION SAUCE

12 *veal scallops, pounded thin*	¼ *cup heavy cream*
2 *cups sliced white onions*	2 *teaspoons salt*
½ *cup butter or margarine*	⅛ *teaspoon nutmeg*
2 *cups chicken stock or consommé*	⅟₁₆ *teaspoon ground white pepper*
2 *tablespoons flour*	6 *ounces pâté de foie gras*
	12 *large mushroom caps butter or margarine*

Sauté onions in 2 tablespoons of the butter until transparent and limp. Add half the chicken stock, cover and cook 2 minutes or until onions are tender. Press through a coarse sieve or purée in an electric blender. Melt 2 tablespoons of the butter in a saucepan, remove from heat, and blend in flour. Add remaining chicken stock and stir over medium-low heat until smooth and thickened. Add onion purée, cream, ¼ teaspoon of the salt, nutmeg, and white pepper. Heat thoroughly. In the meantime, sprinkle remaining salt on both sides of veal scallops and sauté in 2 tablespoons of the butter. Spread 6 of the veal scallops with ⅛-inch layer of pâté de porc or pâté de foie. Top each with one of the remaining scallops in sandwich fashion. Arrange in a 12-inch ovenproof platter. Sauté whole mushroom caps in remaining butter and place in dish with the veal scallops. Pour sauce over veal. If desired place a slice of truffle on each. Place under the broiler 4 to 5 minutes to brown. Serve hot as the main dish. Makes 6 servings.

TRUFFLES

Truffles—the very best black truffles—mean France and Périgord. Marcel Boulestin, in *The Best of Boulestin,* says that truffles are the one thing which man has never managed to improve, force, or grow, which modern science has not been able to interfere with, a mysterious and delectable fungus which, unaided by an animal, man would not even have been able to find.

What are truffles? Where do they come from? How do they grow? They were known in the Roman Empire, in Greece, and Alexandre Dumas says that *"les Barbares en passant sur elles les foulèrent aux pieds et les firent disparaître."* Anyhow, truffles apparently disappeared from Europe and reappeared, just as mysteriously, in the early part of the eighteenth century.

"It is a cruel story of man's selfishness. We are in Périgord, here is an oak forest. There ought to be truffles, but our sense of smell is obtuse; the pig comes to our help; he smells; he hunts; he digs, and when, with delighted gruntings, he has more or less unearthed the truffle, by way of thanks we bang him on the nose with a stick," writes Boulestin.

Truffles perfume foies gras, pâtés, terrines, galantines, turkeys, chickens, and other delicacies.

TURKEY   WITH   TRUFFLES

1 *plump, young 10-pound*	1½ *pounds sausage meat*
turkey	2 *chicken livers, chopped*
10 *truffles, peeled*	*salt, pepper, and*
½ *cup sherry*	*melted butter*

Boil truffle skins for 2 minutes in the sherry, strain and discard the skins. Chop 8 truffles finely and mix them with the sherry, sausage meat, and chicken livers. Season well and stuff the bird with the mixture. Cut the remaining truffles in thin slices and insert them between the skin and flesh of the bird. Rub with salt, pepper, and butter. Roast in a 350-degree oven, basting often with butter. The turkey should be stuffed the day before using.

SOY SAUCE

Soy sauce and the other superb Chinese sauces are complicated blends of many ingredients. The quality of soy sauces differs greatly; it is best, therefore, to buy or order it from Chinese stores. All are worth investigating for use in American as well as Chinese dishes. James Beard, in his *Treasury of Outdoor Cooking*, recommends the following Soy Sauce Marinade:

Mix together equal parts of soy sauce and saké. If this is not available, you may use a dry sherry. Add ¼ cup of peanut or sesame oil if you can obtain it—1 clove of crushed garlic, and some grated fresh ginger.

The Chinese also use juice of abalone as a seasoning.

SASSAFRAS

Sassafras leaves are used as a seasoning. Louisiana's filé powder, which colors, thickens, and seasons their gumbos, is made from sassafras leaves.

Filé powder was originally manufactured by the Choctaw Indians, who also sold bunches of dried sassafras leaves for use in teas, tonics and tisanes.

Botanically speaking, sassafras is related to cinnamon.

GUMBO Z'HERBES

1 bunch turnip greens	2 tablespoons flour
1 bunch mustard greens	1 cup green onions,
1 bunch beet tops	chopped
1 bunch spinach	4 cloves garlic, minced
1 bunch radish tops	½ cup green pepper,
1 small cabbage	chopped
1½ pounds pickled pork or	salt and pepper to taste
slab bacon	1 teaspoon filé powder

Wash all greens. Put in a large kettle with 2 cups water. Cover and let steam until greens are wilted but not cooked. Drain, saving the water. Chop greens very fine (use a blender if possible).

Cut meat into 1-inch cubes. Fry until slightly brown. Add flour to fat. Brown lightly. Add greens, onions, green pepper, garlic, salt, and pepper. Add liquid in which greens were steamed plus water to equal 1½ quarts. Simmer until it becomes a thick puree. Remove from heat. Add filé. Extreme care should be taken with the addition of the filé powder, for once it is added, the gumbo must never be reheated or it becomes stringy. Serve with rice.

WOODS

Woods of various kinds, burning on the barbecue coals, season grilling meats. Both smoke and the kind of fire have their seasoning values.

BONES AND SHELLS

Bones and shells are unequaled seasonings—fresh ones, of course. I do not know what, except gelatin, they put into a broth, a court bouillon, or a roast, but they make all the difference in the final flavor. Even shad is worth the work of eating around all the bones in order to enjoy its superiority to boned shad.

STOCK

The incomparable essence of meat or fish, vegetables, and seasonings, stock is one of the greatest of seasoners. Water is not a substitute for stock.

Goosberry
Bush

RECIPES

Sorrel

Olive Tree

Water Cresses

Chamomile

77. *Whets*

Seventeenth-century Englishmen called them "whets"; they are meant to whet the appetite, not to appease it. Drinks also, when taken in moderation, whet the appetite, and the food that is served with them is designed to tease and alert the taste perceptions for things to come, not to fill the stomach with blotting paper to absorb excessive alcohol.

KÖRÖZÖTT LIPTOI CARAWAY SEED DIP

(Hungary)

> *8-ounce package cream cheese*
> *4 tablespoons (½ stick) sweet, soft butter*
> *1¼ teaspoons salt*
>
> *2 tablespoons sweet paprika*
> *1 teaspoon powdered mustard*
> *4 teaspoons whole caraway seed*

Stir cream cheese until soft and smooth. Add butter, salt, paprika, mustard, and caraway seed. Mix until all ingredients are blended. Chill. Remove from refrigerator about 1 hour before serving. Serve as a dip for crackers, potato chips, or vegetable sticks with cocktails or vegetable juices. Makes 1¼ cups.

CARAWAY-CHEESE POT

1 *pound Cheddar cheese, grated*	1 *teaspoon powdered mustard*
3-ounce package cream cheese	1 *teaspoon caraway seeds*
¼ *cup olive oil*	1 *jigger brandy*
	1 *jigger kirsch*

Combine Cheddar and cream cheese; add olive oil and mix until smooth. Blend in mustard and caraway seed. Stir in brandy and kirsch. Turn into a jar, cover tightly, and store in refrigerator. Remove from refrigerator about 1 hour before serving. Add any cheese, wine, or liqueur to the mixture as desired. Some of the original cheese should be added to act as the "mother" when the jar is renewed. Makes 2 cups. (Other spices or herbs or wines may be substituted in the above recipe.)

BEER-CHEESE DIP AND SPREAD

4 *egg whites, stiffly beaten*	2 *cloves garlic, mashed*
1 *pound (16 ounces) Switzerland Swiss cheese, grated*	1 *tablespoon Worcestershire sauce*
1½ *teaspoons mustard*	8 *ounces (about) beer, ⅔ can*
½ *teaspoon salt*	

Fold cheese and seasonings into egg whites. Add beer gradually while stirring until the mixture is the consistency of whipped cream. Chill. Serves 12.

Stand pretzel thins like porcupine quills in the dip and let guests scoop it out with them; serve on pumpernickel rounds, squares, or oblongs; for a double-taste fiesta serve with Old London triple-rippled corn-chips, "Dipsy Doodles."

DILLY CHEESE STUFFED CELERY

1 cup (8-ounce package) creamy cottage cheese	1 teaspoon dill seed
¼ cup bleu or Roquefort cheese	24 ribs of celery, 3 inches long
1 teaspoon salt	parsley flakes or paprika for garnish

Combine cheeses with salt and dill seed. Mix until smooth. Pile lightly into ribs of celery. Garnish with parsley flakes or paprika. Makes 24 ribs.

SESAME-CHEESE COCKTAIL BALLS

4-ounce package cream cheese	¼ teaspoon salt
4 ounces (1½ cups) grated mild American cheese	¼ teaspoon ground basil leaves
1 tablespoon cooking sherry	2 tablespoons toasted sesame seeds

Combine cheeses, sherry, salt, and basil. Mix well and shape into one large ball. Roll in toasted sesame seed. Chill. Shortly before serving, place on a serving tray. Surround with crackers and serve as an hors d'oeuvre. If desired, shape cheese into ¾-inch balls. Roll each in toasted sesame seed. Serve with cocktail as hors d'oeuvre.

To freeze: wrap cheese balls in waxed paper, then in foil. Place in freezer until ready to serve. These may be kept in the freezer 3 months. Makes 3 dozen ¾-inch balls.

STUFFED PUFFS

PUFFS

3½ cups flour	½ cup butter or margarine
1 teaspoon baking powder	2 eggs
1 teaspoon sugar	1 cup sour cream
1 teaspoon salt	1 egg and 1 tablespoon water for brushing

Sift dry ingredients 3 times. Work in shortening with fingers or cutter. Beat eggs lightly with sour cream; add to flour. Work with the hands into a smooth dough. Roll out on floured board to ¼ inch thickness. Cut into rounds about 2 inches in diameter. Put 1 teaspoon filling on each round. Cover with another round, pressing edges together. Place on well-greased and floured baking sheet; brush with egg and bake in a 400-degree oven for 12 to 15 minutes.

FILLING

½ pound ground beef (or leftover meat of any kind)
¼ cup sausage meat
1 tablespoon minced onion, or 1 teaspoon onion salt
1 tablespoon minced parsley
1 tablespoon Parmesan cheese
2 eggs, beaten
1 slice bread soaked in milk or broth
1 pinch nutmeg
¼ teaspoon monosodium glutamate
pepper and salt to taste

Try out meat in pan; drain off fat. Mix all the ingredients and put through meat chopper. Use to stuff the pastries. There are many other excellent combinations: anchovy and egg; mushroom and onion; meat and rice; shrimp or salmon and egg, etc.

B O E R E K (*Turkish appetizers*)

Use Turkish pastry dough (available in some pastry shops in ready-to-use form), frozen strudel pastry, or puff paste rolled thin as tissue paper. Boerek, with appropriate sizes and fillings, are also used as a main course or dessert. Cut pastry to desired size and brush with melted butter. Place a teaspoon of filling on each piece of pastry and roll up or fold over quickly, handling the dough as little as possible. Place on greased baking sheet and brush with melted butter. Bake in 375-degree oven until golden crisp, about 25 minutes.

FILLINGS

cooked chopped spinach, white (Feta) cheese, and minced parsley in layers.
chicken or fish mixed with egg, a little minced onion and minced parsley.
(for dessert): chopped nuts, cinnamon, sugar and honey.

GARLICKED FRENCH BREAD, OR BORDELAISE FRENCH BREAD

1 crusty French loaf	*1 teaspoon dried mar-*
¼ pound butter	*joram, pulverized*
1 clove garlic, minced and crushed	*⅓ teaspoon coarse black pepper*
3 tablespoons grated Parmesan	*pinch of cayenne pepper*

Cream butter, add garlic and other ingredients. Mix well. Split bread lengthwise. Put under 300-degree broiler until the cut surface is barely yellow, then take out. Spread with the butter mix, return to broiler until the butter bubbles. Transfer bread to a 350-degree oven for about 5 minutes. Serve at once. The first yellowing and spreading with butter can be done ahead of time, rebroiling and heating to serve. Garlic bread is also good as an appetizer: cut bread into cubes and stir them a few times in the soft or melted butter mixture. Broil and toast.

STUFFED GRAPE LEAVES

(Good for a cocktail party, too)

1 can grape leaves, or about 40 fresh grape leaves	*½ cup minced parsley*
	salt and pepper to taste
1 cup cracked wheat	*1 tablespoon salt (optional)*
½ cup canned chick-peas	*1 tablespoon lemon juice*

Soak grape leaves in hot water 15 minutes to soften (or use canned grape leaves). Drain and remove stems. Combine wheat, chick-peas, parsley, and seasoning. Put 1 teaspoon of the stuffing on each leaf and roll. Arrange in rows, seam side down, in pan. Add salt (do not add salt if canned grape leaves are used, as they have been preserved in brine). Weight stuffed leaves with an inverted dish. Add water to reach dish. Cover pan and cook 35 minutes over medium heat. Add lemon juice and cook another 10 minutes. Makes 4 servings.

CHOPPED CHICKEN LIVER

1 *pound chicken livers*
(or use ½ chicken liver
and ½ calves liver)
½ *cup coarsely chopped*
onion
6 *teaspoons chicken fat*
2 *hard-cooked eggs, sliced*

4 *teaspoons chopped*
parsley
1¼ *to 1½ teaspoons salt*
⅛ *teaspoon ground black*
pepper
⅛ *teaspoon garlic powder*

Sauté onions in fat until limp and transparent. Remove onions with a slotted spoon. Add livers to fat and sauté on both sides until well done. Turn into a wooden bowl, add onions and egg and chop thoroughly. Add seasonings and mix well. Serve on crisp crackers as an hors d'oeuvre or as a first-course salad on lettuce with wedges of tomatoes. Makes 1½ cups.

MARINATED SHRIMP *(English)*

1 *pound shrimps, peeled,*
cooked, and deveined
½ *cup vinegar*
¼ *cup oil*
1 *teaspoon salt*
2 *tablespoons chopped*
parsley

few drops garlic juice
few drops Tabasco
2 *tablespoons chopped*
chives
1 *tablespoon chopped dill*

Put the cooked shrimps in a quart jar. Pour remaining ingredients over them. Cover jar tightly and refrigerate for 24 hours before using; shake well and often to blend ingredients.

ROAST PORK (*Chinese*)

1 pound tenderloin pork	*¼ teaspoon onion salt*
¼ cup sherry	*¼ teaspoon cinnamon*
½ teaspoon salt	*¼ cup sugar*
⅛ teaspoon pepper	*½ cup soy sauce*

Combine sherry, salt, pepper, onion salt, cinnamon, sugar, and soy sauce. Pour over the meat and marinate the pork in this mixture for 2 hours, turning and basting frequently.

Preheat oven to 350 degrees and place meat on a rack in a baking pan and roast for 20 minutes. Turn the pork and reduce the heat to 225 degrees and roast for another 15 minutes. Cut into bite-size pieces and serve either hot or cold. May be served on toothpicks as an appetizer with cocktails.

ANTICUCHOS MIXTOS

(*Grilled Peruvian tidbits on skewers*)

Anticuchos are Peruvian appetizers made from beef, veal heart, and chicken livers. One portion of Anticuchos (as served at La Fonda Del Sol in New York City) should contain about 10 skewers of meat, 4 beef, 4 veal hearts, and 2 chicken livers. For first course at dinner, cook at the table on a hibachi.

Dice the beef into squares of about ¾ inch each. Place 4 pieces on 5-inch skewer, about 1 inch apart. (Indonesian Saté, but not shish kebab, is done this way.) Repeat for veal hearts and chicken livers. The veal should be free from all veins and muscles, the chicken livers completely clean. Place skewers in marinade for 2 hours before cooking. The oil in the marinade is the only oil needed for cooking. Since each piece of meat is only ½ ounce, Anticuchos must be cooked quickly over charcoal or on a hot grill and served at once. Serve with Salsa de Anticucho.

MARINADE

¼ ounce crushed aji (dry hot) pepper (about ⅓ teaspoon)
juice from ½ lime
juice from 1 lemon
1 ounce of oil (2 tablespoons)

1 ounce of water (2 tablespoons)
pinch of garlic
half of bay leaf
salt to taste

SALSA DE ANTICUCHO

1 medium onion, chopped
2 cloves garlic, chopped
½ cup oil
½ cup flour

1½ quarts chicken stock
½ cup tomato puree
7 ounces chili powder

Sauté onions and garlic in oil. Stir in flour, add hot chicken stock and tomato puree. Dissolve chili powder in as much water as needed and add to boiling stock. Reduce heat and simmer about 30 minutes, stirring occasionally. Strain and season to taste. Add as much Salsa Picante or Tabasco as your taste requires. Makes about 1 quart.

SATÉS (Chaircoal-grilled meat on skewers)

If you were having a cocktail party in Malaya, you would call in the saté man. Elsewhere in the world, all that is needed is a small hibachi, meat cubes skewered on bamboo sticks, and one or two sauces for dipping.

Bamboo sticks, which can be bought in Chinese and Japanese stores, should be well soaked in water before using them for grilling. Small cubes, ¾ inch, of beef, chicken, pork, lamb, kidney, or liver, are strung 4 or 5 on a stick, leaving a space between each piece of meat. They are soaked in the following marinade:

1 teaspoon ground caraway
1 teaspoon ground coriander
1 clove garlic, mashed

1 tablespoon brown sugar
2 tablespoons soy sauce
1 tablespoon lemon juice
salt and pepper

One hour is enough for marinating. Grill for a few minutes to desired doneness, turning from time to time. Dip in one of the following sauces:

PEANUT BUTTER SAUCE

1 cup water
3 tablespoons peanut butter
1 tablespoon ground hot red pepper
¼ teaspoon salt
2 tablespoons lemon juice
½ cup fried crisp onion flakes

Mix ingredients, serve onion flakes on top.

SOY SAUCE WITH BUTTER

¼ cup butter
½ cup soy sauce
2 tablespoons lemon juice
pinch of salt and pepper
1 tablespoon hot red pepper, ground
½ cup fried crisp onion flakes

Melt butter, mix ingredients. Boil 2 minutes. Serve onion flakes on top.

PICKLED CHIVE BULBS

2 pints chive bulbs
½ sweet red pepper cut in strips
¼ cup salt water and 1 pint boiling water for brine
1 cup distilled vinegar
1 teaspoon sugar
2 teaspoons white mustard seed
2 teaspoons white peppercorns
2 teaspoons whole allspice

Use firm bulbs. Wash and peel. Place bulbs and red pepper in heavy kettle. Blend salt and boiling water to make brine; pour over bulbs. Allow to stand 24 hours at room temperature. Drain. Pour cold fresh water over chives and pepper and let stand 1 hour. Drain well.

Pour distilled vinegar in pan; add sugar and mustard seed, peppercorns, and allspice. Boil 1 minute, stirring well. Pack bulbs with some red pepper strips in small hot sterilized jars. Cover with boiling liquid. Seal well. Allow to cool at room temperature. Store in a cool dark place for two weeks before using. Makes approximately 1½ pints. Serve as condiment or hors d'oeuvre with cocktails.

DILL PICKLES

When dill pickles are made at home in the correct way, they are so superior to the product sold in shops that it is almost like eating a completely different food.

The crispness of the cucumbers and the subtle flavors in the brine are the outstanding qualities of homemade dill pickles (or dill cucumbers as they are sometimes called). To achieve the desired crispness of the cucumber there are certain simple but definite rules to be followed.

First of all it is important to grow your own cucumbers so that they may be freshly picked when they are only 4 or 5 inches long, and put straight into the coldest part of the refrigerator twenty-four hours before putting them into the brine. This is the first step toward crispness.

With twelve little green cucumbers frosting under the ice trays, go into the garden and gather:

4 *sprays of dill about 6 inches long*	1 *sprig of tarragon*
	1 *tiny spike of rosemary*
2 *leaves from the grapevine*	1 *sage leaf*
1 *spray of basil*	

Then go back into the kitchen and place them in the bottom of a large saucepan, together with:

4 *cloves of garlic*	4 *to 6 crushed peppercorns*
½ *dried bay leaf*	*a few caraway seeds*
1 *dry chili*	¾ *cup salt*

Add the cucumbers and cover with boiling water. This is the second step that ensures crisp cucumbers. Put the lid on the saucepan and leave to cool.

When cold pour the contents into a large screwtop jar, making sure the brine covers the cucumbers. Store for about two weeks, and begin to use, first lifting off any mildew from the top. Keep jar in the refrigerator once it is being used.

78. *Soups*

BISQUE DE LANGOSTINA (*Basque*)

about 4 pounds of any white fish, or trimmings (heads, etc.) donated by your fish dealer	*6 carrots, scraped and quartered*
4 pounds langostinas	*6 cloves garlic, sliced*
4 pounds (2 large cans) tomatoes	*2 teaspoons thyme*
	1 tablespoon paprika
2 cups white wine or cider	*8 potatoes, peeled and cubed*
8 onions, 4 sliced and 4 chopped	*½ pound rice*
	6 eggs
4 lemons, 2 sliced and 2 juiced	*1 teaspoon grated lemon rind*
	½ cup chopped parsley salt to taste

Put the white fish and/or heads and trimmings of fish, sliced onions, carrots, potatoes, herbs, garlic, wine, and sliced lemons into a large kettle with 4 or 5 quarts of water. Simmer for at least 2 hours for a strong fish stock. Strain into a clean pan.

Simmer chopped onions and tomatoes with paprika until reduced to a pulp—about 25 minutes. Press through a sieve or food mill into the fish stock. The flavor of the tomatoes is preserved in this way. Stir the soup; bring to a boil and add rice. Cook 20 to 30 minutes. Add langostinas, cut into small pieces; simmer 10 minutes longer. Salt to taste.

Just before serving, reduce heat, beat eggs with lemon juice and stir into soup. Do not allow soup to boil again or eggs will curdle. Add grated lemon rind and chopped parsley. Serve at once with slices of lemon floating on soup.

SPANISH GAZPACHO

Gazpacho is the poor man's summer soup in southern Spain. Cool, cheap, nourishing, delicious.

It is safe to say that no poor man in southern Spain owns a blender or mixer; for them it is chop, chop, chop. But for making this soup a blender is ideal, a mixer, good.

5 *cups ice water*	1/4 *teaspoon pepper*
6 *soft rolls, the insides only*	1 *teaspoon fresh or 1/2*
3 *large tablespoons olive*	*teaspoon dried mint,*
oil	*minced or crushed*
4 *large tablespoons wine*	1/3 *of a very large cucumber,*
vinegar	*diced*
2 *cloves garlic, crushed*	2 *large tomatoes, peeled,*
1 *teaspoon paprika*	*seeded, and minced*
3/4 *teaspoon salt*	

Put all ingredients through a blender or mixer. Serve very cold in soup plates with the following garnishes in small dishes: small cubes of green pepper, minced onion, bread cubes, small cubes of cucumber, seeded grapes. Should make 6 servings. For an outdoor party, present soup on block of ice, surround with garnishes. This makes an attractive dish and also keeps the flies away.

POTAGE GARBURE PAYSANNE (*French*)

3 1/2 *tablespoons butter*
1 *quart chicken broth or water*
3 *ribs celery*   ⎫
1 *leek*   ⎪
1 *onion*   ⎬ *finely*
1 *turnip*   ⎪ *minced*
2 *carrots*   ⎪
1/4 *of a small cabbage* ⎭

Melt the butter in a saucepan and braise all the minced ingredients for ½ hour, stirring frequently. Moisten with chicken broth, season and cook for another hour. One or two potatoes may be added. When cooked, pass through a sieve, bring to a thorough boil, correct the seasoning and serve on toasted French bread. Sprinkle with grated Swiss cheese. Makes 6 servings.

POTATO CHOWDER (*American*)

2 strips bacon	⅛ teaspoon pepper
⅓ cup chopped onion	¼ teaspoon paprika
2 cups diced raw potatoes	1 tablespoon parsley
½ cup sliced carrots	2 cups milk
1¼ teaspoons salt	2 tablespoons flour
¼ teaspoon sage	

Fry bacon until crisp in saucepan large enough for making soup. Remove bacon. Add onions and sauté until limp. Add potatoes, carrots, 2 cups boiling water, and salt. Cover, cook until vegetables are tender (10 to 15 minutes). Add seasonings. Blend ¼ cup of the milk into flour, add with remaining milk to vegetable mixture, stirring constantly. Heat until slightly thickened. Crumble bacon and sprinkle over soup.

WATERCRESS SOUP (*Chinese*)

2 cups watercress leaves, tightly packed	1 teaspoon oil
	1 teaspoon salt
½ pound lean beef, finely diced	3 cups chicken broth
	¼ teaspoon sesame seed oil
1 tablespoon soy sauce	

Wash the watercress thoroughly and discard the hard stems. Mix beef in a bowl with the soy sauce, oil, and salt. Allow to stand for about 30 minutes. Bring the chicken broth and 3 cups water to a boil and add watercress. Stir well, and when it comes to a boil again, add a drop of sesame seed oil and the meat. Stir thoroughly and serve very hot.

POMEGRANATE SOUP (*Persian*)

1 pound mixed fresh green
  onion tops, coriander, or
  parsley, minced
  a few fresh mint leaves,
  minced
1 large onion, minced
1 medium beet, peeled and
  chopped
3 cups hot water

½ pound shoulder of lamb
  or veal, chopped or
  ground
3 ounces yellow split peas
  (⅓ cup)
½ teaspoon each pepper
  and turmeric
1 teaspoon salt
1 cup rice
2 cups pomegranate juice

Put minced vegetables and chopped beet in a deep saucepan with 3 cups boiling water. Add meat. If ground meat is used, form it into balls the size of small walnuts. Add peas, spices, and salt, and stir over medium heat for 15 minutes. Add rice and fruit juice, cover tightly, and simmer for about 2 hours, stirring occasionally, until all the ingredients are well cooked. Add 1 cup hot water or more fruit juice if necessary during the cooking period.

VARIATION—SOUR FRUIT SOUP: substitute 2 cups lemon juice for pomegranate juice, or 2 pounds fresh sour plums or prunes.

THE QUEEN'S MORNING BROTH

(*English, seventeenth century*)

1 fowl
1 medium onion
1 sprig thyme
  a little balm

1 small bunch parsley
3 sprigs spearmint
  salt and pepper
1 clove

Put the fowl in a pot with enough cold water to cover. Bring to a boil. Add the onion, cut in half, the herbs, pepper, and clove.

Simmer until the broth is reduced to 2 cups, and strain. Remove any fat and serve broth in a cup or porringer.

H E R B   S O U P *(English, eighteenth century)*

1 knuckle of veal	*2 onions, halved*
1 pound neck or breast of lamb	*1 bunch sweet herbs ham bone*
1 pound brisket of beef	*⅛ teaspoon mace*
1 lettuce	*4 cloves*
1 bunch sorrel	*4 sprigs parsley*
1 curly endive	*6 or 7 asparagus tips*

"A bunch of sweet herbs": a few sprigs of parsley and 1 sprig of sweet marjoram, winter savory, orange and lemon thyme tied together with string. The equivalent to these in dried herbs would be 1½ teaspoons mixed.

Put veal, lamb, and brisket of beef in a large pan; cover generously with cold water. Bring it to a boil, boil fast 2 minutes, skim and reduce to simmering. Let cook very slowly for 7 hours, skimming occasionally. Then add lettuce, sorrel, endive, onions, sweet herbs, and the shank of a ham bone. Add mace and cloves. Boil quickly for 20 or 30 minutes, until all elements are very tender. Strain, and return broth to the saucepan. Chop a few sprigs of parsley and the tips of some asparagus, add to the soup and let boil about 5 minutes longer. Serve very hot.

M I N E S T R A   A L L A   T R I E S T I N A
(Soup of Trieste)

3 beef bouillon cubes	*2 tablespoons caraway seed*
1 tablespoon flour	*2 eggs*
1 tablespoon butter, melted	*3 tablespoons grated Parmesan cheese*
3 tablespoons olive or salad oil	

Place 5 cups water and bouillon cubes in a 2-quart saucepan. Bring to a boil and boil 5 minutes. Blend flour with butter and oil in a second saucepan, stir and cook until golden brown. Gradually stir in bouillon and caraway seeds. Boil 2 minutes. Beat eggs, add cheese, and beat well. Stir a little hot bouillon into eggs and return to the bouillon. Cook slowly 2 minutes. Serve at once. Makes 5 cups.

MINESTRA ALLA GASTRONOME

2 tablespoons butter
3 tablespoons olive oil
1 onion, minced
  clove garlic, minced
1 rib celery, finely chopped
1 small carrot, finely
  shredded
¼ cup slivered baked ham
  or Canadian bacon
3 cups diced and seeded
  fresh tomatoes
6 cups stock or water
2 cups diced raw potatoes

2 cups sliced zucchini
1 medium green or red
  sweet pepper
1 tablespoon parsley,
  chopped
½ teaspoon ground black
  pepper
2 teaspoons salt
1 teaspoon chopped basil
  leaves
¼ cup grated Parmesan
  cheese

Soften onion in 1 tablespoon water. Sauté in butter and olive oil the onion, garlic, celery, carrots; add ham and tomatoes. Cover and cook 5 minutes. Add stock, potatoes, and zucchini. Cover and cook 25 minutes or until vegetables are tender. Toast peppers 10 to 15 minutes in a 450-degree oven until the skin slips off easily. Remove seeds, slice, and add to soup. Add parsley, black pepper, and salt. Blend basil with Parmesan cheese and sprinkle over the top of each serving. Makes 7 cups.

One Provençal writer claims that Soupe au Pistou has little appeal except in Provence, and even there it is used with restraint. Another writer, with expected French independence of mind, says: "What a delicious dish which, of Genoese origin, has become

Provençal. What a shame that this soup can be prepared only in summer." The people of Provence like strong seasoning, as do most Americans.

S O U P E   A U   P I S T O U *(Basil soup)*

1 pound string beans, diced	*½ pound vermicelli, broken up*
4 medium potatoes, peeled and diced	*salt and pepper to taste* *a pinch of sugar*
4 carrots, scraped and cut in rounds	*3 cloves garlic* *15 to 20 leaves fresh basil*
2 zucchini, washed and diced	*3 tablespoons olive oil* *6 tablespoons grated*
3 or 4 tomatoes, peeled, seeded, and chopped	*cheese (Gruyère and Dutch Gouda)*

Put the vegetables in a large kettle with 2½ to 3 quarts of water. Season. Simmer for an hour, or until vegetables are tender. About 15 minutes before the cooking is finished, add the vermicelli, salt, pepper, and sugar. Stir the soup from time to time while the pasta is cooking.

While the soup is cooking, prepare the "pomade": Crush garlic in a mortar with fresh basil. Gradually work in olive oil and grated cheese. The French, who do not admit the spectacular seasoning qualities of Parmesan cheese, would use here a mixture of half Gruyère and Dutch Gouda cheeses.

Before serving, pour the "pomade" into the soup and stir well. Additional grated cheese should be placed on the table to add to the soup plates.

A big bowl of soup and crisp French or Italian bread are so rich and rib-sticking that the absence of meat is never noticed. Soups like these are good for Saturday suppers and Sunday lunches. But a pot of soup left on the "warm" burner of the stove can be dipped into any day of the week. Low in calories, yet providing quick energy, such a bowl is abundantly popular wherever these are teens and subteens who seem to require constant refilling. There is no more sensible after-school snack.

The following soups from Italy are flexible. They can always be varied to accommodate the best vegetables available at any season.

MINESTRONE ALLA MILANESE

3 tablespoons olive oil	1 cup shredded cabbage
½ cup diced onion	3 medium (1 pound) fresh
1 clove garlic, quartered	tomatoes, peeled, seeded,
1 ham bone	and diced
3 pints water	¼ cup chopped parsley
½ cup sliced carrots	1 tablespoon salt
½ cup diced celery	1 teaspoon basil leaves
1 cup fresh green beans	½ teaspoon ground black
½ cup diced potatoes	pepper
1 cup sliced zucchini	grated Parmesan cheese

Cook onion and garlic in oil, until golden. Add ham bone and water and bring to boiling point. Add carrots, celery, green beans, and potatoes. Cover and simmer 45 minutes. Add squash, cabbage, tomatoes, parsley, and seasonings. Cover and cook 20 minutes or until tender. Serve with grated Parmesan cheese sprinkled over top. Makes 9 cups.

MINESTRONE CON IL PANE

3 tablespoons olive oil	¼ cup chopped fresh
2 tablespoons butter	parsley
1 cup sliced onion	2 teaspoons salt
1 cup diced potatoes	1 teaspoon basil leaves
1 cup cut fresh green beans	½ teaspoon ground black
1 cup diced carrots	pepper
1 cup diced yellow squash	3 cups diced and seeded
2 vegetable bouillon cubes	fresh tomatoes
1 cup sliced zucchini	toasted bread
1 cup shredded cabbage	grated Parmesan cheese

Sauté onion and potatoes in oil and butter until medium brown. Add green beans, carrots, and yellow squash. Add bouillon cubes and 6 cups boiling water. Mix well. Cover and cook 30 to 35 minutes. Add zucchini, cabbage, parsley, and seasonings. Cover and cook 10 to 15 minutes longer, or until vegetables are tender. Add tomatoes and cook 5 minutes. Place a slice of toasted bread in bottom of each soup plate. Fill with soup. Sprinkle with grated Parmesan cheese. Makes 10 cups.

ITALIAN BEAN SOUP

½ pound dried white beans, soaked overnight
1 teaspoon salt
2 tablespoons butter
2 tablespoons olive oil
2 vegetable bouillon cubes
1 clove garlic, minced
1 small onion, minced
1 leek, minced
1 tablespoon parsley, minced
1 teaspoon basil, chopped
1 tablespoon tomato paste
1 cup canned tomatoes, sieved
3 stalks celery, chopped
2 carrots, scraped and diced
2 potatoes, peeled and diced
1 small turnip, diced
½ small cabbage, chopped
1½ quarts of salted water
1 teaspoon freshly ground pepper
1 cup small pasta, such as elbow macaroni
6 tablespoons grated Parmesan cheese

Drain off water in which beans were soaking. Cook beans in 1½ quarts salted water for 1 hour or until tender. In a soup kettle, sauté in butter and olive oil the garlic, onion, leek, parsley, and basil; add tomato paste and sauté 1 minute. Add the beans and their liquid, and all other ingredients except pasta. Simmer 10 minutes; add pasta and cook 10 minutes longer. Serve in warmed bowls and sprinkle with grated Parmesan cheese. Makes 8–9 servings.

79. Eggs and Cheesy Things

ANNIVERSARY EGGS ESCOFFIER

2 medium-size onions	6 hard-boiled eggs, sliced
½ pound mushrooms,	(reserve 2 yolks to put
thinly sliced and sautéed	through sieve)
in butter	1 cup cream sauce
6 large, ripe tomatoes,	2 tablespoons finely grated
peeled and seeded	Swiss cheese
2 garlic cloves, crushed	butter
	salt
	pepper

Slice the onions very thin and let them simmer in a little butter until they are tender; add the tomatoes and garlic. Season and simmer, covered, in a 400-degree oven, until well cooked, about 20 minutes.

Correct the seasoning, which must be sharp, and pour into a gratin dish. Over this mixture place the eggs. To the cream sauce add the mushrooms and spread this mixture over the eggs. Then, sprinkle grated cheese over it and, on top, sprinkle the egg yolks which have been sieved. Brown to a golden color in a 500-degree oven. Makes 6 servings.

SUPPER EGGS

12 eggs	1 teaspoon salt
12 ripe olives, sliced	¼ teaspoon pepper
1 heaping tablespoon	6 slices bacon, fried,
minced onion	drained, and crumbled
1 small green pepper,	4 tablespoons butter
minced (prettier if the	
green pepper has turned	
partly red)	

Beat eggs in a bowl. Combine with all other ingredients except butter. Melt butter in frying pan or double boiler A double boiler is preferred. Add egg mixture, scramble by stirring constantly. They take longer but are lighter. Stir frequently. When cooked, but light and creamy, serve at once with hot French or Italian bread. Makes 6 to 8 servings. Good Sunday night or after-the-dance dish.

SUPPER SANDWICH

3 tablespoons mayonnaise	*36 to 48 spears cooked*
1 teaspoon prepared Dijon-	*fresh asparagus*
type mustard	*1½ cups grated Cheddar*
6 slices bread	*cheese*
6 slices baked or boiled ham	*pimento*

Mix mayonnaise with mustard and spread over one side of each slice of bread. Top each with a slice of ham, and 6 to 8 spears of asparagus. Sprinkle with cheese, completely covering the asparagus. Place under broiler until cheese has melted and is well flecked with brown. Garnish with pimento strips. Serve as a main dish for brunch, lunch, or supper. Makes 6 servings.

CHEESE CASSEROLE

½ pound cubed sharp	*1 cup milk*
Cheddar cheese	*½ teaspoon salt*
4 slices bread	*1 teaspoon paprika*
butter	*¼ teaspoon ginger*
3 eggs	

Butter bread well on both sides and cut it into cubes. Beat the eggs, add the milk, salt, paprika, and ginger. Stir in cheese cubes and bread cubes and pour into a buttered casserole. Bake in a 325-degree oven for about 40 minutes, or until brown and bubbly and cooked through. Makes 4 servings.

CHEESE TIMBALES

1/4 cup butter
2 cups milk
1/2 cup soft bread crumbs
1 teaspoon salt
1 teaspoon powdered
    mustard
1 teaspoon minced chives

1/4 teaspoon freshly ground
    pepper
1 cup sharp Cheddar,
    shredded
3 eggs, lightly beaten
6 teaspoons sharp
    Cheddar, grated
    Mushroom Sauce

Heat butter with milk. Add bread crumbs and set aside to expand. Add salt, mustard, chives, and pepper. Stir in cheese and eggs. Turn into buttered 6-ounce custard cups. Sprinkle each with 1 teaspoon grated cheese. Place cups in pan of hot water. Bake in preheated 325-degree oven for about 1 hour and 20 minutes. Makes 6 servings.

MUSHROOM SAUCE

Heat 1/2 can cream of mushroom soup with 1/2 cup stock or bouillon and 1 teaspoon marjoram. Serve over timbales.

In Spain, tortillas are omelets; there, the delicious Mexican cornmeal pancakes that America calls tortillas are unknown. In fact, in Spain, corn is fed only to animals.

Anything and everything goes into a tortilla, Spanish style, but the Spaniards are especially fond of potato omelets, in which they like a taste of onion. If there is a tomato around—and there usually is—that may go in too. Green peppers are popular and have a long season in Spain, so they invariably find their way into the dish. The result is what we call in English . . .

SPANISH OMELET

8 eggs
1 large onion, minced
1 green pepper, minced
2 medium tomatoes, minced
1 large potato, peeled and
    diced

1 anchovy fillet, minced
3 tablespoons olive oil for
    vegetables
2 tablespoons olive oil per
    omelet
    salt, pepper, and oregano

Use 2 eggs for each omelet. Sauté vegetables and oregano in olive oil until soft and not liquid; stir in anchovy. Heat a small individual omelet pan. Put in 2 tablespoons olive oil to heat. Beat well 2 eggs with seasoning and add ¼ of the cooked vegetables. Pour into hot pan. Cook, scraping away from sides toward the middle until sufficiently set to toss. To turn, toss omelet or turn the Spanish way. Cook ½ minute longer. Turn out on plate. Repeat to make 4 omelets. Butter may be used instead of olive oil.

A professor at Harvard Business School practiced for some time with a folded napkin before attempting to toss an omelet. He did not know how an omelet is turned in Spain.

The Spanish way: cover the tortilla pan with a flat lid. Turn tortilla onto the lid, then slide it back into the pan.

SHRIMP AND TOMATO TORTILLA (*A good one; use small shrimp or cut up big ones*)

FOR 1 TORTILLA

12 small shrimp or 3 chopped big ones, peeled and deveined	2 eggs
	⅛ teaspoon salt
	⅛ teaspoon pepper
1 small tomato, peeled, seeded, and chopped	⅛ teaspoon thyme
	4 tablespoons olive oil

Sauté shrimp, tomato, and thyme in olive oil for 2 minutes. If necessary, add a little water or dry white wine and sauté until liquid is absorbed. Cook according to directions for Spanish Omelet.

SPINACH TORTILLA (*A good example of adding a bit of everything*)

FOR 1 TORTILLA

½ pound spinach, washed	1 teaspoon raisins
5 tablespoons olive oil	¼ teaspoon salt
1 heaping tablespoon cooked white beans	⅛ teaspoon pepper
	dash of cayenne
1 teaspoon pine nuts	

Sauté spinach in 3 tablespoons olive oil. When spinach is almost cooked, add other ingredients except seasonings. Pour off excess oil. Make tortilla according to previous directions. If exceptionally hungry, do as the Spanish do: serve with a fried or poached egg on the side!

MIXED VEGETABLE TORTILLA

Use any combination of vegetables: string beans, peas, artichokes, beet greens, tomato, etc. Proceed as for Spinach Tortilla.

PANCAKES SUISSE

¼ *pound Switzerland Swiss cheese, grated*	1½ *tablespoons flour*
	½ *teaspoon salt*
½ *cup sour cream*	1 *teaspoon mustard*
2 *egg yolks*	1 *tablespoon butter*

Mix ingredients except butter; stir well. Melt butter in frying pan; drop heaping tablespoons of mixture into pan; cook, turning once, until golden brown on both sides. Makes 8 pancakes.

TAMALES DE MAIZ TIERNO
(Corn tamales from Colombia)

12 *ears fresh corn*	½ *teaspoon baking powder*
1 *farmer cheese (1 cup)*	2 *tablespoons sugar*
3 *whole eggs, lightly beaten*	1 *tablespoon salt*
	¼ *teaspoon black pepper*
3 *tablespoons flour*	

Remove husks and silks from corn. Reserve 24 largest strips of shucks for later use. Cut corn from cob and reserve 5 cobs for later use. Measure cut corn. There should be 3 cups. Combine corn, cheese, eggs, flour, baking powder, sugar, salt, and black pepper. Mix well. For each tamale use 2 of the large shucks, placing them side by side lengthwise, overlapping the edges about 1 inch. Place ¼ cup of the corn mixture in center of each. Fold the lengthwise edges over the top as in wrapping a package. Fold ends under the tamales to prevent filling from seeping out. Place tamales in a saucepan with the 5 cobs and 2 inches boiling water to cover. Cook slowly, covered, 1¼ hours or until filling is firm. Serve hot or cold. Makes 12 servings. For leftover tamales, remove shucks and fry in butter until golden brown.

SAILOR'S PIZZA

6 small (1 pound) ripe	*1 teaspoon salt*
tomatoes	*¼ teaspoon ground black*
¼ cup olive oil	*pepper*
1 clove garlic, minced	*4 ounces mozzarella cheese*
1 teaspoon oregano	*pizza crust*

Peel tomatoes, seed, and chop coarsely. Drain well and arrange over unbaked pizza crust. See page 166 for dough recipe. Sprinkle with olive oil mixed with garlic, oregano, salt, and pepper. Dice mozzarella cheese and arrange over the top. Bake in a hot 400-degree oven for 40 to 45 minutes or until the crust has browned. Makes 6 servings.

PIZZA RUSTICA WITH CUMIN SEED

3 cups pizza dough (see	*5 or 6 sage leaves or*
page 166)	*½ teaspoon dried*
⅓ pound thick bacon,	*½ teaspoon cumin seed*
diced quite small	*pizza dough*
1 branch of rosemary or	
1 teaspoon dried	

Mince sage and rosemary and mix well with ½ the bacon. Mix it into the pizza dough. See page 166 for dough recipe. Use a rectangular baking sheet with sides, and oil it well. Roll out dough. Place on baking sheet and pull as thin as possible to fit. Sprinkle with cumin seed and diced bacon. Bake in a 400-degree oven about 25 minutes.

This is a truly rustic pizza, adapted for young people with robust stomachs.

80. Sauces

CUMBERLAND SAUCE

2 shallots or 1 mild onion, minced
shredded peel of 1 orange
6 tablespoons currant jelly
pinch of ginger
pinch of cayenne
juice of 1 lemon
juice of 1 orange

Boil shallots and orange peel for 15 minutes in a little water. Beat in jelly, ginger, cayenne, and juices. Serve with cold ham and other cold meats.

BÉCHAMEL SAUCE

2 tablespoons butter
2 tablespoons flour
1 cup chicken stock, hot
9 tablespoons light cream
3 gratings of onion or a little onion juice
3 egg yolks
¾ teaspoon salt
¼ teaspoon ground black pepper
⅜ teaspoon vanilla
1 large bay leaf

Melt butter in a small saucepan. Blend in flour. Heat chicken stock with bay leaf and onion. Remove flour and butter mixture from heat and stir in chicken stock, after removing bay leaf. Stir and cook over low heat until thickened, about 3 minutes. Reduce heat, add cream blended with egg yolks and vanilla. Add salt and black pepper. Makes 1½ cups. Sauce may be stored in a closed jar in refrigerator.

HOLLANDAISE SAUCE (*made with vanilla*)

¾ *cup butter*	*dash salt*
2½ *teaspoons fresh lemon*	*dash cayenne*
juice	¼ *teaspoon pure vanilla*
3 *egg yolks, well beaten*	*extract*

Divide butter into 3 pieces. Put 1 piece in top of a small double boiler, with lemon juice and egg yolks. Place over hot, not boiling, water and cook slowly, beating constantly with a wire whisk or beater. Add the second piece when first piece of butter has been absorbed. Beat and cook until mixture begins to thicken. Add the third piece. Cook, beating constantly, until sauce is about as thick as mayonnaise. Remove from heat, add salt, cayenne, and pure vanilla extract. Serve immediately over hot cooked vegetables or fish. Makes 1 cup.

TOMATO HOLLANDAISE SAUCE

Add ½ tablespoon tomato paste or sauce to the above hollandaise sauce.

BÉARNAISE SAUCE

1 *cup dry white wine*	1 *sprig tarragon, minced or*
1 *tablespoon tarragon*	½ *teaspoon dried*
vinegar	*pinch of chervil*
1 *tablespoon finely chopped*	3 *or 4 bruised peppercorns*
shallots or mild onion	3 *egg yolks*
2 *sprigs parsley, minced*	*butter*

Simmer all the ingredients, except egg yolks and butter, in saucepan until reduced to half volume. Strain into the top of a double boiler over simmering water. Beat in 3 egg yolks, 1 at a time, beating well after each addition, alternating with as much butter melted to lukewarm as the sauce will hold. Beat until it is the consistency of cream cheese. Excellent with fillet steak; appropriate for any kind of meat or fish.

VARIATIONS

Add 1 or 2 tablespoons of tomato paste with the butter or substitute lobster, shrimp, anchovy, herring, or smoked salmon butter for the plain butter. About ⅛ teaspoon of vanilla extract added to Béarnaise makes a more smoothly blended sauce.

HORSERADISH SAUCE

3 tablespoons butter	*1 tablespoon wine vinegar*
3 tablespoons flour	*½ teaspoon salt*
1 cup hot milk	*¼ teaspoon white pepper*
½ cup stock	*½ cup freshly grated*
¼ teaspoon grated nutmeg	*horseradish*

Melt butter; stir flour smoothly into it. Add hot milk and stock; stir and cook until well blended. Add nutmeg, vinegar, salt and pepper. Mix well. Stir constantly over heat until smooth and thickened. Beat in horseradish just before serving. Makes about 1¾ cups.

TOMATO SAUCE

2 tablespoons butter	*1½ cups stock*
1 carrot, minced	*½ teaspoon salt*
1 small onion, minced	*¼ teaspoon pepper*
3 tablespoons flour	*1 teaspoon sugar*
3 or 4 tomatoes, peeled,	*2 cloves garlic*
seeded, and chopped, or	*½ teaspoon thyme*
sieved	*1 bay leaf, crumbled*
½ green pepper, minced	

Sauté carrot and onion in butter until tender but not brown. Add flour and stir until smooth. Stir and cook until lightly browned. Add other ingredients. Bring to a boil, stirring constantly. Lower heat and simmer for 30 minutes, stirring frequently. Strain and reheat. Makes about 2 cups.

CUCUMBER SAUCE

1 tender cucumber	*juice of 1 lemon*
2 tablespoons creole	*1 egg yolk, beaten*
mustard	*a little salt to taste*

Wash and grate cucumber; it may be peeled or not, as preferred. Mix in other ingredients and beat well. Excellent with fish and on salads.

MUSTARD SAUCE

½ cup butter	*2 cups stock*
½ onion, minced	*2 teaspoons English*
2 tablespoons flour	*mustard*
½ cup dry white wine	

Cook onion in butter, but do not brown. Add flour and mustard and stir until mixed. Gradually add wine and stock, stirring constantly until smooth. Simmer 10 minutes, stirring frequently. Makes about 3 cups.

MINT SAUCE

½ cup fresh mint leaves,	*¼ cup tarragon vinegar*
finely chopped	*1 tablespoon sugar*
1 cup stock	*salt and pepper*

Mix ingredients and heat in double boiler.

SOUR CREAM SAUCE

2 shallots or 1 white onion,   1 cup stock
   minced   ½ cup dry white wine
4 tablespoons butter   1 cup sour cream
2 tablespoons flour   lemon juice

Sauté shallots in butter. Add flour and stir until smooth. Gradually add stock and wine, stirring continually. Simmer and stir until thickened, about 15 minutes. Add sour cream and a squeeze of lemon juice. Mix well. Makes about 2½ cups.

81. Fish

Fish, even fatty fish, has polyunsaturated fat and no carbohydrates. Shellfish contains from 3 to 5 per cent carbohydrates. There are many lean fish, too. So we see fish returning to favor on American tables.

Dry, overcooked, tasteless fish will discourage anyone, but a juicy stuffed fresh fish, baked and basted with a flavorsome liquid, is definitely habit-forming. There are always delicious big fish in season, ready to be baked with a variety of fish stuffings which will enhance the flavor and interest of the dish. The secret is in the seasoning.

The kind of stuffing used depends on the kind of fish chosen. When buying an unfamiliar fish, ask the fish man if it is fat or lean, whether it has a strong or delicate flavor.

For fish of delicate flavor, salt and pepper, a slice of lemon, a large sprig of parsley, and a little butter is enough to put in the cavity before baking. Tarragon, chervil, chives, and fennel all combine well with any kind of fish. For basting fish, dry white wine is usually best; fish broth to which a little lemon juice or wine vinegar has been added will keep the fish moist and flavorsome.

The most delicious stuffing for any fish is another fish, seasoned to bring out the flavors to perfection: boned shad stuffed with its roe; bluefish with fillet of flounder, or red snapper stuffed with oysters. Lean fish can take a rich stuffing.

RICH FISH STUFFING

½ *pound raw fish (boned and skinned) chopped*	1 *tablespoon minced onion or chives*
½ *cup scalded light cream or sour cream*	1 *tablespoon minced parsley*
1 *egg, lightly beaten*	1 *teaspoon minced tarragon, if desired*
½ *teaspoon salt*	
½ *teaspoon paprika*	

Mix all ingredients and put in cavity of cleaned fish. Baste with white wine or cream.

Stuffings to which chestnuts, almonds or brazil nuts have been added are excellent with lean fish. Fat fish like stuffings that cut the fat or the taste of fat. Tart raw fruits are ideal stuffings for fat fish: pineapple, grapes, orange, gooseberries, cranberries. Centuries ago the finest Chinese cooks stuffed shark with half-ripe mulberries.

SEAFOOD STUFFING

3 *tablespoons butter*	½ *teaspoon salt*
12 *medium shrimp, cooked and chopped*	¼ *teaspoon paprika*
1 *cup soft bread crumbs*	12 *oysters, drained*
1 *tablespoon minced parsley*	½ *cup crabmeat*
1 *tablespoon minced onion or chives*	1 *beaten egg yolk (optional)*

Melt butter in large frying pan. Add shrimp, crumbs, and seasonings. Mix over low heat for a few minutes. Add oysters and crabmeat. Mix well. Add egg yolk beaten with a little of the oyster liquor. Use to stuff any fine fish—red snapper, for example. Scallops or lobster meat are also good in a seafood stuffing.

CUCUMBER STUFFING FOR FAT FISH

2 cucumbers, chopped	3 mushrooms, minced
1 tablespoon minced onion or chives	2 tablespoons lemon juice
1 tablespoon minced parsley	1 beaten egg, if desired about 1 cup soft bread crumbs

Mix all ingredients and use to stuff fat fish. For lean fish, 1 slice bacon, chopped, and 2 tablespoons melted butter or margarine may be added to the recipe. *Note:* For Eggplant Stuffing, substitute 1 cup cooked and chopped eggplant for the cucumbers.

OYSTER STUFFING

2 dozen oysters	1 teaspoon minced onion or chives
3 tablespoons butter	
1 cup bread or cracker crumbs	½ teaspoon salt
	⅛ teaspoon pepper
1 tablespoon minced parsley or chervil	2 tablespoons white wine or lemon juice

Drain oysters; retain the liquor. Mix all ingredients. Moisten dressing with oyster liquor if desired; the remaining oyster liquor is excellent for basting the fish.

SEA BASS WITH TOMATO

Spain leans heavily on the luscious Mediterranean tomato, even to "spreading" it on bread. A tomato is cut, then squeezed and rubbed on a large slice of crusty bread until it is permeated with tomato. The bread is then topped with a slice of ham, or even a whole smoked fish. For the sea bass . . .

1 2- to 3-pound sea bass	*1 clove garlic*
½ cup water	*1 onion and 1 carrot,*
½ cup dry white wine	*chopped*
½ cup wine vinegar	*1 fennel, sliced, if avail-*
2 bay leaves	*able or*
2 branches (1 teaspoon)	*6 fennel seeds*
thyme	*10 peppercorns*
4 peeled tomatoes	

Put all ingredients in a large pan and simmer for ½ hour. Remove fish to serving plate. Put sauce through food mill or sieve. Correct seasoning. Pour over fish. This dish is also good cold. Makes 4 servings.

SESAME SEED–RICE STUFFING *(for fish)*

⅓ cup finely chopped celery	*1 tablespoon parsley flakes*
3 tablespoons butter	*3 tablespoons toasted*
⅛ teaspoon ground black	*sesame seeds*
pepper	*2 cups cooked rice*
1 teaspoon salt	*4 pound fish (blue, bass or*
½ teaspoon thyme leaves	*weak fish)*
1 tablespoon instant	
minced onion	

Sauté celery in 1 tablespoon of the butter. Add remaining butter and heat until melted. Stir in seasonings. Add rice and mix gently until blended. Spoon into the cavity of a fish suitable for stuffing. Close cavity with skewers or wooden toothpicks. Brush with salad oil or melted butter. Bake in a greased shallow baking pan, uncovered, in a moderate 375-degree oven for 40 minutes or until fish flakes when tested with a fork. Serve with lemon wedges. Makes 6 servings.

CRABS À LA CREOLE

4 *hard shell crabs per*
person
1 *large onion, chopped fine*
1 *tablespoon butter*
1 *dozen fresh tomatoes*
1 *stalk chopped celery*
sprig of thyme, parsley,
bay leaf, chopped fine

2 *tablespoons minced*
parsley
1 *bay leaf*
1 *clove garlic, chopped fine*
1 *teaspoon salt*
dash of cayenne

To prepare crabs: boil 5 to 6 minutes, remove shells and other inedible portions, crack claws, and cut body into 4 parts.

Brown onion in butter in large kettle. Add finely chopped tomatoes (and their juice). Stir in celery, thyme, parsley, bay leaf, garlic, salt, and cayenne. Cook 10 minutes. Add crabs and cook 10 minutes longer. Serve with boiled rice or boiled potatoes.

STUFFED CLAMS (*Chinese*)

2½ *pounds clams with*
shells
¼ *pound pork, minced*
1 *slice fresh ginger,*
chopped fine
1 *slice scallion, chopped*
fine

3 *teaspoons sherry*
½ *teaspoon salt*
½ *teaspoon sugar*
1 *teaspoon soy sauce*
¼ *cup chicken stock*
2 *tablespoons oil*

Wash the clams well in cold water and then pour boiling water over them to open. Remove clams from shells and retain the juice and shells. Mince clams and combine them with pork and clam juice. Stir in ginger, scallion, sherry, salt, sugar, and soy sauce. Fill the shells with this mixture and arrange in a baking dish containing the chicken stock and the oil. Bake in a 450-degree oven for 15 minutes. Serve very hot in the baking dish.

STUFFED CLAMS (*New England*)

24 littleneck clams
3 fresh mushrooms,
  chopped fine
2 slices cooked bacon,
  chopped fine

1 teaspoon minced parsley
salt and pepper
bread crumbs
2 tablespoons butter

Remove clams from shells. Scrub shells thoroughly to remove all sand and then scald in boiling water. Chop the clams and combine with mushrooms, bacon, parsley, salt and pepper. Stir in enough bread crumbs so that mixture will hold together. Fill shells, sprinkle with additional bread crumbs and dot each shell with butter. Bake in 350-degree oven until browned, about 12 minutes.

KEDGEREE

1 cup uncooked long-grain
  rice
1 teaspoon salt
¾ pound cooked shrimp,
  peeled
1 cup cooked ham, diced
4 hard-cooked eggs
2 tablespoons minced
  onion

1 tablespoon minced
  parsley
½ teaspoon salt
½ teaspoon ground nutmeg
¼ cup butter, melted
⅛ teaspoon garlic powder
⅛ teaspoon ground black
  pepper

Sprinkle rice over 2½ cups boiling salted water. Cover and cook over medium heat until tender. Add shrimp and ham. Peel eggs and dice coarsely. Add with remaining ingredients. Place over hot water or very low heat only long enough to heat through. Since this is a rather dry dish, serve as the main course with a creamed vegetable, green salad, and homemade sweet pickles or chutney. Leftover cooked pork, poultry, or fish may replace shrimp and ham in this recipe. Makes 4 servings.

SCALLOPS LORRAINE

½ *pound cooked scallops,*
  chopped
  pie crust for 9-inch pie
3 *eggs, beaten*
¾ *cup light cream*
2 *tablespoons sherry*

2 *tablespoons chopped*
  parsley
1 *teaspoon salt*
½ *teaspoon celery salt*
  dash of pepper
  paprika

Line 9-inch pie pan with pastry. Combine scallops with all ingredients except paprika. Place mixture in pie shell. Sprinkle with paprika. Bake in a 350-degree oven for 35 to 40 minutes or until firm in the center.

HOW TO BOIL SHRIMP

  a bunch of celery with
  tops, chopped
12 *allspice berries*
2 *blades mace*
2 *cloves*

4 *sprigs each of thyme*
  and parsley
2 *bay leaves*
2 *red pepper pods*
10 *peppercorns*
4 *tablespoons salt*

Put all ingredients in a large kettle and simmer for a half hour or more. Add 5 pounds shrimp. Boil 5 minutes and allow to cool in the same water. Serve on a bed of cracked ice, garnished with parsley and lemon. This is a good way to prepare cooked shrimp for many recipes. The celery discolors the shrimp, but the flavor is excellent. Makes the kitchen smell lovely, too.

DANIEL WEBSTER'S FISH CHOWDER

"Four tablespoons of onion were fried in the kettle, then the other things were added: a quart of well-mashed potatoes, a pound and a half of ships biscuits (Boston crackers) well broken, a teaspoon of thyme, a half bottle of mushroom catsup, half a nutmeg, grated; a few whole cloves and some black pepper, a bottle of port or claret, a little mace, allspice, and some slices of lemon; 6 pounds of blue or whitefish cut in slices, and 25 oysters, with enough water to cover the whole an inch deep." This was cooked slowly and stirred just enough to cook it evenly without burning.

TO BAKE FLOUNDER (*eighteenth century*)

chives—a small handful	*butter*
parsley—one small bunch	*½ cup red wine*
basil—2 or 3 sprigs	*pepper, salt, nutmeg*
tarragon—2 sprigs	*½ cup melted butter*
bread crumbs	

Mince some chives, shred some parsley very fine, cut some savory herbs, including sweet basil and tarragon, very small. Mix them all together with some fresh grated nutmeg, pepper, and salt. Rub the inside of a baking dish well with fresh butter, then strew the seasoning you have just made all over it that it may stick in great quantity on every part of it.

Choose some fine large flounder (medium would be better for this dish), clean them perfectly, cut off the heads and tails, and lay them regularly and evenly in the dish. When this is done, pour in half a cup of red wine. Strew over them a little pepper, salt, and grated nutmeg. Drop in on them some melted butter, in small quantity. Cover with a large quantity of very fine bread crumbs. And bake them a fine brown in a hot oven.

KITTERY BAKED HALIBUT

2½ pounds halibut	*3 tablespoons flour*
4 thin slices salt pork	*1 cup milk*
1 onion, sliced	*1 bay leaf*
3 tablespoons melted	*salt and pepper*
butter	*1 lemon, halved*

Lay slices of salt pork in a baking dish and cover with half the onion slices. Place halibut on them. Pour on half the melted butter. Spread with remaining onion slices and add remaining butter. Sprinkle with flour. Pour milk around fish. Add bay leaf, salt, and pepper. Squeeze juice of lemon over all. Cover and bake 20 minutes in 350-degree oven. Remove cover and bake 15 to 20 minutes longer. Serve with Lobster Sauce. Makes 6 servings.

LOBSTER SAUCE

½ cup diced lobster	1 cup dry white wine
2 egg yolks	reduced to ½ cup or
½ cup cream	½ cup boiling water
⅓ teaspoon salt	juice of ½ lemon
dash of cayenne	lobster roe, if available

Add egg yolks to cream, one at a time, and beat 5 minutes. Add salt, cayenne, and wine or water. Stir over hot water until thickened, 2 or 3 minutes. Add lemon juice, lobster, and roe. Serve at once.

STEAMED FISH WITH MUSHROOMS
(TUNG KU CHEN YÜ—*Chinese*)

1½ pounds porgy	2 teaspoons soy sauce
8 dried mushrooms	⅛ teaspoon monosodium
⅛ pound Smithfield ham, à la julienne	glutamate
	1 teaspoon salt
3 slices fresh ginger, finely chopped	¾ teaspoon sugar
	⅛ teaspoon pepper
1 stalk scallion, sliced fine	3 tablespoons oil

Wash and soak the mushrooms in hot water and when soft, stem and cut them into ¼-inch strips. Cut the ham in strips, à la julienne.

Wash fish and dry it well. Rub inside and outside with oil.

Place on a hot shallow dish (Pyrex, for example) and cover fish with mushrooms, ham, ginger, scallion, soy sauce, seasonings, and the remainder of the oil. Place a rack in a very large covered pan containing 2 inches of water. When the water is boiling furiously, place dish containing the fish on the rack, cover the pan, and steam for 15 minutes. Remove from the steamer and serve very hot.

BAKED SHAD ROE PLANTATION
(Charcutière)

2 *pairs large shad roe or*	1 *bay leaf*
4 *pairs small shad roe*	3 *or 4 slices of onion*
1 *cup dry white wine, as*	1 *clove garlic*
needed	1 *whole clove*
1 *large egg*	½ *cup dry white wine*
½ *teaspoon onion juice*	1 *tablespoon tomato paste*
½ *teaspoon dry mustard*	2 *egg yolks*
salt	¼ *cup cream*
white pepper	*parsley*
dash nutmeg	*lemon quarters*
¼ *pound sausage meat*	

Drop shad roe into pan with equal parts of white wine and water to cover. Simmer for 5 minutes. Drain and let cool. Separate the roes. Beat egg slightly and add onion juice, mustard, salt, pepper, and nutmeg. Brush roe with this mixture and press a cover of sausage meat onto the roe. Brush again with the egg mixture. Place in a shallow pan, add bay leaf, onion, garlic, and clove. Add ½ cup dry white wine mixed with the tomato paste; pour over roe. Bake for 25 to 30 minutes in a 350-degree oven, or until slightly browned, basting occasionally. Transfer the roes to a hot platter. Strain the sauce into a clean saucepan. Remove excess fat. Taste for seasoning. Stir in the egg yolks, slightly beaten with the cream. Cook, without boiling, stirring constantly, until thickened. Pour over the roes. Garnish with parsley and lemon quarters. Makes 4 servings.

STEAMED SOLE IN SAVORY CUSTARD
(CHI TAN CHEN PAN-YÜ—*Chinese*)

2 *pounds fillets of sole*	¼ *green pepper, chopped*
1 *tablespoon oil*	*fine*
1 *tablespoon cornstarch*	4 *eggs*
1½ *tablespoons soy sauce*	1 *cup chicken broth*
2 *stalks scallions,*	1 *teaspoon salt*
chopped fine	

Cut the fillets into 1-inch sections and place in a shallow bowl. Blend the oil, cornstarch, and soy sauce and sprinkle over the fish. Add the scallion and the green pepper. Beat the eggs well and add to the broth with the salt. Mix well and pour over the fish. Place a rack in a pan and add 2 inches of water. Place the bowl on the rack and cover the pan. Steam for 1 hour on top of stove. Serve very hot.

SOLE IN WHITE WINE

Stock: Simmer fish heads, a sliced carrot, onion, parsley, bay leaf, ½ cup dry white wine, and ½ cup water. Simmer for ½ hour and strain.

4 *small sole or flounder,*	2 *tablespoons butter*
filleted	1 *tablespoon flour*
fish stock	2 *egg yolks*
2 *carrots, finely chopped*	*juice of ½ lemon*
1 *onion, finely chopped*	*lemon to garnish*
½ *cup dry white wine*	

Spread the chopped carrot and onion in a fireproof dish and arrange the fillets on top. Pour on white wine; cover and cook in a 375-degree oven for 7 minutes. Melt butter in a saucepan; stir in flour; add fish stock, stirring constantly. When slightly thickened, reduce heat and stir in egg yolks and lemon juice. Stir constantly, without boiling, until thick and smooth. Pour over fillets and serve at once, garnished with lemon.

TONNO CON FAGIOLI

The soup on the stove is tomato. On the table are crisp wedges of Italian bread; dessert is a bowl of cut fruit and a plate of cookies; the main dish is a famous one from Tuscany—Tonno con Fagioli (beans with tuna fish). The tiny restaurant in Florence that served this dish has probably become stylish and expensive.

1 pound dried white beans	*⅛ teaspoon sugar*
10 tablespoons olive oil	*1 clove garlic, minced*
½ teaspoon leaf sage	*1 large sweet onion, thinly*
¾ teaspoon salt	*sliced*
¼ cup wine vinegar	*¾ pound chunk tuna fish*
¼ teaspoon freshly ground	*2 tablespoons minced*
black pepper	*parsley*

Prepare beans according to directions on package. Simmer very slowly in unsalted water to cover until soft, adding 2 tablespoons of the olive oil and the sage to the water. Add ½ teaspoon of the salt for the last half hour of cooking. Cool. Mix remaining olive oil with wine vinegar, remaining salt, pepper, sugar, garlic, and onion. Pour over beans and mix well. Allow to marinate at least 2 to 3 hours. Do not refrigerate. Before serving, add chunks of tuna, toss loosely and sprinkle with parsley.

82. *Meats*

LONDON BROIL CHAMPAGNE SUPREME

2½ pounds flank steak	*½ teaspoon pepper*
2½ cups champagne	*½ teaspoon dried rosemary*
½ teaspoon salt	*½ minced onion*
¼ teaspoon celery salt	*2 tablespoons butter*

Place steak in bowl. Combine remaining ingredients, except for butter. Mix well and pour over steak. Cover and chill for

3 hours, turning steak frequently. Drain steak, preserving wine mixture. Broil steak 2½ minutes on each side. Cut into thin slices across grain of meat.

Add butter to wine mixture and boil rapidly until reduced one-fourth; stir well and strain over meat. Makes 6 servings.

HUNTER'S BEEF

4 5-ounce slices round steak, pounded	1 teaspoon capers
1 onion, minced	1 dill pickle, sliced
2 anchovies, minced	3 tablespoons butter
4 rashers bacon, chopped	1 tablespoon flour
	½ cup sour cream

Mix onion, anchovies, bacon, and capers and spread on meat. Cover with slices of pickle. Roll steaks and tie with string. Heat butter in heavy frying pan and brown steaks on all sides. Cover tightly and simmer for 1½ hours, turning from time to time. Add a little water or white wine, if necessary. When meat is tender remove to warmed serving platter. Stir in flour and sour cream and simmer until slightly thickened. Serve sauce with meat.

BRAISED BEEF OF BRESCIA

(*Manzo Braciato alla Bresciana*)

2 pounds top or bottom round	2 cloves garlic, crushed
3 tablespoons butter	½ onion, chopped
2 tablespoons bacon or salt pork	salt and pepper
	sprinkle of spice blend
	2 cups dry red wine

Put all ingredients except wine in a heavy pan or kettle and brown well with the cover on. Turn meat occasionally. After ½ hour, add wine. Let it simmer, covered, for about 2½ hours. This dish should be served with noodles or risotto in order to make good use of the delicious sauce. Makes 4 to 6 servings.

BAVARIAN POT ROAST

5 *pounds beef chuck, rump* *or round*	1 *can (12 ounces) beer*
2 *tablespoons bacon* *drippings*	1 *can (8 ounces) tomato* *sauce*
1 *tablespoon sugar*	½ *cup chopped onion*
1 *tablespoon vinegar*	1 *bay leaf*
2 *teaspoons cinnamon*	1½ *teaspoons salt*
2 *teaspoons ginger*	⅛ *teaspoon pepper*

Brown meat on all sides in bacon drippings. Combine sugar, vinegar, cinnamon, ginger, 2 cups water, beer, tomato sauce, onion, bay leaf, salt and pepper; pour over meat. Cover, simmer 2 hours or until tender. Thicken gravy if desired. Makes 12 servings.

CARBONNADE OF BEEF FLAMANDE

(from the Brussels Restaurant, New York City)

12 **thick slices lean beef,** **cut from the round**	2 **tablespoons flour**
4 **onions, sliced**	1 **cup stock**
3 **tablespoons butter**	1 **small bottle beer**
2 **tablespoons bacon fat**	1 **faggot made of 3 sprigs**
1 **tablespoon salt**	**parsley, 2 ribs celery,**
¼ **teaspoon pepper**	**1 bay leaf, 1 sprig thyme**

Brown the onions in butter. Push onions to one side and add the flour. Gradually add the stock and cook, stirring well until thickened. Season slices of beef with salt and pepper and sauté in bacon fat. Remove from pan and place on onions. Pour off fat from the pan and add the beer. Cook until reduced to ⅓ of original quantity. Add all the ingredients to the pan with beer. Simmer for 1½ to 2 hours or until meat is tender. Remove faggot and serve meat with boiled potato. Makes 6 servings. (Sauce may be strained if desired.)

POTATO MEAT LOAF

1 *pound ground beef*	1 *small onion, chopped*
1 *cup bread crumbs*	1 *teaspoon salt*
1 *tablespoon chopped*	¼ *teaspoon pepper*
parsley	4 *tablespoons olive oil*
½ *cup grated Parmesan*	2 *cups mashed potatoes*
cheese	½ *pound mozzarella cheese*
2 *eggs*	

Mix meat with 14 tablespoons bread crumbs, ½ cup water, parsley, Parmesan cheese, eggs, onion, salt, and pepper. Mix thoroughly. Brush a 10-inch Pyrex baking dish with 1 tablespoon of the olive oil. Sprinkle lightly with remaining bread crumbs. Place half the meat mixture in the dish, then a layer of mashed potatoes, then a layer of mozzarella. Top with balance of meat. Close edges firmly so potatoes and cheese do not ooze out. Brush with remaining oil. Bake ½ hour in 375-degree oven until meat is golden brown but not dry. Invert on hot platter, slice and serve hot. This is a wonderful variation of an economical dish.

LAMB AND FRUIT

3 *pounds boneless lamb,*	2 *cloves*
cut in 3-inch pieces	3 *cardamom seeds*
3 *cups rice*	1 *tablespoon salt*
¼ *pound butter*	1 *teaspoon saffron*
3 *onions, sliced thin*	½ *cup sliced mixed nuts*
4 *cups sour milk, butter-*	*(almonds, pistachios,*
milk, or yogurt	*cashews, etc.)*
2 *cloves garlic, minced*	2 *oranges peeled,*
1-inch piece ginger,	*segmented and pitted*
crushed, or 2 teaspoons	½ *cup seedless grapes, or*
powdered ginger	*grapes with seeds*
1 *teaspoon coriander*	*removed*
½ *teaspoon pepper*	

Although Orientals like to bite into whole fresh spices, Westerners are not accustomed to this, so it is recommended to crush or grind the coriander, pepper, cloves, and cardamom.

Wash the rice thoroughly, then soak in cold water for 15 minutes; drain well. Melt the butter in a large saucepan; add the lamb and onions and brown on all sides. Add the milk or yogurt, garlic, ginger, coriander, pepper, cloves, cardamom, and salt. Mix well. Place the rice over lamb mixture. Dissolve the saffron in 2 tablespoons boiling water and add to saucepan. Stir mixture well. Arrange nuts and fruit on top. Cover and cook over medium heat for 10 minutes. Reduce heat and cook for 30 minutes, or until lamb and rice are tender. Makes 6 servings.

RAGOÛT D'AGNEAU PARISIAN

2 pounds lean lamb or mutton cut for stew	6 small onions
2 tablespoons butter salt, pepper	2 turnips, cut lengthwise in parts
½ tablespoon flour enough stock or water to cover ⅔ of the meat	2 carrots, cut lengthwise in parts
1 bouquet made of 1 sprig parsley, 1 rib celery, ½ sprig thyme, ¼ bay leaf	½ cup shelled peas ½ cup cut-up string beans 6 small potatoes
2 cloves garlic, crushed	½ teaspoon freshly chopped parsley
1 fresh tomato, coarsely chopped	1 pinch sugar

Heat butter in a saucepan. When sizzling hot, add meat; season with salt and pepper and when well browned on all sides, remove excess fat, add flour, blend with meat and cook, stirring, for 1 or 2 minutes; pour in stock and stir constantly with a wooden spoon until it starts to boil. Add the bouquet, garlic, and tomato and simmer gently. Add onions and turnips, but brown first in fat, to which a pinch of sugar should be added to secure caramelization of these two vegetables. Then add carrots, peas, string beans, and potatoes and cook for 40 minutes. Before serving, remove the bouquet and garlic and skim off fat which appears on surface of stew. Serve piping hot with coarsely chopped parsley sprinkled over the top.

LEG OF LAMB ARETINA

1 leg of lamb	1 tablespoon red wine
salt	vinegar
ground black pepper	1 teaspoon rosemary
3 tablespoons olive oil	1 clove garlic

Rub lamb with salt and pepper. Pour olive oil and vinegar over it. Prick fat on the leg here and there with the point of a knife. Leave in marinade for several hours, turning meat from time to time. Add rosemary and garlic and roast in a 350-degree oven for about 1½ hours, basting occasionally, until cooked to a faint pink color.

WINE–BAKED LAMB SHANKS WITH DILL GRAPES

4 lamb shanks	¼ teaspoon dried dill seed
celery tops	flour
1 clove garlic, peeled and	salt
split	pepper
1 bay leaf	1½ cups dry red wine
10 peppercorns	¼ cup oil
1 teaspoon salt	Dill Grapes

Place lamb shanks in large kettle with water to just cover. Add celery tops, garlic, bay leaf, peppercorns, salt, and dill seed. Cover and simmer 1 hour. Remove shanks from broth. Strain broth; skim off excess fat. Dust shanks with flour seasoned with salt and pepper. Arrange in single layer in greased baking pan. Combine part of the wine, some stock, and oil and pour evenly over lamb. Bake in a 375-degree oven for 1 hour or until shanks are crisp and brown (turn once and baste frequently during baking). Remove shanks to serving platter; keep warm, discard excess fat from drippings. Make gravy from pan drippings and strained broth. Boil briskly, scraping pan well, until well reduced. Serve gravy separately. Accompany shanks with Dill Grapes. Makes 4 servings.

DILL GRAPES

In a small frying pan, melt 2 tablespoons butter. Add 2 cups seedless white grapes (or halved and seeded red grapes) and a pinch of dried dill seed. Sauté grapes, stirring gently, just until heated through.

SAGE-CURED LAMB

Wrap a leg of lamb, or any other cut, in a large quantity of fresh sage leaves and let stand for 2 days before putting in the roasting pan.

To cook: Remove sage leaves, insert clove of garlic near the bone and roast in uncovered roasting pan in 350-degree oven. Cook 30 minutes to the pound, basting occasionally with dry red wine.

SWISS SOUR LIVER

1 pound liver	*salt and pepper*
flour	*½ cup dry white wine*
3 tablespoons butter	*1 bay leaf, crumbled*
3 tablespoons olive oil	*1 cup sour cream*

Cut liver into strips about 1 inch wide and 2 inches long and roll strips in flour. Heat butter and oil in frying pan and when hot add the liver and sauté quickly, a minute or so. Sprinkle liver with salt and pepper and remove to a hot platter. Add wine, bay leaf, and sour cream to the pan. Blend thoroughly with pan juice. Heat but do not boil after addition of sour cream. Return liver to pan and reheat before serving.

LOIN OF PORK ALSATIAN

loin of pork	1 large head cabbage, shredded
salt	2 bay leaves
pepper	6 juniper berries, crushed
ginger	3 white onions, quartered

Rub the meat with salt, pepper, and ginger. Place in roasting pan and cook 1 hour in a 350-degree oven. Remove from oven and pour off most of the fat. Mix cabbage, bay leaves, crushed juniper berries (these can be bought in any drugstore), and quartered onions. Spread around the roast. Pour in 1 cup hot water. Cook another hour or until roast is well done.

ROAST PORK TENDERLOIN

2 pork tenderloins	grated raw beet
salt and pepper	½ teaspoon salt
pinch of thyme	½ teaspoon black pepper
2 or 3 strips bacon	2 teaspoons wine vinegar
grated horseradish	sour cream

Season tenderloins with salt and pepper and a pinch of thyme. Place in baking pan and top with strips of bacon. Place in a 325-degree oven and allow about 35 minutes to the pound roasting time. This is a delicious meat with no waste, but don't let it become dry. Roast slowly in a pan very little larger than the meat and baste frequently. Sweet potatoes, boiled and peeled, may be browned with the tenderloins.

Mix horseradish, beet, salt, pepper, vinegar, and sour cream. Serve with the pork. Makes 6 servings.

COSTOLETTE DI MAIELE ALLA
MODENESE *(Pork chops of Modena)*

4 or 5 pork chops
1 teaspoon fresh sage (½
   teaspoon dried)
1 teaspoon fresh rosemary
   (½ teaspoon dried)

1 clove garlic, crushed
   salt and pepper
½ cup dry white wine

Lay the pork chops without overlapping in a greased frying pan. Sprinkle with sage, rosemary, garlic, salt, and pepper. Cover with water and simmer on a slow fire. When the water is evaporated, allow chops to brown. Turn and brown on the other side. Add the wine and cook briskly, scraping juices from sides of pan, until wine is reduced to half. Pour sauce over chops and serve at once. Makes 4 or 5 servings.

HAM STEAK MONTMORENCY

3 pounds ham steak
   salt and freshly ground
   black pepper
1 can Bing cherries
2 thin slices lemon
1 bay leaf
1 whole clove
1 clove garlic

4 thin slices of onion
2 tablespoons finely
   chopped fresh mush-
   rooms
½ cup red wine
1 tablespoon butter
½ teaspoon flour
¼ teaspoon anchovy paste

Rub mixed salt and pepper on both sides of the ham and brown well on both sides. Transfer to casserole. Add cherry juice and other ingredients except butter, cherries, flour, and anchovy paste. Remove ham to heated platter; slice slantwise as for London broil, and reshape. Strain gravy from baking dish into a saucepan, taste for seasoning; stir in butter creamed with flour and anchovy paste. Bring to a boil, stirring well. Stir in cherries. Pour half of this sauce over the carved ham and serve remainder separately.

OXFORD SAUSAGES

1 *pound pork, ground*   1 *teaspoon salt*
1 *pound beef suet, ground*   1 *teaspoon thyme*
1 *pound bread crumbs*   1 *teaspoon marjoram*
  grated rind of 1 lemon   *flour*
¼ *teaspoon nutmeg*   1 *egg, beaten*
½ *teaspoon chopped sage*   *bacon or beef fat*
  leaves
1 *teaspoon black pepper*

Mix together pork and suet, ½ pound of the bread crumbs, lemon rind and other seasonings. Roll out into sausage shapes on a floured board. Dip each one into egg and bread crumbs. Sauté in a small amount of bacon or beef fat until pork is well cooked.

SCALLOPS OF VEAL WITH RIPE OLIVES

8 *scallops of veal, cut about*   ½ *cup chopped ripe olives*
  ¼ *inch thick*   ¼ *cup dry white wine*
3 *tablespoons butter*   1 *teaspoon lemon juice*
  salt, pepper, and mono-
  sodium glutamate

In a heavy skillet, brown veal in butter. Sprinkle with salt, pepper, and monosodium glutamate. Cover and let cook very slowly for 30 minutes. Add the chopped ripe olives 15 minutes before the meat has finished cooking. Remove veal to a warm serving dish and arrange olives on top. Add white wine and lemon juice to the gravy in pan. Cook until reduced by half; pour over meat and serve at once. Makes 4 servings.

ROAST CHICKEN

Roast chicken can be a quick and easy specialty if prepared in this way. The bird must be young and well-fed—the lovely broiler-fryers weighing 3 to 3½ pounds are ideal for roasting in this way.

Wash chicken and season it inside and out with salt, pepper, and lemon juice. Inside put a large lump of butter and a piece of lemon peel. Lay chicken on its side in a roasting dish not too much larger than the bird. Put butter (or some bacon fat) all around. Cover with buttered aluminum foil. Cook in a 350-degree oven. After 15 minutes turn bird over and cook another 15 minutes. Now turn chicken breast up, remove foil and cook another 30 minutes or so until bird is golden brown and tender, basting well. Serve the gravy from the pan to which has been added a little more butter, lemon juice, and a touch of tarragon. Garnish with watercress. A piece of bread rubbed with garlic and placed inside the chicken also gives a delicious flavor.

OX TONGUE WITH HORSERADISH SAUCE

1 ox tongue	*4 tablespoons cream*
2 onions stuck with a clove	*1 tablespoon white bread*
1 clove garlic	*crumbs*
bouquet garni	*2 tablespoons grated*
6 peppercorns	*horseradish*
1 teaspoon salt	*½ teaspoon mustard mixed*
1 cup liquor in which	*with*
tongue was cooked	*1 teaspoon wine vinegar*
2 tablespoons butter	*2 egg yolks*

Parboil tongue for about 15 minutes. Skin and clean well. Put tongue, onions, garlic, salt and pepper, and bouquet garni in a heavy kettle and simmer for 1½ to 2 hours, until meat is tender. In a saucepan melt butter, add crumbs, cream, remaining seasonings; stir well. Gradually add a cup of liquor in which tongue was cooked. Cook, stirring well, until slightly thickened. Remove from fire and beat in egg yolks. Return to heat; stir until thick, but do not boil. Serve tongue, sliced, with sauce poured over.

NEW ENGLAND ROAST CHICKEN
WITH CORNBREAD STUFFING

1 chicken, 3½ to 4½   flour
  pounds   salt and pepper
Cornbread Stuffing   strips of salt pork
butter

Wash and dry chicken, salt the cavity and stuff, then truss. Rub the chicken with butter and flour mixed with salt and pepper. Fasten strips of salt pork across breast and back. Use a shallow uncovered pan with a rack. Do not add water. Place chicken on one side, and when the flour is brown, turn. Baste with pan drippings. Roast 2½ to 3 hours in a 350-degree oven. Serve with corn on the cob.

CORNBREAD STUFFING

¾ cup chopped celery   3 or 4 cups cornbread
¼ cup chopped parsley   crumbs
1 small onion, chopped   ½ teaspoon thyme
6 tablespoons fat   1 teaspoon salt
                              ¼ teaspoon pepper

Cook celery, parsley, and onion in fat until onion is light brown. Mix in cornbread and seasonings. Spoon into chicken—not too full, leave room for swelling.

RED–COOKED DUCK (Hung Shao Ya)

1 3-pound duck   3 teaspoons salt
2 slices ginger   3 teaspoons sherry
1 stalk scallion   3 teaspoons soy sauce
5 dried mushrooms, soaked   2 teaspoons sugar
2 teaspoons sesame-seed oil

Wash the duck, remove the tail and oil sacs and discard. Place duck in a saucepan with enough water to cover. Add the rest of the ingredients and bring to a boil. Turn down the heat and simmer for 1½ hours. Serve in a deep bowl with the gravy.

NOODLES WITH CHICKEN, HAM, AND OYSTERS (*Chi Jo Huo T'ui Li Luang Mien*)

¼ *pound medium broad egg noodles*	¼ *pound chicken, thinly sliced*
2 *ounces Smithfield ham*	6 *mushrooms, soaked and sliced*
2 *cups chicken stock*	
1 *cup oysters*	2 *stalks leeks, quartered and thinly sliced*
¼ *teaspoon salt*	
1 *slice ginger, chopped fine*	4 *pieces tree fungus, soaked (optional)*
2 *stalks scallions, finely chopped*	2 *tablespoons soy sauce*
1 *tablespoon oil for chicken*	2 *tablespoons sherry*

History, or legend, tells us that early Virginia traders to the Orient learned the secret of making "Smithfield" ham there. Other ham may be substituted in this recipe, but of course it is not the same. Tree fungus, or woodear, may be bought in Chinese stores, or omitted.

Boil noodles in a generous amount of water for about 10 minutes. Turn into a colander, rinse in cold water, and drain well.

Cut Smithfield ham into shreds 1½ inches long, and simmer in chicken stock for 5 minutes. Add oysters, salt, and ginger and continue to simmer for another 10 minutes. Add noodles and scallions and when it becomes hot, cook for another 2 minutes. Set mixture aside and keep it warm. Just before serving divide the noodles into individual bowls and keep warm.

Heat a pan with the oil and sauté the chicken and mushrooms. Add the leeks, woodear, and soy sauce and sauté for 5 minutes, stirring well. Sprinkle with sherry, arrange over noodles in individual bowls and serve very hot.

TURKEY, BRAZILIAN STYLE

1 turkey	*4 green peppers, chopped*
1½ tablespoons salt	*½ cup chopped parsley*
2 teaspoons pepper	*1½ cups vinegar*
3 cloves garlic, minced	*1 pound thinly sliced*
1 cup olive oil	*smoked ham*
4 tomatoes, cubed	

The turkey should be seasoned the day before it is used. Mix salt, pepper, and garlic into a paste and rub into the turkey both inside and out. Place turkey in roasting pan. Combine olive oil, tomatoes, green peppers, parsley, and vinegar. Pour over turkey. Marinate turkey overnight, basting occasionally.

If turkey has been refrigerated, remove 4 hours before roasting and baste frequently. Place in 350-degree oven and cook 20 minutes to the pound, basting now and then. Carve turkey and arrange slices on a platter with a slice of ham for every 3 slices of turkey. Force gravy through a sieve and serve separately.

TURKEY À LA BERRICHONNE

1 8- to 12-pound turkey	*1 tablespoon flour*
butter	*1 cup red wine*
1 onion, cut up	*¼ pound bacon, diced*
1 carrot	*1 pound small mushrooms*
1 clove garlic	*salt and pepper*
bouquet of thyme,	
parsley, bay leaf	

Have the butcher cut turkey, dividing legs and wings into 2 pieces each and the breast into 4 pieces.

Prepare a stock by browning the giblets and neck in butter with onion, carrot, garlic, and bouquet; mix in flour and let it brown a little. Add half the red wine and 2 cups water. Simmer 1 hour. Season turkey with salt and pepper and brown in butter in a heavy casserole until golden on all sides. Remove turkey. Put in bacon and mushrooms. Cook slowly until lightly browned; add remaining red wine and stock put through a strainer. Return turkey to casserole. Cover and simmer for 1½ hours. Serve garnished with triangles of fried bread.

GAME: Venison and hare should always be hung for a few days so that it becomes seasoned, but never so long that it becomes tainted. Care must be taken that game does not become dry in cooking. For this reason game is often larded or marinated, though with very young and tender animals this is not desirable as it changes the special flavor of the meat. And for very old, tough animals nothing will do any good.

SADDLE OR RACK OF VENISON OR HARE

Lard the saddle with strips of salt pork or bacon and roast in a 350-degree oven. Remove and keep warm. Swirl into the roasting pan a small glass of gin and set it alight; add 1 crushed juniper berry and ⅓ cup of heavy cream. Boil the cream to reduce by half; add 5 tablespoons of Poivrade Sauce and a few drops of lemon juice. Serve this sauce with meat and hot stewed apples, very lightly sugared.

POIVRADE SAUCE

1 pound raw mirepoix (dice fairly fine: 2 carrots, 2 onions, 2 ribs celery, 1 tablespoon raw ham or bacon or salt pork, sprig of thyme, ½ crushed bay leaf)
¼ cup butter or margarine
¼ cup oil
1 pint vinegar
1 pint white wine or stock or water
3 quarts game stock
2 tablespoons tomato puree or paste

Brown mirepoix in butter and oil; drain off grease. Add other ingredients. Put pan in a slow oven and leave, stirring now and then until the stock has reduced to 4 cups. Strain before serving. Excellent with all game.

FOURTEENTH–CENTURY GAME PIE

Make a firm short piecrust—using some eggs with the water to mix the flour, and a little salt. Roll it out not too thin, and then line a deep springform pan with it (or a large earthenware casserole or bowl). Put in the middle of the pie 3 young partridges (boned) and round them put 6 fine quail, boned and stuffed. Round these put 12 larks boned. Cut a little bacon into dice and sprinkle them into the pie. Pour in some grapes and a very little salt. And fill up with boned thrushes and other small birds. Put in neither spice, nor cheese, nor water.

Cover with pastry, ornament with pastry leaves, etc., and make a hole in the middle. Brush it over with yolk of egg and bake in a very moderate oven (300 degrees) slowly for several hours according to size. Meantime make some good clear nicely flavored game stock that will be a firm jelly when cold; strain it, and directly the pie comes from the oven pour it, hot, into the pie by means of a funnel placed in the middle of the lid. This pie may be eaten hot or cold.

The following recipe is not quite the Argentine Asado described by Gerald Durrell in *The Whispering Land*:

. . . a great stake had been stuck upright in the ground, on this a whole sheep, split open like an oyster, had been spitted. We lay on the ground around the fire and drank red wine while waiting for our meal to cook. . . . The wonderful smell of burning brushwood, mingling with the smell of roasting meat . . . above us the night sky, trembling with stars. . . . To gulp a mouthful of soft, warm red wine, then to lean forward and slice a fragrant chip of meat from the brown, bubbling carcass in front of you, dunk it in the fierce sauce of vinegar, garlic and red pepper, and then stuff it, nut-sweet and juicy, into your mouth, seemed one of the most satisfying actions of my life.

CARNE ASADO

4 *pounds beef*	1 *cup chopped green*
4 *teaspoons salt*	*pepper*
2 *teaspoons ground mace*	1 *cup chopped onion*
1 *teaspoon minced garlic*	1 *can (6¼ ounces) concen-*
½ *teaspoon pepper*	*trated tomato juice*
½ *cup vinegar*	¼ *cup water*
1 *tablespoon oil*	3 *tablespoons flour*

Combine salt, mace, garlic, and pepper and rub thoroughly into meat. Place meat in bowl; pour in vinegar; refrigerate 12 to 14 hours, turning several times. Remove meat from marinade, dry thoroughly and brown in oil in a Dutch oven. Combine marinade, pepper, onion, tomato juice, and water; spoon over meat. Roast meat, covered, in a 375-degree oven for 2½ to 3 hours, or until tender, basting occasionally. For a smooth gravy, put sauce through food mill or sieve. Thicken with mixture of flour stirred with 3 tablespoons water. Serve gravy separately. Makes 8 to 10 servings.

VINDALOO

Vindaloo is a dish of West India, from Bombay, the gateway of India. Meat and spices are marinated in vinegar; the spices used are ground, not whole, as is often the way spices are used in India. The meat is then cooked in the marinade. A Vindaloo is usually prepared with pork, lamb, chicken, or shrimp.

2 *pounds meat*	2 *ounces vinegar*
1½ *pounds potatoes*	½ *ounce mustard seeds*
6 *ounces tomatoes*	½ *ounce red chilies*
12 *ounces onions*	6 *ounces clarified butter*
¼ *ounce ginger*	*(ghee) or fat*
⅛ *ounce turmeric*	*stock*
⅛ *ounce garlic*	

Cube meat. Grind spices and mix with some of the vinegar. Smear on meat and let stand for an hour. Heat fat and brown meat. Add remaining vinegar and a little stock. Simmer. When half cooked, add potatoes. Cook until meat and vegetables are tender.

To be more economical in the use of meat, there are many hearty and well-seasoned dishes in the Middle Eastern cuisine which substitute other high-protein foods for meat. Much Syrian food is nourishing as well as flavorsome, using yogurt, cracked wheat, sesame seeds, and olives. Mint, neglected in most cooking, is a favorite seasoning. Not only has mint a delicious flavor of its own, but it also combines beautifully with other seasonings and foods; its powerful capacity to sting the taste buds opens them to greater taste and appreciation of all food. Vegetables with various stuffings are the most popular dishes.

SQUASH WITH YOGURT SAUCE

2 dozen medium to small zucchini, hollowed with apple corer	1 teaspoon salt
	4 tablespoons butter

Rinse squash in water with 1 teaspoon salt. Stuff squash with Lamb Stuffing. Fry in butter until tender. Remove from skillet and drain off butter. Place in pan and set aside.

LAMB STUFFING

1 pound lamb, chopped fine	dash of allspice, cinnamon, and nutmeg
1/4 pound butter	salt and pepper to taste
1 onion, chopped	1/2 cup pine nuts

Sauté lamb in butter. Add onion and stir until brown. Add spices. Remove from skillet. Sauté pine nuts in butter until slightly browned. Mix all ingredients together. Set aside to cool before stuffing squash.

YOGURT SAUCE

2 quarts yogurt	1 teaspoon salt
1 tablespoon flour or cornstarch	1 tablespoon dried mint, crushed
1 clove garlic	

Stir yogurt. Mix flour or cornstarch with water to make a paste (an egg may be used instead of cornstarch or flour). Add to yogurt and cook on a low fire, stirring until it boils. Crush garlic with salt. Add garlic and dried mint to sauce. Pour over squash and cook 40 minutes in a covered pan. Makes 6 servings.

L E C O U S C O U S *(for about 20 people)*

4 *pounds fine semolina*	1 *pound turnips*
2 *pounds lamb or mutton*	*several sprigs fresh*
cut from the shoulder	*coriander, chopped,*
1 *pound beef*	*or 1 tablespoon dried*
1 *chicken (plus wings and*	*several sprigs of parsley,*
gizzards of another if	*minced*
available)	1 *pound squash or*
1 *tablespoon pepper,*	*pumpkin*
freshly ground	2 *cups broad beans*
½ *tablespoon saffron*	3 *ripe tomatoes*
1 *pound onions, chopped*	*heart of 1 cabbage*
1 *cup chick-peas, cooked*	1½ *cups raisins*
1 *pound carrots*	1 *teaspoon paprika*
1½ *teaspoons salt*	*a few artichoke hearts,*
1 *cup olive oil*	*if in season, cooked*
about ½ pound butter	*apart with*
	2 *cups peas*

For cooking couscous one needs a large kettle which will contain the meat, vegetables and water, on which is fitted a colander or steamer (a utensil with holes) in which to steam the semolina (the couscous itself). Put 1½ quarts water in the kettle, add lamb, beef, whole chicken rubbed with pepper and saffron, onions, pepper, chick-peas, carrots, ½ teaspoon salt, saffron, and olive oil and let it boil at least an hour. A ⅓ cup butter may also be added, also chicken wings and gizzards, if available.

Spread semolina in the steamer to a depth of about ½ inch —not too much at a time because the grains must all become damp with steam, staying light and separate. It can be stirred lightly with the hands from time to time. Seal with a damp floured cloth so that the semolina does not fall through the holes or the steam escape. Cook about ¾ of an hour. When the semolina is cooked, wet it well with cold water, allow it to drain, then remove it from the steamer with the handle of a wooden spoon.

Add to the bouillon the turnips, coriander, parsley, squash, beans, tomatoes, and cabbage (artichokes and peas, if available). Simmer about ½ hour.

Now take the semolina and put it in a bowl with about ½ cup of water which has been salted with 1 teaspoon salt. Pull it apart so that the salted water penetrates each grain, aerates and swells the couscous. Repeat this operation until the semolina is saturated with water, then cool. Add the raisins to the bouillon.

Start cooking another batch of semolina as before, but adding in 4 or 5 batches the cold couscous until it is assimilated. Let the bouillon reduce on a hot fire. Take out the couscous and stir in gently about ¼ pound of butter.

In Morocco the couscous is served on a large round platter; the semolina is formed into a cone with a good-size well in the center in which the meat is placed and the whole well dampened with the bouillon. The vegetables and raisins are arranged around and on the couscous. One of Morocco's best-known chef's, M. Zakaria, arranges the vegetables in sections on each plate, "as in a garden," he says. He then sprinkles the raisins over everything.

A hot sauce is usually served with couscous. Grind together a dry hot red pepper (seeds removed), 1 teaspoon cumin seed, about 3 sprigs of parsley, ½ slice of bread, and a pinch of saffron, if wished. Moisten with the bouillon. Add the juice of 1 lemon, 2 tablespoons olive oil, and ½ cup bouillon, and mix well.

Le Couscous can be made with only vegetables and dates or with pigeons or other fowl. The Moroccans like leftover couscous, heated over steam, and sprinkled with cinnamon and sugar.

Couscous may be ordered from the Northwest Trading Company, 366 Broadway, New York City.

KEBAB

Meat-on-a-skewer is known by many names: kebab, shashlik, brochette, anticuchos, the saté. Since flames of the first fires drew forth succulent juices from slabs of prehistoric meat grilling on eucalyptus sticks, causing Cro-Magnon noses to twitch and mouths to water, this most universal way of cooking meat is still one of the best.

In Tangier, beside the steep winding streets of the old town and the Casbah, one finds iron braziers grilling a half dozen brochettes. Eat them Tangier style. Take a good hunk of freshly baked bread (everybody in town takes his bread to a nearby central oven to be baked), slide the juicy kebab off its skewer onto the bread, fold the bread over the meat and eat it like the best sandwich ever, the bread deliciously anointed with the flavorsome juices. When eating kebab in a restaurant, break off a small piece of bread and with it draw off one piece of meat—one bite.

TANGIER KEBAB

1 pound beef, lamb, or liver cut in 1½-inch squares (In Morocco fillet is suggested, but less expensive cuts, well-marinated and meat-tenderized, are often more flavorsome.)

beef or lamb fat, cut in smaller pieces
1 large onion, finely chopped
1 tablespoon minced parsley
1 teaspoon salt
1 teaspoon freshly ground pepper
1 teaspoon cumin, crushed

Put all ingredients together on a plate. Mix and squeeze together with the hands in order to incorporate the spices and leave to marinate for some time—hours if possible. String on a skewer, putting a small piece of fat between each piece of meat. Cook for a short time over a hot fire, turning frequently.

The symmetrical elegance, the formality of design and manner in a well-to-do Moroccan home is a restful foil for the savage independence of their character. A meal for guests involves elaborate protocol—the sequence and manner of serving and eating each dish is a ritual—so that when the Moroccan national dish, the couscous, is finally served at the end of a plentiful meal, the sated guest can do no more than try to eat a few bites.

But if you are fortunate enough to be seated around a table with friends, eating a delicious couscous as the only main dish, you know that "you can with impunity stuff yourself with this semoline—each grain detached, light, unctuous, perfumed, and swallowed and digested with incredible ease," as said in *Fez Vu Par Sa Cuisine,* by Guinaudeau. You take in the hollow of the right hand a chick-pea or a raisin with a small amount of semolina. With precaution you toss just a little of the semolina and form it into a light ball that one stroke with a practiced thumb pops into the mouth.

As you, a novice, will probably only make a great mess trying to accomplish this difficult way of eating, it is best to ask for a spoon. But learn to savor the contrast of the dry raisin with the brutality of the pungent semolina.

83. Vegetables

ARTICHOKES

Americans have not yet fully explored the possibilities of the succulent artichoke.

The artichoke, a member of the same family as the sunflower and lettuce, has long been famed for medicinal properties. It is a good food for diabetics, and the sugars extracted from artichokes are used in diabetic therapy. The leaves, stems, and to a lesser extent, the flower, contain an ingredient which aids the normal functioning of the liver.

The usual manner of preparing and serving artichokes in the United States is the French way: boiling in water, then, at table, taking off each leaf and dipping it in sauce or melted butter. Many think this makes them work too hard for little meat. Actually, in its native habitat, the artichoke is cooked with olive oil, from which it should never be separated, until the whole vegetable is tender and edible.

Artichokes are in particularly good supply from October through May. Select rounded artichokes with compact heads with a visible hole in the middle, and green, fleshy scales.

STUFFED FRESH ARTICHOKES

6 medium-size fresh
  artichokes
½ fresh lemon
½ pound ground beef
1 tablespoon butter
3 tablespoons grated
  Parmesan cheese

½ cup Béchamel Sauce (see
  page 260)
1 whole egg
1 egg yolk
1 teaspoon salt
⅛ teaspoon ground black
  pepper
⅔ cup olive oil

Remove any coarse discolored outer leaves. Cut off stems. Cut off top third of artichokes to remove thorny tips. Spread open by placing the artichoke upside down on the table and pressing down firmly. Dig out the fuzzy choke with a teaspoon. Let stand in water to cover with juice of ½ lemon until ready to use. Mix beef, cheese, Béchamel Sauce, eggs, and black pepper. Mix well. Drain water from artichokes, place them in a saucepan or skillet just big enough for them to fit snugly and deep enough to come above the tops of artichokes. Add stems to pan. Salt and pepper the inside of each artichoke and put a spoonful of olive oil in each. Fill each with the stuffing. Spoon more olive oil over the top. Dot with butter. Cover artichokes and bake in 375-degree oven 1 hour or until tender. Remove cover last 10 minutes to brown. Makes 6 servings.

CARCIOFI ALLA TRIESTINA

6 medium-size fresh
  artichokes
½ fresh lemon
  artichoke stems, peeled
  and cut in pieces
2 cloves garlic, minced
⅔ cup olive oil

¼ cup soft bread crumbs
½ cup finely chopped fresh
  parsley
½ teaspoon salt
⅛ teaspoon ground black
  pepper

Remove any coarse discolored outer leaves from artichokes and wash well. Cut off the top third of the artichokes to remove the thorny tips. Scoop out chokes with a spoon (optional). Spread artichokes open by placing them upside down on a table and pressing down firmly. Cut off stems and place artichokes in water to cover with the juice of 1/2 lemon to prevent discoloration. Peel artichoke stems, cut into pieces. Sauté 5 minutes with garlic in 1 tablespoon olive oil. Add bread crumbs, parsley, salt, and black pepper. Remove artichokes from water and drain well. Place them in a saucepan or skillet just big enough for them to fit snugly and deep enough to come above the tops of artichokes. Spread leaves a little to open them enough to put in stuffing and pour a teaspoon olive oil over each. Put stuffing in center cavity and down between the leaves and sprinkle each with an additional teaspoon olive oil. Add enough water to come halfway up around the artichokes and the remaining olive oil. Cover and cook 1 1/2 hours or until artichokes are tender and water nearly evaporated. Use juice from pan as a sauce. Makes 6 servings.

FRESH ARTICHOKE FRITTATA

4 small fresh artichokes
1 tablespoon lemon juice
2 tablespoons butter
1/4 cup olive oil
1 clove garlic, minced
1/2 cup chopped parsley
1/2 teaspoon salt

1/8 teaspoon ground black pepper
1/2 cup white wine
6 eggs, well beaten
3/4 teaspoon salt
1/4 teaspoon ground black pepper

Cut off stems from artichokes and remove discolored outer leaves. Wash well and cut off top third of artichokes to remove thorny tips. Cut each into lengthwise quarters and remove center bristles. Let stand in cold water with 1 tablespoon lemon juice added to prevent discoloration. Heat butter and oil in a 9-inch skillet. Add artichokes, garlic, parsley, salt, and black pepper. Cover and cook slowly adding 2 tablespoons wine at a time as the liquid evaporates, turning artichokes to cook uniformly, until they are tender (30 to 40 minutes) and liquid has evaporated. Combine eggs, remaining salt and black pepper. Pour over artichokes. Cover and cook over very low heat until eggs are puffed and set. Makes 6 servings.

SPANISH BEANPOT

2 large cans red kidney
beans or 1 pound dried
red kidney beans cooked
until tender
2 large tablespoons bacon
fat
1 large clove garlic,
chopped fine
1 small bay leaf
2 whole cloves
2 teaspoons dry mustard

2 tablespoons strong cider
vinegar
1/8 teaspoon thyme
1/8 teaspoon rosemary
1 teaspoon salt
1/4 teaspoon cayenne pepper
1/2 cup juice from pickled
pears or peaches
4 slices bacon
1 onion, sliced thin
1/4 cup strong black coffee
1 jigger brandy

Put beans in beanpot or earthenware casserole. Mix together all other ingredients, except bacon, onion, coffee, and brandy. Pour over beans, stir, and bake 1 hour in a 275-degree oven. Cover with onions, and top with bacon. Bake for 15 minutes in a 400-degree oven. Add coffee and bake a few minutes more until bacon is crisp. Add brandy and leave in hot oven until brandy is heated. Makes 5 to 6 servings.

SESAME SEED–LEMON BUTTER
FOR VEGETABLES

1/3 cup butter, melted
1 tablespoon fresh lemon
juice
2 tablespoons toasted
sesame seeds (see page
180)

salt to taste
1/16 teaspoon ground black
pepper

Combine all ingredients and heat. Serve on hot cooked Brussels sprouts, broccoli, cabbage, cauliflower, potatoes, or asparagus. Makes ⅓ cup or enough for 6 servings of vegetables.

MRS. CHURCHILL'S PURÉE OF BRUSSELS SPROUTS

(*from the* Overseas Press Club Cookbook)

2 *pounds Brussels sprouts*	2 *egg yolks beaten with*
1 *piece stale white bread*	¼ *cup cream*
4 *tablespoons butter*	¼ *teaspoon ground cloves*
1 *tablespoon flour*	¼ *teaspoon ground nutmeg*
1 *cup meat broth*	*pinch of mace*
	salt and pepper

Cook the sprouts quickly in salted water in an uncovered pan with a piece of dry bread for about 10 minutes. The bread serves to absorb some of the stronger flavor of the sprouts and is removed as the sprouts are drained. If the sprouts are exceptionally young, fresh, and sweet-tasting, a little of the water in which they were cooked may be added to the meat broth. If the taste of the water is strong, it must be discarded even if it means losing some vitamins and minerals.

While the sprouts drain, melt the butter and blend in flour, adding the meat broth before the flour begins to take on color. Cook a few minutes until the mixture is slightly creamy. Add the spices and the sprouts and cook over low heat until the sprouts are very soft, 12 to 15 minutes. Force the sprouts through a sieve.

Since the strength of spices varies, the mixture must be tasted carefully at this point to make sure that no flavor predominates. Add salt and pepper and make whatever corrections your taste buds suggest: a pinch of turmeric, a mere hint of saffron or curry may prove enjoyable additions.

Beat egg yolks into cream. Slowly stir in sprout purée. Taste once more. Heat thoroughly without allowing mixture to boil. Makes 6 servings.

SWEET AND SOUR NEW CABBAGE

1 cabbage, shredded	1 tablespoon flour
4 tablespoons chicken or beef fat	½ teaspoon ground allspice
2 tablespoons sugar	1 teaspoon salt
1 tart apple, peeled and sliced	5 tablespoons vinegar

Cook all ingredients together, except cabbage, for 10 minutes, stirring frequently. Add cabbage and 2 cups boiling water; stir to mix ingredients. Cook 8 minutes. Serve at once. Makes 5 or 6 servings.

CREOLE CABBAGE

1 head cabbage, shredded	1 green pepper, diced
2 teaspoons salt	1 cup ham, diced
2 tablespoons butter	3 cups tomatoes, peeled and mashed
1 small onion, diced	2 cloves garlic
6 pods okra, cut	1 bay leaf

Cook cabbage with 1 teaspoon of the salt in 1 inch boiling water in a covered saucepan for 8 to 12 minutes. Drain well. Sauté onion, okra, green pepper, and ham in butter, add tomatoes and cook 5 minutes longer; add garlic, bay leaf, and remaining salt. Simmer uncovered for 15 minutes. Remove garlic and bay leaf. Pour over cabbage, toss lightly, and serve.

CABBAGE IN WINE (*Chou au Vin*)

3 cups shredded cabbage	½ cup dry white wine
2 tablespoons butter	salt and pepper to taste

Melt butter; add cabbage and wine, salt, pepper. Cover tightly and cook over medium heat for 7 minutes or until cabbage is just tender.

CAULIFLOWER AND TOMATO CASSEROLE

1 head cauliflower	1/4 teaspoon dill seed
2 teaspoons salt	2 large fresh tomatoes,
3 strips bacon	sliced
2 cups soft bread crumbs	1/8 teaspoon black pepper

Wash cauliflower and break into flowerettes. Cook, covered, in 1 inch boiling water with 1 teaspoon salt for about 10 minutes or until almost tender. Fry bacon crisp; crumble and mix with the bread crumbs, dill seed, and 3 tablespoons of the bacon fat. Arrange sliced tomato, cauliflower, and bread crumbs in a 6-cup casserole, sprinkling tomatoes with the salt and pepper. Repeat until all ingredients are used, having bread crumbs as the top layer. Bake in preheated 400-degree oven 30 to 40 minutes or until crumbs are brown. Makes 6 servings.

CELERY, VINAIGRETTE

Wash 3/4 of a stalk Pascal celery and cut ribs into 3-inch pieces. Place in a saucepan with 1/2 inch boiling water or stock, 1/2 teaspoon salt, and a pinch of sugar. Cover and boil 10 minutes or until celery is tender. Drain. Serve cold with Vinaigrette Sauce.

VINAIGRETTE SAUCE

1/2 teaspoon salt	1/3 cup wine vinegar
1/2 teaspoon pepper	1 cup olive oil
1/2 teaspoon sugar	1/4 cup minced chives, parsley,
dash of monosodium	and shallot
glutamate	2 hard-cooked eggs, finely
1/2 teaspoon English	chopped
mustard	

Mix seasonings well with vinegar. Stir in oil. Add greens, and sprinkle with egg.

BRAISED CELERY HEARTS

3 ribs celery
1 inch boiling meat stock or
water

1½ teaspoons salt
Browned Butter-
Almond Sauce

Remove outside ribs of celery, leaving the hearts intact. Cut celery hearts into 5-inch lengths, measuring from root ends. Split lengthwise in halves. (Save tops and outside ribs for use in soup, salads, sauces, and sandwich fillings.) Place the hearts flat in a 9-inch or 10-inch skillet. Add 1 inch boiling stock and salt. Cover and cook slowly 12 to 15 minutes or until barely crisp-tender. Serve with Browned Butter-Almond Sauce. Makes 6 servings.

BROWNED BUTTER-ALMOND SAUCE

Place ⅓ cup butter or margarine and 2 tablespoons slivered blanched almonds in a saucepan. Heat until butter is golden and almonds begin to turn color. Makes ½ cup.

CONNECTICUT BAKED CELERY

2 cups diced celery
Cream Sauce

grated cheese

Cook celery 10 to 15 minutes in boiling salted water. Drain, save some of the water.

CREAM SAUCE

1 cup milk, scalded with
½ bay leaf
2 tablespoons butter
water from cooking celery

2 tablespoons flour
1 teaspoon grated onion
salt, pepper to taste

Melt butter over low heat, stir in flour and onion but do not brown; add scalded milk, stirring constantly, then add a little celery water, season with salt and pepper.

Put celery in buttered baking dish, pour sauce over celery, sprinkle with grated cheese and brown in 350-degree oven.

SWOONED PRIEST

(Persian—so good that it makes even a priest swoon; also known as Imam's Delight)

1 eggplant, peeled and
sliced ½ inch thick
2 large onions, sliced
3 large tomatoes, sliced
salt and pepper

1 small bunch of fresh
coriander or parsley,
minced
2 tablespoons oil
2 cloves garlic, sliced

Arrange eggplant, onions, and tomatoes in alternate layers in a frying pan, sprinkling each layer with salt and pepper and the minced greens. Add ⅓ cup hot water, oil, and garlic. Cover tightly and simmer for about 30 minutes or until the liquid is reduced to a rich gravy. Serve hot with bread or rice.

HERB PIE

2 hearts of head lettuce
1 bunch parsley
½ cup spinach, packed
a few shiny new beet
leaves
1 bunch watercress
½ cup mustard greens

¼ cup chopped chives
pepper, paprika, salt
2 eggs
1 cup cream
1 cup milk
¼ cup flour

Bring large kettle of water to boil, toss in the hearts of lettuce and other greens. Boil hard for a few minutes until tender; drain well, chop fine, and season with freshly ground pepper, plenty of paprika, and salt.

In a separate pan beat eggs into cream and milk, stir in flour and mix briskly with wooden spoon to make thin smooth batter. Mix this thoroughly with the chopped herbs and pour everything into a baking dish. Cook in a 350-degree oven until a good crust is formed on top. Spread with butter before serving.

POPPY-SEED NOODLES (*Mohnnudeln*)

½ pound egg noodles	*1 tablespoon sugar*
4 tablespoons butter	*grated rind 1 lemon*
½ cup ground poppy seed	

Boil noodles in salted water 10 to 13 minutes. Drain well. Shake to separate them. Add softened butter, sugar, poppy seed, and lemon rind. Toss until well mixed. Serve in heated dish. Makes 4 servings.

ONIONS MADÈRE

1½ pounds white onions,	*dash of powdered cloves*
peeled	*or mace*
¼ cup brown sugar or	*salt and pepper*
honey	*½ cup Madeira wine*
¼ cup butter	*¼ cup seedless raisins*
	2 tablespoons currants

Glaze onions in sugar and butter until they are syrupy and evenly browned; shake pan frequently. Put them in a shallow baking dish and add the spices, a light sprinkle of salt and pepper, wine, raisins, and currants. Cover tightly and bake in a 375-degree oven for about 40 minutes or until they are just tender. If there is a quantity of liquid after 20 minutes, uncover for the last half of the cooking. These are excellent with game or beef. Makes 4–5 servings.

SOUR POTATOES (*Pennsylvania Dutch*)

2 cups diced, cooked	*2 tablespoons vinegar*
potatoes	*½ teaspoon salt*
2 slices bacon	*⅛ teaspoon pepper*
¾ cup chopped onion	*1 teaspoon sugar*
¼ cup chopped pepper	*2 hard-cooked eggs*
1 egg	

Pan-fry bacon. Remove bacon and cook chopped onion and green pepper in bacon fat for 3 minutes. Beat egg and add to it the vinegar, salt, pepper, sugar. Pour into bacon fat and cook until thickened, stirring constantly. Add potatoes to sauce. Chop 1 egg and add to sauce. Serve garnished with slices of the other egg. Especially good with liver. Makes 4 servings.

NEW POTATOES

Early or "new" potatoes are shipped directly from the field after harvesting. Because they are dug before complete maturity, new potatoes must be marketed immediately. The skins are very delicate, likely to get a bit scuffed in handling. Because they are so young and fresh they are rather perishable, especially if stored at room temperature.

The flavor of new potatoes is so good they can be prepared very simply. Scrape off a patch of peel so that salt can penetrate the inside, then cook with the remainder of the jacket intact. Serve them whole with fresh parsley butter or minced chive butter. New potatoes are extra high in vitamin C.

When thinking of good ways to cook new potatoes, remember they are immature, low in starch. For this reason they shouldn't be used for baking, mashing, or deep-fat frying. Such potato dishes need the mealy mature potato.

There are little cooking tricks which will make boiled potatoes more inviting. To make sure potatoes cook uniformly, select potatoes of the same size. Once the potatoes are tender and have been drained, set the pan of potatoes, uncovered, over low heat and shake them gently for a few minutes. This dries potatoes and makes them flaky. Do this whether potatoes are cooked peeled or in their jackets.

NEW POTATOES WITH FRESH PEAS

2 pounds raw new potatoes	⅛ teaspoon ground black pepper
1¼ teaspoons salt	2 tablespoons butter
1 pound (1 cup shelled) fresh green peas	¼ cup top milk or light cream
½ teaspoon ground basil	

Scrape new potatoes. Place in a saucepan with ½ inch boiling water and salt. Cover. Bring to boiling point and boil 25 minutes or until done. (The cooking time depends upon the size of the potatoes.) Add peas and basil about 5 minutes before end of cooking time. Drain, if necessary. Add black pepper, butter, and top milk or cream. Heat a few seconds only. Serve at once. Makes 6 servings.

SAVORY NEW POTATOES

18 *small new potatoes*
1 *inch boiling chicken or beef stock*
½ *teaspoon salt, if desired*
¼ *teaspoon finely chopped garlic*
1 *tablespoon flour*
½ *cup light cream*
⅛ *teaspoon ground black pepper*
1½ *tablespoons parsley, chopped*

Wash new potatoes well and scrape them if skin is not tender and thin. Place in a heavy-bottomed saucepan with chicken or beef stock, salt and garlic. Cover and boil 30 minutes or until potatoes are tender. (Cooking time depends upon size of potatoes.) Remove potatoes. Blend cream into flour. Cook 5 minutes or until sauce is slightly thickened. Add black pepper. Return potatoes to sauce. Garnish with chopped fresh parsley. Makes 6 servings.

BAKED CREAMED NEW POTATOES

12 *(2 pounds) small new potatoes*
1 *teaspoon salt*
½ *cup heavy cream*
¼ *teaspoon salt*
⅛ *teaspoon ground black pepper*
½ *teaspoon turmeric*
3 *tablespoons chopped green onion*
1 *tablespoon chopped parsley*

Wash potatoes well. Do not peel. Place in a saucepan with 1 inch boiling water and salt. Cover, bring to boiling point and cook 15 to 20 minutes until potatoes are about half done. Drain off water. Bake in a 375-degree oven for 20 minutes or until potatoes are tender. Remove from oven, cut potatoes in half and put them in a serving dish. Do not peel. Combine cream, salt, black pepper, turmeric, onion, and parsley. Cook *only* until boiling point is reached. *Do not boil.* Pour over potatoes. Serve hot. Makes 6 servings.

CREAMED NEW POTATOES AND HAM

12 small new potatoes	½ teaspoon salt
1 teaspoon salt	⅛ teaspoon basil leaves
¼ cup (½ stick) butter	⅛ teaspoon ground black
4 tablespoons flour	pepper
½ cup potato water	1 cup diced cooked ham
1½ cups milk	1 cup cooked green peas

Wash and scrape potatoes. Place in a saucepan in 1 inch boiling water with salt. Cover, bring to a boil and cook 25 minutes or until potatoes are tender. Drain, if necessary, saving ½ cup of the potato water to use in cream sauce. Melt butter. Blend in flour. Cook about ½ minute or until bubbly. Add potato water mixed with milk. Add the butter. Stir and cook until medium thick. Add salt, basil, black pepper, ham, and peas. Heat 1 to 2 minutes. Makes 6 servings.

SAVORY RICE

1 cup raw rice	1 cup celery, diced
2 bouillon cubes	¼ pound mushrooms or
½ cup beer or ale	1 4-ounce can
	½ teaspoon salt

Put 2 cups water with bouillon cubes (if canned mushrooms are used include liquid and use less water), beer, celery, mushrooms, and salt in a heavy pan. Bring to a boil; add rice slowly. Cover and reduce heat. Simmer 25 minutes. Drain and dry rice. Makes 4 servings.

RICE AND PEAS (*or Red beans*)

1 cup split peas (or red beans)	1 small onion, minced
1 clove garlic	1 tomato, peeled and minced
½ pound soup meat, cubed	½ teaspoon thyme
1 tablespoon bacon fat or cooking oil	½ teaspoon minced parsley
1 cup rice	1 teaspoon salt
2 blades chives	¼ teaspoon pepper

Wash peas or beans and soak overnight in 2 cups water. Next day add meat and garlic to the peas. Simmer until peas begin to soften. Brown the seasoning, onion, and tomato in the fat to develop flavor. Add seasoning mixture, rice, and 2 cups boiling water to peas. Cook until rice and peas are soft but grainy.

ÉPINARD À LA BOURGEOISE

2 pounds spinach	pinch of nutmeg
¼ pound butter	½ cup croutons (small cubes of bread fried in butter or bacon fat)
salt and pepper to taste	
½ cup cooked ham, cubed	

Wash spinach well. Do not drain. Cook it in a heavy saucepan with the butter and salt, stirring well, over fairly high heat. When cooked, stir in ham, pepper, and nutmeg, and just before serving, the croutons. Serve at once. Serves 4 as a side dish.

SPINACH WITH ANCHOVIES

2 pounds fresh spinach	1 pinch freshly grated nutmeg
1 clove garlic, minced	
2 tablespoons olive oil	1 fillet of anchovy
¾ teaspoon salt	1 teaspoon basil, chopped
freshly ground pepper	grated Parmesan cheese

In a heavy kettle, cook garlic in olive oil without browning. Add well-washed spinach with only the water that clings to the leaves. Sprinkle with salt. Cook, covered, 6 to 8 minutes. Halfway through cooking, turn and loosen spinach with a fork. Drain off excess water. Sprinkle with pepper and nutmeg. Add anchovy fillet and basil. Mix well with spinach and turn into a hot serving dish. Sprinkle with grated Parmesan cheese. Makes 4 or 5 servings.

ANNA'S ZUCCHINI

5 (about 1¼ pounds) zucchini	*1 tablespoon minced fresh parsley*
1 medium clove garlic	*½ teaspoon salt*
2 tablespoons butter	*¼ teaspoon ground black pepper*
3 tablespoons olive oil	

Peel garlic and quarter. Fry until golden in butter and olive oil. Wash zucchini and slice ⅛ inch thick. Cook quickly in the hot oil until tender, stirring from time to time. Add parsley, salt, and black pepper just before squash is done. Serve hot with the main course. Makes 4 servings.

ZUCCHINI ALLA MEDITERRANEA

TOMATO SAUCE

4 medium (1½ pounds) fresh tomatoes	*1½ teaspoons salt*
½ cup chopped onion	*¼ teaspoon ground black pepper*
1 clove garlic, minced	*8 (2¼ pounds) zucchini*
⅓ cup chopped celery	*flour*
½ teaspoon basil leaves	*3 hard-cooked eggs*
6 tablespoons olive oil	*¼ cup finely chopped fresh parsley*
1 tablespoon capers	

Combine tomatoes, onions, garlic, celery; cover, cook slowly until vegetables are soft, about 20 minutes. Put through a food mill or sieve. Add basil and half the olive oil. Cook 10 minutes or until thickened. Stir in capers, salt, and black pepper. Keep warm while preparing zucchini. Wash zucchini, cut unpeeled into lengthwise slices ¼-inch thick. Sprinkle with flour. Cook slowly in remaining olive oil until lightly browned on both sides. Remove to serving platter. Spoon the tomato sauce over top. Chop hard-cooked eggs finely, mix with parsley and sprinkle over the top. Makes 8 servings.

84. Salads

In sixteenth-century England as in twentieth-century California, salads were popular as a first course. And in many ways this is right—a salad is an appropriate hors d'oeuvre, a fresh and appetizing opening to a meal.

But something hot and aromatic, an enticing odor, may be even more appropriate. Holland-America Line's magnificent white-haired Chief Steward, the great Rietbergen of the *Nieuw Amsterdam,* has said that he will not even plan a meal for someone who wants to skip the soup.

Wholesome though it may be to serve greens at the beginning of the meal, salads—crisp, clean, astringent—have a definite function later on. Their cool crispness is a happy contrast to soft, hot foods; their light, clean astringency cleanses the palate after the heaviness of the main course.

Salads should never be limp, soggy, or watery. Greens should be well washed, shaken dry in a towel, loosely folded in the same towel, and placed in the refrigerator to become crisp.

An amusing old saying maintains that one cook alone cannot make a salad—four persons are needed: a spendthrift for oil, a miser for vinegar, a counselor for salt, and a madman to stir it up. Dressing should be used sparingly. Green salad needs only enough dressing to coat the leaves after lightly tossing them many times. No watery solution should lap at the bottom of the bowl, washing out flavor and limping the lettuce. A salad of cooked vegetables, on the other hand, needs more dressing. The vegetables like to sit in the dressing, absorbing its flavors, being turned occasionally.

Mayonnaise is a sauce, quite a heavy sauce, not a salad dressing. It is most appropriate with an hors d'oeuvre or a main-dish salad.

Watery fruits and vegetables, such as very ripe tomatoes, destroy the flavor in a salad. Such juicy fruits should be well drained before adding to crisp lettuce; or less ripe fruits can be used. Tomatoes gain in acidity with ripeness; they can have a salad all to themselves, with perhaps some thinly sliced sweet onion to point up taste.

SEAFOOD DRESSING

1 cup olive oil	¼ teaspoon garlic powder
3 tablespoons wine vinegar	½ teaspoon onion powder
	1 teaspoon salt
2 tablespoons lemon juice	¼ teaspoon sugar
grated rind of 1 lemon	¼ teaspoon monosodium
1½ teaspoons chervil	glutamate
1½ teaspoons tarragon	⅛ teaspoon cayenne

Combine all ingredients and mix well.

The following dressings are excellent condiments for green salads, cooked or raw vegetables, leftover meats, and fish salads. A green salad for 6 people will require only 3 to 4 tablespoons of dressing. All these dressings are better with a sprinkle of MSG and a touch of garlic or garlic powder.

WITH EGG

3 tablespoons wine vinegar	3 fresh mint leaves
9 or 10 tablespoons olive oil	¾ teaspoon salt
	¼ teaspoon freshly ground
2 hard-cooked egg yolks, mashed	pepper
	⅛ teaspoon sugar
½ teaspoon capers	

Before using, shake these ingredients well in a jar or cruet.

WITH COGNAC

9 or 10 tablespoons olive
oil
1 tablespoon wine vinegar
2 tablespoons lemon juice
½ teaspoon Worcestershire
sauce

2 tablespoons cognac
¾ teaspoon salt
¼ teaspoon freshly ground
pepper
⅛ teaspoon sugar

Before using, shake all ingredients well in jar or cruet.

WITH CELERY

9 or 10 tablespoons olive
oil
1 tablespoon catsup
½ teaspoon celery seed
6 small pickled onions,
and 1 tablespoon of
their juice

2 tablespoons wine vinegar
2 tablespoons minced
parsley
1 teaspoon salt
¼ teaspoon freshly ground
pepper
⅛ teaspoon sugar

Before using, shake all ingredients well in a jar or cruet.

WITH AROMATIC HERBS

9 or 10 tablespoons olive oil
1 tablespoon wine vinegar
2 tablespoons lemon juice
5 fresh basil leaves,
chopped, or ½ teaspoon
dried
5 fresh mint leaves,
chopped, or ½ teaspoon
dried

2 tablespoons minced
parsley
1 tablespoon fresh chervil,
chopped, or ½ teaspoon
dried
1 tablespoon onion (or
chives), minced
1 teaspoon salt
¼ teaspoon freshly ground
pepper
⅛ teaspoon sugar

Before using, shake all ingredients well in a jar or cruet.

WITH ANCHOVY

9 tablespoons olive oil
1 clove garlic, minced
3 anchovies, mashed
3 tablespoons wine vinegar

¼ teaspoon freshly ground
   pepper
⅛ teaspoon salt

Before using, shake all ingredients well in a jar or cruet.

MIXED FRESH MELON SALAD

2 cups fresh cantaloupe
   balls
1 cup fresh honeydew balls

1 cup fresh watermelon
   balls
1 cup fresh berries in season
   Fruited French Dressing

Combine all the melon balls and heap in the center of a salad bowl lined with lettuce leaves. Sprinkle berries in season over the top. (If strawberries are used, slice them.) Pass a cruet of Fruited French Dressing (see page 315). Makes 8 servings.

ACCORDION SHRIMP–TOMATO SALAD

6 large fresh tomatoes
1 cup cooked shrimp, cut
   up
½ cup chopped celery
¼ cup chopped green
   pepper
⅓ cup mayonnaise

1 teaspoon salt
1 teaspoon fresh lemon
   juice
¾ teaspoon curry powder
   pinch of black pepper
   lettuce

Wash tomatoes and cut a very thin slice off the blossom end. Stand upright on stem and make 3 vertical slits of uniform thickness with a sharp knife, being careful not to cut all the way through. Drain juice and spread slices apart. Combine other ingredients except lettuce. Mix lightly and spoon mixture between tomato slices. Serve on lettuce with additional mayonnaise, if desired. Makes 6 servings.

FRUITED FRENCH DRESSING

1 cup olive oil	*¼ teaspoon vanilla*
¾ teaspoon salt or salt to taste	*½ teaspoon sugar*
⅓ cup fresh lemon or lime juice	*1 teaspoon tarragon leaves*
½ cup diced orange or grapefruit sections	*½ teaspoon ground white pepper*
	⅛ teaspoon garlic powder

Combine all ingredients in a jar. Shake well. Serve over fruit salads. Makes 1⅔ cups.

SESAME SEED, APPLE, AND CELERY SALAD (*First course*)

3 cups diced, unpeeled raw apples	*3 tablespoons toasted sesame seeds (see page 180)*
3 cups diced celery	*3 tablespoons mayonnaise head lettuce*

Combine apples, celery, 2 tablespoons of the toasted sesame seeds, and mayonnaise. Toss lightly. Serve on lettuce leaves. Garnish each serving with an additional ½ teaspoon toasted sesame seeds. Makes 6 servings.

ITALIAN TOSSED GREEN SALAD

½ head escarole	*2-ounce can anchovies, diced*
¼ head romaine	*⅓ cup Herbed French Dressing*
¼ head lettuce	*1 hard-cooked egg, sliced*
¼ head curly endive	

Wash salad greens. Tear into smaller pieces and dry thoroughly. Turn into a salad bowl. Add anchovies. Add salad dressing. Toss lightly. Garnish with hard-cooked egg slices. Makes 6 to 8 servings.

HERBED FRENCH DRESSING

1 cup olive oil
1/3 cup wine vinegar
1 tablespoon chopped
chives or green onion
tops
1/2 teaspoon chervil
1/2 teaspoon crumbled basil
leaves

1/2 teaspoon crumbled
tarragon leaves
1 teaspoon salt
1/4 teaspoon sugar
1 clove garlic (remove
before serving)

Combine all ingredients. Mix well. Makes 1 1/3 cups.

COOKED COLE SLAW

1 medium head cabbage
2 teaspoons salt
1/4 teaspoon ground black
pepper

1 teaspoon dill seeds
1/2 teaspoon sugar
1/2 cup sour cream
2 tablespoons wine vinegar

Shred cabbage and immerse in boiling water to cover for 1
minute. Drain well. Remove to another bowl and cool. Combine
salt, black pepper, dill seeds, sugar, sour cream, and vinegar and
add to cabbage. Toss and serve. Makes 6 servings.

AVOCADO SALAD ON COLE SLAW

2 ripe avocados
1/2 cup tomato, chopped
1/2 cup onion, chopped
1 small chili pepper,
crushed
2 hard-cooked eggs,
chopped
1/2 teaspoon salt

1/4 teaspoon ground cumin
dash black pepper
dash thyme
dash chili powder
lemon juice
fresh parsley, chopped
Cole Slaw

Peel avocados. Cut off the small ends of avocados, sprinkle
with lemon juice, and set aside. Cut remainder of avocados into

rings ½ inch thick. Arrange over cole slaw. Chop avocado ends finely and mix with remaining ingredients. Pile in centers of avocado rings. If desired, garnish with pimento strips or fresh parsley. Makes 6 to 8 servings.

COLE SLAW

5 cups finely shredded cabbage	½ teaspoon paprika
1 cup sour cream	⅓ cup sugar
1½ teaspoons salt	¼ teaspoon garlic powder
¼ teaspoon ground black pepper	⅓ cup wine vinegar
	¼ teaspoon celery salt

Combine all ingredients except cabbage. Beat well, combine with cabbage. Turn into a salad bowl and top with Avocado Salad.

COTTAGE CHEESE AND TOMATO SALAD

1 pound package cream-style cottage cheese	¾ teaspoon salt
4 medium (1¼ pounds) fresh tomatoes	¼ teaspoon cracked black pepper
¼ cup olive oil	1 tablespoon finely chopped chives
4 teaspoons wine vinegar	½ teaspoon chervil leaves
½ teaspoon basil leaves	

Combine oil, vinegar, basil, ½ teaspoon of the salt, and black pepper. Wash tomatoes (do not peel), cut into slices ¼ inch thick. Arrange on a large platter or plate; spoon over the dressing. Let stand at least 30 minutes at room temperature. Combine cottage cheese, chives, chervil, and the remaining salt. Mix well. Place in center of platter. Surround with marinated tomato slices. Garnish cheese with chervil leaves. Sprinkle tomatoes with additional black pepper, if desired. Makes 6 servings.

LOW–CALORIE SALAD

salad greens (about 1½
quarts)
2 tablespoons garlic vinegar
1 tablespoon olive oil
1 tablespoon water
1 teaspoon grated lemon
rind
1 teaspoon parsley flakes

1 whole bay leaf, crumbled
1 teaspoon celery salt
½ teaspoon chervil leaves
¼ teaspoon fennel seed
¼ teaspoon basil leaves
¼ teaspoon oregano leaves
⅛ teaspoon ground black
pepper

Place salad greens in bowl. Add oil and toss until all greens are thoroughly coated. (This will take quite a while.) Add remaining ingredients. Toss. Makes 6 to 8 servings.

ORANGE AND ONION SALAD

2 large oranges
1 large sweet onion
4 tablespoons olive oil
1 tablespoon orange juice

1 tablespoon lemon juice
salt and pepper
rosemary

Peel oranges and onions and cut into thin slices. Arrange alternating slices on a large platter or salad plate. Mix oil, fruit juices, salt, pepper, and a pinch of crushed rosemary. Pour over salad.

A GRAND SALLET OF WATER CRESSES
(Old English)

1. Watercress, finely picked, washed, and laid in the middle of a clean dish.
2. Sliced oranges and lemons, finely carved, one against the other in partitions, or around the dish.
3. Garnish with some celery, boiled or raw, currants, capers, oil and vinegar, sugar or none.

RAW SPINACH SALAD

½ *pound raw spinach*
½ *cup onion rings*
1½ *tablespoons fresh
lemon juice*
4 *tablespoons olive oil*
½ *teaspoon tarragon
leaves*

½ *teaspoon salt*
pinch of sugar
⅛ *teaspoon ground black
pepper*
hard-cooked eggs
anchovies

Thoroughly wash spinach, drain and wrap in a clean towel to absorb excess water. Tear leaves into bite-size pieces and put into a salad bowl. Add onion rings, lemon juice, salad oil, tarragon leaves, salt, sugar, and black pepper. Toss lightly. Garnish with hard-cooked eggs and anchovies.

TOMATO SALAD PROVENÇAL

Combine tomato wedges, cucumber slices, green and red pepper rings, anchovy fillets, and chopped onions. Add French dressing and mix together lightly. Garnish with small ripe and green olives. If desired, garnish with chopped basil and hard-boiled egg.

BRANDIED TOMATO SALAD

2 *or 3 tablespoons brandy*
4 *sliced tomatoes*
salt and pepper
1 *tablespoon olive oil*

1 *teaspoon wine vinegar*
*minced onion and parsley
and basil*

Pour brandy over sliced tomatoes, season with salt and pepper and let stand. Mix oil and vinegar and pour over tomatoes. Sprinkle with minced onion, parsley, and a pinch of basil to taste. Serve with pâté de foie gras, smoked meat, such as ham, smoked turkey sandwiches, or hot smoked sausages.

NASTURTIUM SALAD

1 head lettuce	*green nasturtium seeds,*
French dressing	*chopped*
6 fresh nasturtium leaves	*nasturtium flowers*

Add nasturtium leaves to lettuce, add seeds to dressing, toss together, and decorate with flowers.

WINTER SALADS

Here are some ideas for winter salads. Dressings, too, may be varied—a cream seasoning, for instance, made with three parts thin cream, one part vinegar or lemon juice, salt and pepper. Egg seasoning is a pleasant change: add a pounded, hard-cooked egg yolk and a little mustard to the usual olive oil and vinegar to make a smooth dressing. Before serving, sprinkle the salad with the chopped white of egg.

NEW WORLD SALAD

Take equal quantities white cabbage and red cabbage. Shred them and keep them separate. Season the red cabbage with salt and pepper and pour boiling vinegar over it. Let it marinate for a day. Dress the white cabbage with ordinary French dressing of olive oil, vinegar, salt, and pepper. To serve, drain the red cabbage; arrange alternating wedges of red and white cabbage in a salad bowl for a pretty effect. Sprinkle with riced hard-cooked egg. Mix at the table after it has made its effect.

SALAD OF APPLE WITH CELERY

Cut celery into thin julienne strips about 2 inches long. Cut peeled eating apples into similar strips. The dressing is made with cream and lemon juice instead of oil and vinegar with the addition of 1 teaspoon tomato catsup. Sprinkle a few finely chopped celery leaves (the tender ones) over the salad.

FLEMISH SALAD

Wash and drain Belgian endives well. Cut them across in 1-inch slices. Mix with the same quantity of cold boiled potatoes. About 15 minutes before serving add French dressing mixed with ¼ teaspoon English mustard. Chop 1 small onion very fine with a sprig of parsley. Sprinkle over the salad as it is served.

SALAD CREOLE

Cut slices of fresh pineapple in short, thin pieces. Cube some not-too-ripe tomatoes. Allow ⅔ of pineapple to ⅓ of tomatoes. Add a sprinkling of finely chopped onion. The dressing is made (for 1 cup tomatoes, 2 cups pineapple) with ½ cup light cream, 1 tablespoon lemon juice, 1 teaspoon catsup, and ½ teaspoon salt. Season the salad ½ hour before serving. Serve on lettuce leaves.

BEET AND CELERY SALAD

The celery and beets are cut in thin julienne strips, 1½ to 2 inches long. Watercress or fresh leaves of spinach are then added. It is dressed at the last minute with a simple French dressing. The salad is even better if the beets are baked rather than boiled.

CABBAGE SALAD

1 medium cabbage,	*2 tablespoons wine vinegar*
cleaned	*2 tablespoons sour cream*
boiling water	*½ teaspoon each salt, sugar,*
1 small onion, minced	*and pepper*
1 teaspoon caraway seeds	*2 tablespoons chopped*
½ teaspoon marjoram	*parsley*
4 tablespoons olive oil	

Shred cabbage into large bowl. Pour boiling water over and leave 7 minutes. Drain. Mix all other ingredients, except parsley, with the cabbage. Cool. Before serving, sprinkle with parsley.

ORANGE AND CELERY SALAD

Mix inch-long strips of celery with orange sections and dress with a very little olive oil and lemon. A very good accompaniment to chicken or duck.

85. Sweets

PERSIAN RICE PUDDING

2 cups (1 pound) rice	1 cup sugar
1 quart milk	1 teaspoon cardamom
½ cup rose water	

Wash rice in several changes of hot water, then put it in a deep saucepan with the milk and 2 cups water. Bring quickly to a boil, then reduce heat and cook over very low heat, stirring and folding occasionally to prevent rice from sticking, for 2 hours or until liquid has been absorbed. Combine sugar, rose water, and cardamom and stir into the pudding. Cook, stirring, for 5 minutes. Pour into a serving dish and serve either hot or cold. If it is to be served cold, use honey instead of sugar.

PERSIAN YELLOW PUDDING

½ pound rice	2 cups sugar
½ teaspoon prepared saffron	½ teaspoon cardamom
½ teaspoon turmeric	¼ cup blanched shredded almonds
2 tablespoons butter	½ teaspoon cinnamon
1 cup rose water	

To prepare saffron: Pound a pinch of saffron in a small mortar until it turns to a fine powder. To this add a few drops of hot water to make a thick liquid.

Wash rice in several changes of water. Bring 6 cups cold water to a boil. Add rice and turmeric, stir well, then simmer, covered, for about 30 minutes, or until most of the water has boiled away and the rice is puffed and tender. Stir the rice with a large perforated spoon while gradually adding 3 cups hot water. Add shortening and continue to cook the rice for about 2 hours, stirring occasionally. Then add the rose water mixed with sugar and stir again until well blended. Stir in the prepared saffron and cardamom, and cook, stirring, for about 10 minutes longer. Stir in nuts. Pour into a serving dish and sprinkle with cinnamon, making crisscross lines over the surface. Serve hot or cold. It will keep in the refrigerator for a week.

ENGLISH BAKED RICE PUDDING

¼ *cup rice*	2½ *cups milk*
¼ *cup sugar*	*nutmeg*
2 *tablespoons butter*	

Wash the rice and put it in a casserole. Sprinkle with sugar, add butter, and pour in the milk. Stir well, grate some nutmeg over the top and put the dish into a 275-degree oven. Let cook without further attention for 4 hours unless it looks as if it is getting too dry, in which case add a little more milk. The secret of this pudding is very slow and prolonged baking—it should come out of the oven golden brown and creamy.

For a flavor variation the peel of half a lemon or grated lemon peel may be added with the sugar.

SPANISH CINNAMON RICE

1½ *cups rice*	*peel of 1 lemon*
1 *teaspoon salt*	½ *cup sugar, or to taste*
1 *quart milk*	*powdered cinnamon*
1 *3-inch stick cinnamon*	

Bring 4 cups water to a boil, add rice and salt. Let simmer for 15 minutes. Drain off water, add milk, cinnamon, and lemon peel.

Let the rice cook slowly until it absorbs all the milk. This will take about 20 minutes more. The rice should now be smooth and white and creamy in consistency. If it is not, add another cup of milk and let it cook until it is absorbed.

Take out the lemon peel and the cinnamon and add sugar to taste, at least ½ cup, which makes it not very sweet. Powdered cinnamon should be thickly sprinkled on a platter or shallow glass bowl. Pour rice on it, and sprinkle top thickly with cinnamon. Chill thoroughly before serving. Will keep 3 or 4 days in refrigerator. May be served with fresh cream.

SPANISH RICE PUDDING

1 cup pearl rice	¼ teaspoon powdered anise
1 can evaporated milk	¼ cup sugar
½ cup grated coconut and its milk	¼ teaspoon salt
2½ cups coconut milk * or water	½ teaspoon vanilla
¼ cup raisins	1 teaspoon grated lemon rind
1 2-inch cinnamon stick	powdered cinnamon

TO MAKE COCONUT MILK: Place a whole grated coconut in a strainer in a bowl and pour over it the required amount of boiling water; let soak a few minutes, then squeeze through strainer or cheesecloth. Only the liquid is used.

PUDDING: Cook all ingredients except powdered cinnamon together for 25 to 30 minutes or until liquid is absorbed and rice is tender. Arrange in serving bowl or individual dishes. Sprinkle with powdered cinnamon. Good hot or cold. Makes 6 servings.

HOT RICE PUDDING (*Dutch*)

2 cups milk	½ cup rice

Bring milk to boiling point. Sprinkle in washed rice. Simmer without stirring until thick.

½ stick vanilla or vanilla
    sugar
⅓ cup sugar (vanilla sugar,
    if desired)
    grated rind of 1 lemon

3 eggs, separated
2 tablespoons butter
¼ cup chopped almonds
    bread crumbs

Mix sugar, lemon, vanilla, egg yolks, butter, and almonds into the rice. Beat egg whites until stiff and fold into mixture. Butter a pudding mold and sprinkle with bread crumbs. Cook pudding over hot water for 2 hours. Serve hot with or without a sauce. The Dutch say that a hot sauce goes with a hot pudding. (See *dessert sauces* on page 74.)

AFRICANELLA

¾ cup sugar
3 squares (1 ounce each)
    bitter chocolate, grated
    grated rind of 1 lemon
⅛ teaspoon cinnamon

2 teaspoons baking powder
2 cups milk
    butter and crumbs for
    casserole

Combine all ingredients in a double boiler and add milk slowly, stirring constantly until the consistency of cream. Butter a casserole with rather high sides and sprinkle it with fine bread or cracker crumbs. Pour the chocolate mixture into this. Bake in a 400-degree oven for ½ hour. Serve at once. It should be a little creamy inside. Makes 6 servings.

REGAL CHOCOLATE MOUSSE

2½ ounces unsweetened
    chocolate
¾ cup sugar
⅛ teaspoon salt

3 egg yolks, well beaten
2 cups whipping cream
1 teaspoon vanilla
¼ teaspoon allspice

Melt chocolate in ⅓ cup water over low heat; stir well. Add sugar and salt and simmer 3 minutes, stirring constantly. Blend a little of the mixture into the egg yolks. Then blend egg-yolk mixture back into chocolate mixture. Cool. Whip cream; fold with vanilla and allspice into chocolate mixture. Spoon into freezing tray. Freeze for 3 to 4 hours. Makes 8 to 10 servings.

LINCOLN LOG

6 ounces sweet chocolate	5 egg whites
3 tablespoons strong coffee	cocoa
5 egg yolks	1½ cups cream, whipped
¾ cup sugar	1 teaspoon vanilla extract
1 tablespoon cognac	or 1 tablespoon dark
	rum

Grease jelly-roll pan and line with buttered waxed paper. Melt chocolate in the coffee over low heat; remove from fire and mix in cognac. Beat egg yolks, gradually adding sugar. Mix in chocolate and cognac. Beat egg whites until stiff and fold into chocolate mixture lightly but thoroughly. Spread on jelly-roll pan. Bake in preheated 350-degree oven for 15 minutes. Do not overbake. Cover cake with damp towel and place in refrigerator 1 hour.

Sprinkle a piece of waxed paper (a little larger than the cake) with cocoa. Turn cake onto this and peel off waxed paper. Mix whipped cream with vanilla and spread over cake. By raising edge of waxed paper, roll up the long way. If roll cracks, patch with cocoa. Makes 10 servings.

MAPLE COTTAGE PUDDING

1 cup maple syrup	1½ cups flour
1 tablespoon butter	2 teaspoons baking
3 tablespoons sugar	powder
1 egg	¼ teaspoon salt
¼ cup milk	chopped nuts

Bring syrup to boil and pour into baking dish. Cream together butter and sugar; beat in egg. Add milk. Sift dry ingredients and fold into mixture. Pour batter into the syrup and bake in a 400-degree oven for 25 minutes. Remove from oven and turn cake upside down on serving plate. Sprinkle with nuts. Serve plain or with whipped cream.

PRUNES IN RED WINE

1 *pound prunes*
1 *bottle dry red wine*
½ *cup sugar*

thin rind of 1 lemon
1 *stick cinnamon*

Soak prunes in red wine. Boil all together until prunes are soft. Remove prunes to serving dish. Boil juice a little longer. Pour over prunes. Serve very cold. Makes 6 servings.

APPLES ZABAGLIONE

3 *baking apples, peeled, cored, and quartered*
1 *cup sugar*
¼ *teaspoon salt*
1 *stick whole cinnamon*

1 *tablespoon fresh lemon juice*
Zabaglione Sauce
mint leaves

Combine sugar, 2 cups water, salt, cinnamon, and lemon juice in a saucepan. Bring to a boil. Add apples to hot syrup. Cover and cook slowly until tender, 8 minutes. Cool and chill in syrup. To serve, fill parfait glasses with alternating layers Zabaglione Sauce and apple slices. Garnish with mint leaves. Makes 6 servings.

ZABAGLIONE SAUCE

8 *egg yolks*
½ *cup sifted confectioners' sugar*
⅛ *teaspoon salt*
½ *cup fresh orange juice or cream sherry*

¾ *teaspoon grated lemon rind*
½ *teaspoon pure vanilla extract*

Beat egg yolks until light and lemon-colored. Gradually beat in sugar and salt. Place over hot water (not boiling). Beat until foamy. Heat orange juice or sherry and gradually beat into the egg and sugar mixture, continue beating to a thick custard consistency. Remove from heat and stir in lemon rind and pure vanilla extract. Cool at room temperature. Makes 2 cups.

APPLE SOUFFLÉ

1 cup (2 medium)
  shredded raw apples
¼ cup butter
¼ cup flour
1 cup milk
3 eggs, separated
½ cup granulated sugar

1 tablespoon fresh lemon
  juice
½ cup macaroon or cake
  crumbs
1 teaspoon pure vanilla
  extract
⅛ teaspoon almond extract
  Lemon Sauce

Melt butter, stir in flour and mix until smooth. Add milk and cook over low heat, stirring constantly, until thick. Beat egg yolks with half the sugar until thick and lemon-colored, gradually adding ¼ cup of the raw apples (shredded into lemon juice), almond extract, vanilla, and cake crumbs. Beat egg whites until soft peaks are formed. Gradually beat in remaining sugar and continue beating until stiff. Gently fold whites into apple mixture. Turn into an ungreased 1½-quart casserole. Place in a pan of hot water. Bake in a 325-degree oven for 1 hour or until done. Serve at once with Lemon Sauce. Makes 6 servings.

LEMON SAUCE

½ cup sugar
1 tablespoon cornstarch
¹⁄₁₆ teaspoon salt
¼ cup fresh lemon juice

½ teaspoon pure vanilla
  extract
¼ teaspoon grated nutmeg

Combine first three ingredients in a saucepan. Stir in ¾ cup water. Cook, stirring constantly, until thick and transparent. Remove from heat. Cool. Stir in fresh lemon juice, vanilla, and grated nutmeg. Serve over Apple Soufflé. Makes 1½ cups.

SOUR CREAM APPLE TART

pastry for 1 9-inch crust	*1 egg*
1 cup sour cream	*2 cups diced tart apples*
¾ cup sugar	*½ cup brown sugar*
2 tablespoons flour	*⅓ cup flour*
½ teaspoon cinnamon	*¼ teaspoon nutmeg*
¼ teaspoon salt	*¼ cup butter*
1 teaspoon vanilla	

Line pie pan with pastry. Beat together sour cream, sugar, flour, cinnamon, salt, vanilla, and egg. Fold in apples and pour into the pie shell. Bake in a 400-degree oven for 25 minutes. Mix together brown sugar, flour, butter, and nutmeg. Remove pie from oven; sprinkle with the brown sugar mixture, then bake for 20 minutes more.

BEIGNETS AUX ANANAS (*Pineapple fritters*)

FILLING

1 small pineapple	*1 tablespoon brandy or rum*
½ teaspoon powdered sugar	*deep frying fat*

BATTER

2 tablespoons flour	*1 tablespoon warm water*
1 pinch salt	*1 tablespoon brandy or rum*
1 teaspoon melted butter	*2 egg whites, beaten stiff*
1 tablespoon beer	

Pare, core, and cut pineapple in thick slices and marinate with powdered sugar and brandy for ½ hour in a pie plate. Meanwhile, make batter by blending batter ingredients, except the egg whites, in a bowl. Fold stiff egg whites into the batter just before making the fritters. Dip each slice of pineapple in this batter and drop in the deep fryer in moderately hot fat. When delicately browned on both sides, remove and drain on absorbent paper, sprinkle with confectioners' sugar and serve as is, or glaze under a grill for one minute. Serve very hot.

CHESTNUTS

Although chestnut purée from France may be bought in a can, at a price, a far better purée can be made in the kitchen. The smooth soft shell of fresh chestnuts comes off quite easily while they are hot. Boil the nuts with 1 or 2 bay leaves 15 to 20 minutes in lightly salted water to cover. When peeling them, take them out of the hot water one by one. Both the outer and inner layers come off easily as long as the chestnut is fairly hot. Cold chestnuts are exasperatingly difficult to peel.

The cooked, cleaned chestnuts may be puréed with a potato ricer or food mill, but the most deliciously satisfactory results are obtained with a blender. The liquid required by the blender to accomplish a fluffy purée should be a flavorsome liqueur designed to point up and blend with the special taste of the chestnuts. Ginger liqueur accents chestnut flavor; crème de cacao goes well and so does coffee. An orange liqueur such as Triple Sec, or a mixture of these flavors makes an ambrosial combination.

For the cook who does not use liqueurs, the flavors of ginger, orange, chocolate, and coffee, mixed with whipped cream, are ideal accents for the bland flavor of chestnuts.

CHESTNUT SWEET

2 *pounds chestnuts*	½ *cup slightly softened*
liqueur, at least ½ cup	*butter*
1 *cup diced candied fruit*	½ *pound powdered sugar*
½ *cup chopped blanched*	1 *cup whipping cream*
almonds	

Put candied fruit in bowl and cover with liqueur. Boil chestnuts in lightly salted water until soft. Peel and purée. Cream butter in a bowl. Add chestnuts, ¾ of the sugar and 4 tablespoons of the liqueur in which the candied fruit is soaking. Put aside 2 tablespoons of this mixture.

Butter a mold of the desired form, or shape the chestnut mixture into a mound with the hands. Whip the cream; fold in the reserved chestnut mixture, 1 tablespoon of the powdered sugar and the drained candied fruit. Mix delicately.

If mold is used, press chestnut mixture into it with a spoon dipped in liqueur. Chill until firm. Unmold on serving plate. Sprinkle with the chopped almonds. Cover with whipped cream. Cool in the refrigerator. Before serving, mix the rest of the powdered sugar with liqueur and pour over. Decorate with candied fruit. Makes 6 or more servings.

HALF–COLD CHESTNUT SWEET

2 *pounds chestnuts*	*3 eggs*
½ *pound candied chestnuts*	⅓ *cup granulated sugar*
(marrons glacé)	⅓ *cup bitter cocoa*
liqueur, at least ½ cup	¾ *cup powdered sugar*
1 *or 2 bay leaves*	⅓ *cup butter*
salt	1 *cup whipping cream*
1 *cup milk*	1 *envelope gelatin*
1 *vanilla bean or 1*	
teaspoon vanilla	

Put the candied chestnuts in a bowl, add liqueur, and marinate. Boil chestnuts with bay leaves in lightly salted water until soft; peel them while hot and purée in a food mill or sieve.

Dissolve gelatin in ¼ cup milk. Heat remaining milk with vanilla bean or vanilla extract. If bean is used, remove after 10 minutes and wash and dry. Beat the eggs in a bowl. Beat in granulated sugar and add vanilla milk slowly. Return to fire and heat, stirring constantly, but do not boil. Add gelatin. Allow to cool in refrigerator, stirring from time to time.

To the chestnut purée add the cocoa, powdered sugar, softened butter, and 4 tablespoons liqueur. Press into a buttered mold or shape with the hands. Whip cream and mix with 2 or 3 of the chopped candied chestnuts. Fold into gelatin mixture. Before serving, unmold chestnut purée on serving platter. Cover with the whipped cream-gelatin mixture and decorate with candied chestnuts.

CHRISTMAS DESSERTS

Christmas desserts ought to be perfectly scrumptious—richly satisfying and undeniably fattening.

The Imperial Torte is a spectacular dessert that is in keeping with Yuletide gatherings. It is made of thin crisp cookie-like cake layers, put together with Vanilla Cream Filling.

These layers may be 8 inches in diameter or they may be made into 3-inch layers for individual cakes. As a time-saver for the day of the party, layers may be made the day before. Wrap them in foil or store in an airtight cake box to keep crisp until needed. Put them together with Vanilla Cream Filling about 2 hours before serving. Decorate with shaved unsweetened chocolate and green and red candied fruits, if desired.

Another unusual Christmas cake with good keeping qualities is the Savarin alla Frutta (see below), an Italian fruit cake. It is neither too rich nor too sweet, keeps well, and is ideal to serve with coffee or wine when unexpected callers arrive.

TORTE ITALIANE

1 can (4½ ounces) blanched almonds
1¼ cups sugar
3 cups sifted all-purpose flour
½ teaspoon salt

1 teaspoon grated lemon rind
1 envelope active dry yeast
3 egg yolks
⅔ cup butter
⅓ cup cold water
2 teaspoons vanilla extract

Put almonds through a food chopper, using the fine blade and adding sugar, a little at a time. Mix well. Dissolve yeast in water. Blend together flour, salt, lemon rind, and yeast. Add to almonds.

Add egg yolks, butter, and vanilla extract. Mix well and knead until well blended. Shape into a ball. Wrap in wax paper. Chill 1 hour. Divide dough into 10 equal parts. Place 2 parts of the dough on an ungreased 17 × 14 inch cookie sheet and roll each into 8-inch circles.

Bake in a 400-degree oven for 6 minutes or until browned around the edge. Remove from oven and immediately trim edges with a sharp knife, using an 8-inch cake pan as a guide. Cool on wire racks. Put layers together with Vanilla Cream Filling. Decorate top with shaved unsweetened chocolate; for an additional decoration if desired, garnish with angelica and glacé cherries. Let stand 2 hours before serving. To serve, cut into wedges. This is a 10-layer cake. Makes 12 servings.

For individual servings: Roll dough $\frac{1}{16}$-inch thick on ungreased cookie sheets. Shape with 3-inch cookie cutters. Push all excess dough left from cutting cookies off the sheet to re-roll. Bake in a preheated hot 400-degree oven for 5 to 6 minutes or until browned around the edges. Cool on wire racks. For each serving, put together in layer-cake fashion with Vanilla Cream Filling, using 5 or 6 layers per serving. Makes 10 to 12 servings.

VANILLA CREAM FILLING

1½ *envelopes unflavored gelatin*	¾ *cup Marsala*
¼ *teaspoon salt*	1½ *teaspoons pure vanilla extract*
¾ *cup sugar*	1½ *cups heavy cream, whipped*
8 *egg yolks*	

Soften gelatin in 6 tablespoons cold water. Combine salt, sugar, and egg yolks in the top of a double boiler. Beat until the mixture is frothy. Beat in Marsala and vanilla extract. Beat and cook over hot water (not boiling) until light and fluffy. Stir in softened gelatin. Cool until mixture begins to thicken but not until it is stiff, stirring frequently. Fold in whipped cream. Spread between Imperial Torte layers and over the top layer. Decorate with candied cherries and shaved unsweetened chocolate. Makes 4 cups filling.

SAVARIN ALLA FRUTTA

1⅓ cups (½ pound) mixed glacé fruit	¼ teaspoon salt
⅔ cup Cointreau	2 teaspoons pure vanilla extract
1 package active dry yeast	6 egg yolks
1⅔ cups flour	⅓ cup milk, scalded
1 cup sugar	about 1 tablespoon fine
½ cup softened butter	dry bread crumbs

Soak fruit in half the Cointreau overnight or some hours. Soften yeast in lukewarm water. Add ½ cup of the flour and let rise in a warm place until double in size (10 minutes) to form a sponge. Blend in ½ cup of the sugar, butter, salt, vanilla extract, sponge, and egg yolks. Beat until the batter falls in sheets from spoon. Add soaked fruit. Cool milk until lukewarm and add to batter with remaining flour. Grease a 6½-inch tube cake pan well and sprinkle thoroughly with dry bread crumbs. Fill with batter. Let rise in a warm place (80 to 85 degrees) until batter reaches the top of the pan (1 hour).

Bake in a 400-degree oven for 25 minutes or until browned. While cake is baking, place the remaining sugar and ½ cup water in a small saucepan. Mix well and bring to boiling point. Cook 2 to 3 minutes. Remove from heat and stir in remaining Cointreau. Remove cake from oven. Let stand in pan 5 minutes. Turn out onto a serving plate and spoon Cointreau syrup over the cake. Serve warm or cold. Makes one cake 11½ inches in diameter.

MINT PASTY—YORKSHIRE (English)

pie pastry	fresh finely chopped mint leaves
currants	
seedless raisins	brown sugar
candied peel (chopped very fine)	butter
	nutmeg or spice

Roll out pastry about ¼-inch thick. Cut into large rounds or squares. On ½ put a layer of currants, raisins, and candied peel.

Sprinkle with the chopped mint, then with brown sugar. Add some more currants, raisins, and candied peel, then some dabs of butter and grated nutmeg. Wet the edges of the pastry, turn plain half to cover fruit. Press edges together and bake in 350-degree oven until brown. Serve hot or cold.

FLOWER FRITTERS

elderberry blossoms (the whole cluster)

clary sage (the tender top leaves and blossoms)

acacia or locust blooms (the whole cluster)

squash blossoms (serve as a vegetable, omitting sugar from batter)

FRITTER BATTER

2 *egg yolks, beaten*
⅓ *cup water*
⅓ *cup rich milk or evaporated milk*
1 *tablespoon lemon juice or wine*
1 *tablespoon melted butter*

1 *cup all-purpose flour, sifted*
¼ *teaspoon salt*
2 *tablespoons sugar (optional)*
⅛ *teaspoon salt*
2 *egg whites*

Beat milk, water, juice, and butter into egg yolks. Combine liquid and dry ingredients with a few swift strokes. Whip egg whites with salt until stiff. Fold into batter. Dip flowers in batter. Sauté in butter or olive oil (or fry in deep oil) until golden. Drain on absorbent paper. Serve sprinkled with sugar.

REAL HUNGARIAN STRUDEL (*according to Hungarian Anne Sekeley, whose Artistic Cooking School for Cooking is in New York City*)

11 *ounces unbleached all-purpose flour, such as Hecker's or King Arthur*
½ *egg*

3 *tablespoons melted Crisco*
¼ *teaspoon salt*
2 *drops of white vinegar in ¾ cup lukewarm water*

Put the flour on a pastry board. Make a well in it and fill it with remaining ingredients. Mix together by hand or by machine until the dough forms a tight ball. Put on a floured board, rub top of dough with melted oil or fat; cover with a lukewarm pan. Allow to set for ½ hour. Keep windows closed and room free from drafts. Cover a large, hard table with a floured cloth. Slowly, carefully pull the dough until it is very thin, paper-thin, all over the table. Cut off thick ends. Open window and allow dough to dry. Sprinkle with melted butter. Fold back on all sides to form a 4-layer rectangle. Don't spare the butter. Fill and roll like a jelly roll. Bake on a greased baking sheet in a 400-degree oven for about 45 minutes, or until golden brown, basting from time to time with melted butter. Strudel is best when served warm with unsweetened whipped cream. Makes about 12 slices.

FILLINGS

APPLE STRUDEL

2 to 2½ cups apples, sliced as for pie	1 cup finely ground walnuts
1 cup granulated sugar	½ teaspoon cinnamon grated rind of 1 lemon

Sprinkle strudel well with butter; spread long side with nuts, then with apples and seasoning. Roll up, and bake as directed. Raisins may be added if wished.

CHERRY STRUDEL

1 large can pitted sour cherries, drained	½ cup cracker meal
	1¼ cups granulated sugar

Use same method as for apple strudel.

CHEESE STRUDEL

1 pound pot cheese, forced through strainer	¾ cup sugar
½ pint sour cream	3 eggs separated grated rind of 1 lemon
¼ cup seedless white raisins	¼ cup cream of wheat

Beat egg whites until stiff and fold into cheese, which has been mixed with the remaining ingredients. If creamed cottage cheese is used, use less sour cream. Sprinkle ¼ cup cream of wheat on the strudel slices under the filling. Proceed as for apple strudel.

POPPY SEED STRUDEL

12 ounces finely ground poppy seeds	pinch of salt
1 cup (or a little less) sugar	½ cup scalded milk
	grated rind ½ lemon
	½ cup grated apple

Pour hot milk over poppy seeds. Mix all ingredients. Add more milk if too thick and stiff. Proceed as for apple strudel.

ORANGE JELLY

4 oranges	¼ cup sugar
¼ cup sherry or Marsala	whipped cream
1 envelope unflavored gelatin (or 1 tablespoon)	1 lemon

Wash the oranges and dry them. Peel one very thinly and steep the peel in the wine for 1 hour. Sprinkle gelatin in ¼ cup cold water to soften. Stir sugar into ½ cup boiling water, take from heat and stir in gelatin until dissolved. Stir in the juice and pulp of the oranges, the juice of the lemon. Add the sherry or Marsala, first taking out the orange peel. Turn into a moistened mold and leave in a cool place to set. To serve, turn out carefully onto a glass dish and garnish with whipped cream.

Orange Jelly is a very old English dessert traditionally associated with Christmas in many parts of the country.

As served in the sixteenth century: The jelly may be put into the emptied cleaned skins of half oranges and when set these may be again halved to form quarters of oranges.

VIOLET JELLY (*Old English*)

> ⅔ *cup sugar*   *1 envelope gelatin*
> ¾ *to 1 cup fresh violets*   *(1 tablespoon)*
> ½ *cup orange juice*

Bring to boil ⅔ cup sugar in 2 cups water and boil gently 10 minutes to make syrup. Add to boiling syrup ¾ to 1 cup fresh violets, without stems. Cover, simmer 30 minutes. Strain, measure, add ½ cup orange juice and sufficient gelatin to thicken (1 package gelatin to 1 pint liquid). Chill in a mold.

ROSE SHERBET (*Spanish*)

> *1 pint rose petals (fragrant*   *2¼ cups granulated sugar*
> *ones, preferably red)*   *6 oranges*

Wash the rose petals and pound them to a paste in a mortar, adding gradually ¼ cup of the sugar. Dissolve remaining sugar in 4 cups boiling water and stir in the rose paste thoroughly. Boil 10 minutes, without stirring. Allow mixture to cool and add the strained juice of the oranges. Freeze. Serve in punch glasses garnished with fresh rose petals.

VIOLET SHERBET (*Spanish*)

> *2 cups granulated sugar*   *2 tablespoons powdered*
> *juice of 2 lemons, strained*   *sugar*
> *1 pint grape juice*   *fresh violets*
> *1 egg white*

Mix 2 cups water with sugar, boil for 10 minutes, add lemon juice. Take from heat and cool. Then add the grape juice and freeze. When partly frozen, remove from freezer, mix in the egg white beaten with the powdered sugar. Finish freezing. Serve in glasses set on plates. Decorate with fresh or candied violets.

FROSTED MINT

mint leaves or sprigs	*sugar*
egg white whipped with	*peppermint oil*
water	

Select fine large leaves or whole sprigs of as many different flavored mints as possible, rinse them and dry well. Dip in egg white whipped with a bit of water, or use a small soft brush to paint the egg white on the mints—this last method necessary for frosting whole sprigs. Hold by the stem and sift granulated sugar over until well coated; then shake gently, lay on sheets of waxed paper and let stand in a sunny window or low oven to dry slowly and crisply. Add peppermint oil in the proportion of 1 drop to each tablespoon of sugar used, if desired. These are perishable and will keep only a few days.

They will improve with age, and keep green for a year, if candied. Immerse in heavy syrup, let dry, immerse again and repeat until well candied. These can go with tea or fruity cocktails or substitute for after-dinner mints.

CHERVIL JELLY

3 tablespoons chopped	*4½ cups sugar*
chervil leaves	*3 drops green food*
¼ cup cider vinegar	*coloring*
2½ ounce box powdered	
pectin	

Combine chervil and 2½ cups boiling water. Cover and let stand 15 minutes. Strain and measure 2 cups into a 2½-quart saucepan. Add vinegar and powdered pectin. Place over high heat and bring to a rapid boil. Stir in sugar at once. Bring to a full rolling boil and boil hard for 1 minute, stirring constantly. Remove jelly from heat and stir in green food coloring. Skim off foam with a metal spoon and pour into hot sterilized glasses. Seal at once. Makes three 8-ounce jars.

ROSE–PERFUMED HONEY

½ pound fresh rose petals,   2½ pounds strained honey
preferably damask rose

Put fresh damask rose petals in an earthenware dish, add 3 cups boiling water, cover and let stand overnight. Next morning strain, stir the liquid into strained honey and cook until thickened.

ROSE PETAL JAM (*from* The Vicomte in the Kitchen *by the Vicomte de Mauduit, who developed it*)

25–30 large red roses   juice of half a lemon
* 5 cups granulated sugar   butter, the size of a walnut*
* 4 cups spring (or distilled) (1 tablespoon)*
*   water*

For this preserve they must be red roses, picked in the early morning before touched by the sun. Best varieties: General MacArthur, Victory, Richmond, Étoile de Hollande, George Dickson, and especially Red Provence.

Separate the petals, inspect each one, removing the yellow or white parts in the centers, and any parts which have been marked by rain or insects. Rub the petals with best veri-fine sugar.

Make a syrup of the water and sugar: boil until it candies slightly. Then add the juice of half a lemon and the rose petals. Boil again, with the addition of the butter, then simmer very gently under a lid for an hour and fifteen minutes. Every ten minutes or so stir with a wooden spoon. Pour into dry warm jar to cool, then seal as usual.

SHREWSBURY CAKES (*Eighteenth-century cookies*)

4 cups flour	*half nutmeg grated, or*
1 pound butter	*¼ teaspoon*
2 cups sugar	*3 eggs*
caraway seeds—½ ounce	*¼ cup sherry*
or 2 or 3 tablespoons	*¼ cup rose water*

Rub the flour, butter, sugar, caraway seeds, and nutmeg well together. Beat the eggs well, and add the wine and rose water to them. Mix the liquid with the dry mixture, a little at a time, so as not to overdo it. Chill until slightly stiff and easy to handle, then roll out thin and cut into desired shapes. Put on slightly greased and floured cookie sheets and "prick with a pin." Bake in a 300-degree oven until light brown around the edges.

TURKISH FLOWER PUDDING

1 cup sugar	*4 cups milk*
4 teaspoons cornstarch	*5 teaspoons rose water*
6 tablespoons rice flour	*4 almond macaroons*

Mix cornstarch, sugar, and rice flour thoroughly in a saucepan. Add milk and mix well; cook over medium heat, stirring constantly, for 10 minutes. Then, *without stirring,* cook slowly to allow flour paste to settle and to caramelize. Occasionally test bottom of mixture with spoon for signs of caramelization. When bottom layer becomes firm and sticks to spoon, turn flame slightly higher to speed up process. When spoon gives off a caramel odor, the cooking is done. Remove from heat and add rose water. Place macaroons in bottom of Pyrex dish and pour hot mixture over them, scraping caramelized bottom into pudding. The macaroons will quickly disintegrate and rise to form a crumblike surface. Allow 2 to 3 hours to cool and set.

86. Drinks

CAFÉ DIABLE WITH BENEDICTINE AND B & B

Have ready 1 broken stick cinnamon bark, 1 tablespoon whole cloves, heads removed, 2 teaspoons coriander seeds, 1 tablespoon whole roasted coffee beans, grated rind 1 orange, and 12 lumps of sugar. Standing at hand are the Benedictine and B & B bottles and enough freshly made after-dinner coffee for 6 persons. Light the flame beneath the chafing dish and let the bowl warm slightly before dropping in cinnamon stick, headless cloves, coffee beans, coriander, sugar, and orange rind. Let all warm together cozily a minute or so, then stir in ⅓ cup Benedictine, and get the liqueur hot, then touch it with a match. The ice-blue flames should lick around the bowl. Ladle the liquid fire gently to mix well, then add 1 quart of hot, strong coffee. Wait! It's not ready yet. Next pour a little B & B into the coffee ladle, let it burn a moment, then dip this up and down in the coffee till the flames are extinguished. Add more B & B to the ladle and repeat the performance till ⅓ cup B & B has been added and well blended through the deviled brew. Serve hot in demitasse cups.

CAFÉ BRÛLOT CRÉOLE WITH BENEDICTINE

Place in chafing dish the outer rind of ½ orange cut into 5 or 6 pieces and the thin peel of a quarter lemon. Add 2 sticks of broken cinnamon bark, 10 whole cloves, heads removed, 8 lumps of sugar, and 2 demitasse of Drambuie. Light the burner under the chafing dish, stir constantly with a punch ladle or gravy ladle, till the contents are warm, then ignite. A spectral flame in the darkened room ensues. Burn about a long minute, then slowly pour over the blaze 5 demitasses of freshly made double-strength black coffee. Ladle out at once into demitasse cups.

CAFÉ CORRETTO WITH STREGA

Prepare coffee in espresso machine or, for lack of one, brew a good pot of double-strength coffee. While it perks or boils whip one egg white stiff; add 2 teaspoons sugar and ½ cup stiffly whipped cream. Pour coffee into warmed cups containing 1 small lump sugar and 1 tablespoon Strega. Float a spoon or two of the "fluff" on top and sip coffee through the cool foam.

CAFÉ ROYAL WITH COGNAC OR PERNOD ANIS

This French after-dinner coffee is very popular and easy to prepare. Drop a lump of sugar into each little after-dinner coffee cup, then fill but halfway with double-strength coffee. Fill up with good cognac or Pernod Anis poured in very slowly and carefully. Touch it with a lighted match and let it burn a few seconds, never too long or the flame destroys all the alcohol. Stir and drink very hot.

SPICY DRINKS

After skating or skiing—or even after school—a cup of hot milk which has been sweetened with a little maple syrup, honey, or molasses tastes better for the addition of a flick of spice—ginger or nutmeg, allspice, cinnamon or cloves.

The fruity flavor of hot fruit toddy is heightened if properly seasoned with sweet spices or herbs. Whole spices or leaves of rosemary steeped in hot fruit juices give off an aroma so comforting that winter seems a joyful time.

A bit of spice transforms the commonplace into something new. To a pot of hot cocoa, chocolate, or tea, a few whole cloves are added (a slice of lemon also to the tea); in each cup, a cinnamon stick to stir with. A small decanter of rum is a welcome addition to the hot-drink tray.

MOCHA–COCOA

¼ cup sugar	4¾ cups milk
¼ cup cocoa	2 teaspoons pure vanilla
1 teaspoon instant coffee	extract
¼ teaspoon salt	cinnamon stick
2 cloves	

Mix sugar, cocoa, salt, cloves, coffee, and ¾ cup water in a saucepan. Bring to boiling point. Add milk and heat until hot, stirring to prevent a skin from forming over the top. Add vanilla extract. Mix well with cinnamon stick. Serve hot, topped with whipped cream or marshmallow, if desired. Makes 8 servings.

BRAZILIAN HOT CHOCOLATE

2 squares unsweetened	2 cups hot coffee
chocolate	2 cups milk
¼ cup sugar	1½ teaspoons pure vanilla
¼ teaspoon salt	extract
¼ teaspoon ground	
cinnamon	

Melt chocolate in a double boiler over hot water. Add sugar and salt and cinnamon. Mix well. Stir in ¼ cup of the hot coffee and cook ½ minute, over low, direct heat. Add remaining coffee and bring to boiling point. Scald milk and add. Heat, stirring to prevent a skin from forming over the top. Stir in vanilla extract. Serve hot. Makes 4½ cups.

PUNCH

Vodka is ideal for wedding punch. Colorless, it allows the punch to stay light and sparkling; nearly tasteless, it combines with champagne without taking away the champagne flavor.

WEDDING PUNCH

1 bottle vodka	*juice of 1 lemon mixed*
2 bottles champagne	*with*
1 cup Triple Sec	*1 tablespoon sugar*
	1 quart soda water
	cucumber peel

Mix lemon juice, sugar, and soda water. Combine with other ingredients. The cucumber peel, which blends the other ingredients as well as adding a pleasant, elusive flavor, should be removed before serving. The punch may be decorated with showy flowers, like gladiolas or violets nestling in their leaves, or with fragrant herbs such as mint, costmary, lemon balm, or lemon verbena.

SANGRIA

In Spain, Sangria is the favorite summer drink, and it is inexpensive. There it is made with red wine, mineral or soda water, pieces of lemon (sometimes oranges), very little sugar, and ice cubes. In Colombia there's no picnic without it. Sangria is made with red or white wine sweetened with very little sugar. The pitcher should contain lots of ice cubes and lemon slices. Add soda at the last moment.

CREMAT used to be only a fisherman's drink on Spain's Costa Brava, but now it lights up night beach parties and warms the after-swimming chill. The name is Catalonian, meaning "something which has been burned."

1 cup brandy	*½ teaspoon cinnamon*
2 cups caña (similar to	*2 lumps sugar per person*
anisette)	*peel of 1 lemon*
3 cups black rum	*1 cup of strong coffee*
1 teaspoon Cointreau	

Put all except coffee in a large pottery bowl. Heat it over the beach fire. Set the liquids alight and keep them burning for 10 to 15 minutes. One minute before taking off the fire add 1 cup of strong coffee. Serve very hot in pottery cups.

A PERRY OR CIDER CUP

1½ quarts perry or cider	*grated peel of 1 lemon*
3 slices toasted bread	*1 cup sherry*
½ nutmeg	*juice of 1 lemon*
3 tablespoons sugar	*1½ quarts soda water*
ginger	*sprigs of borage*

Put toast in a gallon jug, grate nutmeg over it, add sugar, ginger, and grated lemon peel. Pour in sherry, lemon juice, perry (a cider with a delicate champagne flavor, made from pear juice) or cider, and soda. Decorate with sprigs of borage.

ORGEAT (*A drink from Colonial days, still to be found in the South*)

1-inch stick cinnamon	*1 tablespoon rose water*
¼ pound blanched almonds	*sugar to taste*
1 quart rich milk	

Crush cinnamon and almonds with a rolling pin and add to milk; add rose water and sweeten to taste. Bring slowly to the boiling point; strain through a fine sieve and serve hot in punch cups for supper, or icy cold on a warm afternoon.

MINT JULEP

1½ ounces bourbon	*finely crushed ice*
1 teaspoon sugar	*5 or 6 sprigs fresh mint*
water to taste	

Keep silver mugs or thick cut-glass tumblers in refrigerator until required. Fill each mug with finely crushed ice, add whisky and stir with a spoon or adjust a shaker top over the mug and toss 5 minutes or more, until a heavy coating of frost is formed on the outside of the mug. Then stir in the sugar and water, if any. Arrange 5 or 6 perfect mint sprigs so the stems are lightly held by the ice slush and the tops stick up about 2 inches above the cup rim. Short straws are used, only an inch longer than the mug, so that in sipping the drinker buries his nose in the mint bouquet, for the mint should be smelled rather than tasted. For this reason in a proper julep neither stem nor leaf of mint is ever crushed or bruised.

FROZEN MINT PUNCH (*Spanish*)

1 dozen mint leaves	*1 quart water*
½ cup granulated sugar	*juice of 3 lemons, strained*

Pound mint leaves to a paste in a mortar, adding half the sugar gradually. Boil 4 cups water with remaining sugar for 5 minutes. Remove from heat, add lemon juice and stir in mint paste. Cool and freeze. Leave punch in the freezer to season 4 to 5 hours before serving.

SYRUP OF ORANGE FLOWERS

Boil equal quantities of sugar and water to a thick syrup; clarify while boiling with the beaten white of an egg, and add fresh orange flowers (or extract of orange). Rose, violet, and other flowers may be treated the same way.

ROSE WATER (*from the Vicomte de Mauduit,* The Vicomte in the Kitchen)

Half fill a silver basin with red rose petals. Fill to 2 inches of the rim with rainwater, cover the basin and set it into a pan of boiling water. In 1 hour take out the petals, wringing out all their liquor into the silver basin, then put in more fresh petals, in the same water. Repeat the process 6 more times, then bottle.

SYRUP OF ROSES

Proceed as for Rose Water, but instead of bottling at the end of the seventh iteration, pour the hot liquor over a quantity of granulated sugar in a saucepan (1 cup sugar to 1 cup rose water). Stir well, and when the sugar is dissolved (without heating) bottle up the syrup.

PISCO SOUR *(from La Fonda del Sol)*

> 1¼ ounces Peruvian pisco
>   (white grape brandy)
> 2 ounces fresh lemon
>   juice
>
> egg white—½ teaspoon
>   per cocktail
> 1 level teaspoon (or less)
>   sugar
>   Algarrobina bitters

Shake all ingredients except bitters together with ice. Top with Algarrobina bitters, which is a vegetable tonic made from a Peruvian plant. It adds highlights to the drink.

MATÉ Y CAÑA *(from La Fonda del Sol)*

> 4 ounces tea made from
>   toasted Brazilian maté
> 1½ ounces white rum
>
> ½ ounce pineapple liqueur
>   (Leroux)
>   wedge or juice of lime

Combine all ingredients with ice in a tall glass. Stir well. This innocent-seeming drink is extremely intoxicating. The herb tea is a very strong stimulant as well as a smooth blender.

Measures and Temperatures

Oven Temperatures are Fahrenheit
250–275 very slow
300–325 slow
350–375 moderate
400–425 hot
450–475 very hot
500–525 extremely hot

For those who like to experiment with an international selection of cookbooks, the following table of conversions is included.

Liquid Measures

FRENCH	BRITISH	AMERICAN
1 litre	1¾ pints	4½ cups or 1 quart, 2 ounces
1 demilitre	¾ pint (generous)	2 cups (generous) or 1 pint (generous)
1 decilitre	3–4 ounces	1 cup (scant) or ¼ pint (scant)

Weight

FRENCH		BRITISH AND AMERICAN	
1	gram	.035 ounce	
28.35	grams	1 ounce	1 tablespoon (approx.)
100	grams	3½ ounces	
114	grams	4 ounces (approx.)	½ cup (approx.)
226.78	grams	8 ounces	
500	grams	1 pound, 1½ ounces (approx.)	
1	kilogram	2.21 pounds	

Bibliography

American Spice Trade Association. *How to Use Spices.*
———. *Heritage of Spices.*
———. *Spices, What They Are.*
———. *Seasoning on Therapeutic Diets.*
———. *Seasoning for Children.*
———. *Spices as Anti-Oxidents.*
Amerine, Roessler and Filipello. *Modern Sensory Methods of Evaluating Wine.*
Anderson, E. E. *The Role of Flavor in Today's Food Picture.* Arthur D. Little, Inc.
Atiyeh, W. *Scheherazade Cooks.* Manhasset, New York, Channel Press, 1960.
Bacon, Francis. *Essays.* Mt. Vernon, New York, Peter Pauper Press, 1964.
Bennett, Harry. *Substitutes.* New York, Chemical Publications, 1943.
Blakeslee, A. F. and A. L. *American Journal of Heredity* 23:97, 1932.
Boni, Ada. *Il Talismano della Felicita.* Rome, Carlo Columbo.
Borustein, W. S. *Yale Journal of Biological Medicine* (December, 1940), p. 719.
Boulestin, X. Marcel. *The Best of Boulestin.* London, Heinemann, 1952.
———. *The Finer Cooking.* London, Cassell & Co., Ltd., 1957.
———, and Jason Hill. *Herbs, Salads and Seasonings.* London, Heinemann, 1930.
Bowen, Elizabeth. *A Time in Rome.* New York, Alfred A. Knopf, 1959.
Bowles and Towle. *Secrets of New England Cooking.*
Breasted, James H. *The Conquest of Civilization.* Harper, 1938.
Brillat-Savarin, A. *Physiologie du Gout.* Paris, Garnier.
Brunet and Pelleprat. *La Cuisine au Vin.*
Butler's Recipe Book. Edited by Philip James. Cambridge University Press, 1935.
de Candolle, Alphonse. *Origins of Cultivated Plants.* New York, D. Appleton Co., 1885.

Carnes and Yale. *History of Spices.*

Caul, J. F. *Sugar as a Seasoning.* Arthur D. Little, Inc.

———. *The Profile Method of Analyzing Flavor.* Arthur D. Little, Inc.

———. *Effect of Glutamate on Flavor and Odor of Foods.* Arthur D. Little, Inc.

———. *Methodology of the Flavor Profile.* Arthur D. Little, Inc.

———, L. B. Cairncross and L. B. Sjostrom. *The Flavor Profile in Review.* Arthur D. Little, Inc.

———, L. B. Sjostrom. *Consumer Food Product Acceptance.* Arthur D. Little, Inc.

Chang, I. C. *Chinese Cooking Made Easy.* New York, Paperback Library, 1961.

Clark, E. Phyllis. *West Indian Cookery.* London, Thomas Nelson & Sons, 1958.

Clarkson, Rosetta, E. "Magic Fragrance," *Herb Journal,* 1937.

Conti, Niccolo. *Marco Polo.*

Cookery by the Bayou. Episcopal Churchwomen of Slidell, Louisiana.

Cooper, R. M., I. Bilash, and J. P. Gaberk. *Journal of Gerontology,* 14:56, 1959.

Culpeper, Nicholas. *Herbal.*

La Cucina Italiana.

De Gouy, Louis P. *The Gold Cookbook.* Philadelphia, Chilton Co., 1947.

Dodge and Alcott. *News.*

———. *Laboratory Reports.*

Erken, Henriette S. *Stor Kokebok.* Oslo, Forlajt au H. Asckhaug & Co., 1951.

Escoffier, Á. *La Guide Culinaire.* Paris, E. Flammarion.

Escudier, Jean-Noel. *La Veritable Cuisine Provençale & Niçoise.* Toulon, Editions Gallia.

Fergusson, Erna. *Mexican Cookbook.*

Ficken, M. S., and M. R. Koore. *Individual Variation in the Ability to Taste.* 1961.

Finnemore, Horace. *The Essential Oils.* London, E. Benn Co., 1926.

Flower, B., and E. Rosenbaum. *Apicius Roman Cookery Book.* London and New York, Peter Merrill, Ltd., 1958.

Ford, Ford Madox. *Provence.* Philadelphia and London, J. B. Lippincott Co., 1935.

Geldard, F. A. *The Human Senses.* New York, John Wiley & Sons, 1953.

Gibbon, Edward. *Decline & Fall of the Roman Empire.* New York, The Heritage Press.

Gray. *In a Surrey Garden.*

Gray and Boyd. *Plats du Jour.*

Grieve. *Herbal.*

Guinaudeau. *Fez Vu par Sa Cuisine.* Ousaia, Rabat, J. E. Laurent, 1957.

Guser, N. K. *Intellectual Mediation y Tarte Sensations.* 1940.

Handbook of Experimental Psychology. Edited by S. S. Stevens. New York, John Wiley & Sons.

Harris. *Flavor's the Thing.*

Haynes. *This Chemical Age.* New York, Knopf, 1942.

Heath, Ambrose. *The Book of the Onion.* London, Methuen, 1933.

Hekmat, F. *The Art of Persian Cooking.* New York, Doubleday & Co.. 1961.

Hemphill, Rosemary. *Fragrance & Flavor.* Sydney, Australia, Angus & Robertson, Ltd., 1961.

Histories of Herodotus.

Huizinga, J., *The Waning of the Middle Ages.* Anchor Books, 1954.

Indian Cuisine. Indian Government Publication.

Inglett, G. E. *New Aspects of Food Seasoning.* International Mineral & Chemical Corporation, 1964.

———, B. Dowling, J. J. Albrecht, and F. A. A. Hoglan. *A New Concept of Sweetness.*

Journal American Medical Association, v. 104, p. 2060–63, 1935.

Kaare and Halpern. *Psychological and Behavioral Aspects of Taste.* University of Chicago, 1961.

Kirvan, A. V. *Host and Guest.*

Kookboek van de Amsterdamse Huishoudschool. Edited by C. J. Wanee. Amsterdam, H. S. W. Becht.

Lucia, S. P. *Wine as Food and Medicine.* New York and Toronto, Blakeston Co., Inc., 1954.

Luke, Sir Harry. *The Tenth Muse.* London, Putnam, 1954.

Marco Polo. *Travels.*

Meyer. *Food Chemistry.*

Miloradavitch, Milo. *Art of Cooking with Herbs and Spices.*

Moncrieff, R. W. *The Chemical Senses.* New York, John Wiley & Sons, Inc., 1951.

Le Monde au Table.

Montaigne. *Journal de Voyage en Italie.* Paris, Editions Garnier Frères.

Moriarty, J. H. *The Role of Flavor in Food Acceptance.* Arthur D. Little, Inc.

———. *Flavor Research and Food Acceptance.* Arthur D. Little, Inc.

Murray. *Oyster and Fish.* Philadelphia.

New Orleans *Times Picayune. Creole Cookbook.*

Ouei, Mimi. *The Art of Chinese Cooking*. New York, Random House, 1960.

Plimouth Antiquarian Society. *Plimouth Colony Cookbook*.

Power, Eileen. *Medieval People*. Penguin Books.

Ptolemy. *Cosmography*. Yale Collection.

Rosin, Jacob, and Max Eastman. *The Road to Abundance*. New York, McGraw-Hill, 1953.

Scandinavian Cookbook.

Schneider, Max A., Vincent DeLuca, Jr., and Seymour J. Gray. "Effect of Spice Ingestion Upon the Stomach," *American Journal of Gastroenterology* (December, 1956).

Sjostrom, L. B. *The Descriptive Analysis of Flavor*. Arthur D. Little, Inc.

———. *Flavor in Baked Foods*. Arthur D. Little, Inc.

———. *Adding Zest to Foods*. Arthur D. Little, Inc.

———, and S. E. Cairncross. *What Makes Flavor Leadership?*

Sollman, Torald. *A Manual of Pharmacology*. Philadelphia & London, W. B. Saunders Co., 1957.

Spice Islands Co. *Spice Islands Cookbook*. Lane, 1961.

Spry, Constance. *Come into the Garden, Cook*. London, J. M. Dent & Sons, 1946.

Starling, E. H. *Principles of Human Physiology*. Lea and Febiger.

Stillwater Gardens. *Herb Plants*.

Titcomb. *Native Use of Fish in Hawaii*.

Toklas, Alice B. *Cookbook*. New York, Doubleday & Co., 1954.

Treasured Armenian Recipes. New York, Armenian General Benevolent Union, Inc., 1959.

Tuberville, A. S. *English Man and Manners in the 18th Century*. New York, Oxford University Press, 1957.

Two Fifteenth-Century Cookbooks, Yale Library Collection.

U.S. Department of Agriculture, Farmers' Bulletin. *Savory Herbs*. 1946.

Van Loon, Henrik. *Lives*. New York, Simon & Schuster, 1942.

White, Gilbert. *Natural History of Selborne*. London, Oxford University Press, 1937.

Yule, Sir Henry. *Cathay and the Way Thither*. London, printed for the Hakluyt Society, 1866.

Index

Index